Art,
Style,
& History

JON D. LONGAKER

Randolph-Macon College

Art,
Style,
& History

A Selective Survey of Art

SCOTT, FORESMAN AND COMPANY

Library of Congress Catalog Card No. 70-90090

Acknowledgments

Colorplates

Drawings and diagrams by Jon D. Longaker.

Preface

Some years ago a cartoon in the *New Yorker* magazine depicted two men in an art gallery, one of whom confided to the other: "I know all about art but I don't know what I like." If we find this confession amusing, it is partly because it contains a seeming paradox: with most things in life, the more we know about them the surer we are whether we like them or not. *Art, Style, and History* has been written for introductory art history, humanities, and art appreciation courses in the belief that the intellectual process of learning *about* art is unsatisfactory and impermanent when the student does not, at the same time, learn to respond emotionally to a painting or a piece of sculpture. All too often, whatever it is that the student learns about art leaves him unprepared for what is, after all, the chief function of all the arts—the communication of an emotion.

During the fifteen years the author has taught introductory courses in art to liberal arts students, he has sought ways of making the study of art a creative rather than a passive act. Often, especially if the class is large, the student does little more than to learn by rote a series of names, dates, and judgments from his teacher and his text, all of which he returns to the teacher at test time. It is hoped that this book will help the student respond creatively to a given piece of art, so that he can then bring this awareness to other works and other styles.

Art, Style, and History differs from textbooks usually used in introductory art courses in that instead of including several hundred works of art, each of which is allotted one or two paragraphs, the author has chosen thirty-eight art objects, each of which is discussed at considerable length. The discussion is supplemented by full color reproductions, black and white photographs, or diagrams of the work of art examined.

The teacher who uses *Art, Style, and History* will find that its selective method of presentation offers a degree of flexibility in teaching not possible with other textbooks, and its "in depth" approach will be welcomed by those who have struggled, sometimes vainly, to cover the material crowded into the usual art history textbook of the encyclopedic type. Here, on the contrary, there is opportunity for the teacher to introduce material of his own choice—something he has seen in his travels, something he has done research on, or something about which he has a special personal enthusiasm.

The specific emphasis of this discussion, as suggested by the book's title, is first to consider the specific work of art, second to characterize its style, and then to place it in its historical context. Paintings and sculpture, for example, are discussed to simulate, insofar as it is possible to do so with words, the emotional experience which the reader might have if he were confronting the actual object. In the case of architecture, the reader is conducted on an imaginary excursion into and around each of the buildings discussed, and by means of plans, elevations, and photographs he is made aware of the aesthetic effects which that building makes upon the receptive spectator.

While acquainting the reader very intimately with works from 470 B.C. to 1952 A.D., from various cultures, Eastern and Western, and in a variety of techniques and materials, *Art, Style, and History* seeks above all to impress the reader with the importance of discovery in the enjoyment of art. Through this dual process of exploration and discovery the student will learn to relate the art object to his own experience so that all subsequent study of art, especially the factual aspects of art history, will become more meaningful and permanently satisfying.

The projects listed at the end of each chapter are intended to impel the student to make his own investigations, to combine what he reads with what he is able to see in works of art, and to use what he has learned in connection with one art object by applying it to another. Since most of these projects require the student to make judgments about specific works of art, many of the books listed at the end of each chapter have been chosen primarily for the excellence of their illustrations. Color slides and reproductions of nearly all works referred to may be obtained from either the National Gallery of Art in Washington, D.C. or from University Prints in Boston. The latter has available a spiral-bound set of illustrations specifically selected by the author to accompany *Art, Style, and History.*

The author is grateful to a number of friends and colleagues who read parts of this manuscript and offered him their advice and criticism, among them Herschel B. Chipp, Frederick Hartt, Richard S. Hasker, Julius S. Held, Robert D. Kinsman, Edgar Munhall, and Adolph K. Placzek. As he thanks them for their help, he absolves them of responsibility for the imperfections that remain herein.

J. D. L.
Ashland, Va.

Table of Contents

List of Illustrations

List of Colorplates
following page 260

Art,
Style,
& History

1 | Two Images of Power
Statues from Africa and Greece

No one knows for certain, but it is quite possible that sculpture was the first of the visual arts invented by man. Before he learned to build his own house or even before he derived satisfaction from scratching a pattern of some sort on the earth or on the walls of a cave, primitive man may have found a stone that resembled a human being or animal. And when he found another stone that was not quite as real to him as the first, perhaps he made some clumsy effort to correct that deficiency, and the art of sculpture was born.

The Concept of Style

There are many different ways in which a stone may be carved to resemble a man. We call these different ways style. Since men in a given community at a given time tend to share certain ideas and ideals, they also tend to share a way of seeing things and, consequently, a certain style, although we must guard against putting too rigid a definition on that word. It is possible, for example, to speak of a Renaissance style, but we must realize that various sculptors in that era worked very differently, depending on whether they were Italian, German, or Flemish, what part of Italy or Flanders they worked in, with whom they studied, and so on. Moreover, each of these artists shows personal characteristics in his style as well. Still, the very fact that we can speak of a Renaissance style proves that all the artists of this period had certain common ways of working which the artists of the preceding Middle Ages and the later Baroque era did not have.

In many ways sculpture is the most realistic of the visual arts in reproducing natural appearances. A painting, for example, can suggest a third dimension but a statue actually possesses it. One might think, therefore, that the statue of a man would be easy to make, that all the

1

sculptor has to do is to look at a man's arm or head and carve a piece of stone to conform to what his eyes see. He might even reach out and touch the arm, feel the convexities and concavities of a head, and then duplicate them in his stone. One might even think that there should be no variety of style in sculpture at all, that if an artist really duplicates the human body in stone, then there is no such thing as style. How then have men managed to represent the human form in so many ways?

The answer to this question is twofold. First, art in its finest moments has never settled for mere imitation. An actual mold made of a human face is very disappointing from an artistic standpoint. To "come alive" a portrait needs an artist to select this and omit that facial feature. Art, as the French writer Émile Zola put it, is a fragment of life seen through a temperament. Two portraits of the same model done by two different sculptors should, therefore, if the artists are creators and not mere craftsmen, be two very different statues.

Secondly, the style of a statue is determined also by the collective outlook on life—the *Weltanschauung* as the German language puts it—of a group of people at a given time in a certain place. And so, the style of a particular artist is the product of two factors: his own personal vision and the collective vision of the culture in which he works. To illustrate this point let us look at a wooden statue from the French Sudan region of West Africa, the region now called Mali, which is illustrated in figure 1.

Ancestral Figure from Mali

In our first glance at this carved wooden statue we may not even realize that it represents a human figure, so far is it removed from nature in proportion and detail. Slowly we begin to decipher some recognizable details—the eye and the mouth, for instance—that allow us to "read" this part of the statue as the head, this as the arms, the legs, and so on. But our feeling for the head as a head or the arms as arms is really not as important here as our awareness of the separate units, the individual volumes that make up the statue as entities in themselves.

In this respect the statue is like the theme and variation form in music in which a composer repeats a melody over and over, each time with changes in tempo, instrumentation, mood, and contrasts of loudness and softness, so that the listener sometimes loses the melody completely but is delighted by the transformations he hears.

Although inventing variations on a theme may serve to show how clever a composer or an artist is, it offers little satisfaction of a lasting kind unless these transformations add up to some cumulative effect which heightens the power of the work as a whole. Such effects might be called

Figure 1 | Ancestral Statue, Dogon tribe,
from Mali, Africa. Late nine-
teenth century. Wood, 14″ high.
University Museum, Philadelphia

aural ideas in the case of music and *visual ideas* in the case of the visual arts. Unlike intellectual ideas, which appeal primarily to our reason, such visual ideas are relayed through our eyes directly to the seat of our emotions, so that we respond to these ideas not by means of rational logic but through a logic that may sometimes even defy reason.

Among the visual ideas communicated to us by the Dogon statue, for example, is a vertical elongation, as if the thighs at one end of the spindly trunk and the shoulder-and-breast mass at the other were being pulled apart. This attenuation produces the illusion of a tension between the two extremities like that of an extended rubber band. The unnaturally thin arms serve to augment this tension, as do the multiplied vertical forms that support the figure from below. Such elongations and tensions do not conform to our rational concept of a human body, but in the case of the African statue they serve very effectively to dramatize the human form.

The same force which elongates the torso, moreover, seems to thrust upward through the shoulders and ram itself into the head which, in its compactness and complexity, becomes the culmination, the explosive climax of the whole construction. "Construction" is an apt word here, for the statue is not so much a representation of a human figure as it is a construction in wood derived from the human form. But what compensations are there for its loss of humanity and the denial of the beauty of the female body as we know it in nature? The above reference to music may not be inappropriate to our answer. In listening to a musical composition we hear melodies which we follow with our ear as they appear and disappear and intertwine with other melodies. We also respond to the combinations of several sounds which we call harmony and which consist of tensions built up between pleasant consonant chords and less pleasant dissonant sounds. We also respond to the element of rhythm in music, both the repeated, patterned beats we call meter and the freer, irregular inflections which are inherent in any melodic line.

As our eye wanders over the surface of the Sudanese figure, we sense, among other things, the importance of its outline: how sharply everything is edged, how abruptly that outline changes from horizontal to vertical, from relatively straight to curved. Like melodies in music, these lines are perceived singly and in combination; now separating from, now combining with one another; here flowing side by side; there opposing one another in an angular, often perpendicular relationship. Angularity, as a matter of fact, is a word that epitomizes this statue. Instead of flowing smoothly over the form, our eyes collide with unexpected protrusions and abrupt changes in direction. If this were a piece of music we might imagine it as a jumpy, angular tune with surprising, dissonant harmonies and sudden, perhaps syncopated rhythms.

There are, of course, visual rhythms as well as musical ones. A row of buttons on a coat, a line of columns on the side of a building, or the repeated shapes of trees in a landscape produce rhythms for our eyes just as the beat of a drum does for our ears. In the African statue, there are tiny beats in the notched legs of the bench and in the saw-toothed knobs on the head. There are clusters of small accents in the parallel grooves on the wrists, arms, shoulders, and face. There is a larger rhythmic interplay between the long thin shapes and the rounder, more voluminous ones. The diversity of these rhythms and the complexity of their interrelationships makes us think of the intricate interplay of rhythm, pitch, and volume in African drum music performed by the people for whom statues such as this were made. We have looked at only some of the more salient relationships and interrelationships. We can discover others for ourselves—visual ideas, as we have called them—which build on one another to provide the eye with a wealth of sensations. Only a suggestion of these sensations can be gathered from the photograph of this statue, of course, for in the original freestanding, three-dimensional carving, all these relationships change as we move around it.

For some, the enjoyment of these relationships is not enough to compensate for the lost beauty of the human body as it appears to the eye. "Why," some may ask, "need the human figure be retained here at all? Why not just carve notches and grooves in a piece of wood and dispense with any reference to nature?" Before we find an answer to these questions, let us examine one of the handsomest of Greek statues from the early fifth century B.C., the bronze figure of Zeus (fig. 2) which was discovered in the ocean near Artemision just a few decades ago.

Zeus from Artemision

Even a cursory glance at this statue, which is slightly larger than life, will convince us that the sculptor has succeeded admirably in reproducing the human body as it appears to the eye. It may seem ludicrous, therefore, to suggest that both this statue and the African carving exert their power over us by some of the same means, but this is true. The flowing lines that our eye pursues as we follow this statue's form, though less complicated and much subtler than those in the African statue, lead our eyes along its graceful and subtly varied surface. Instead of the insistent and vehement contrasts of verticals and horizontals we saw in the Mali carving, we have here one major confrontation of vertical and horizontal elements whose impact, however, is softened by innumerable small and gentle changes of direction. The surface of the bronze undulates in sinuous curves that flow smoothly into one another.

Figure 2 | *Zeus,* from Artemision, Greece. c. 470 B.C. Bronze, 6′ 10″ high. National Museum, Athens

As far as their rhythms go, these changes in direction suggest not the percussive thumping of drums, but rather the mellower sound of a bowed instrument such as a violin. Across the rib cage the pectoral muscles relate to each other as repeated and varied volumes, but ever so quietly so as not to interrupt the slow and simple curves of the chest as a unit. The whole, in other words, is more important than its parts. And so, if the Dogon carving communicated visual ideas of tautly compressed energy, everywhere in opposition to itself, the Greek statue speaks to us of fluid movement, of lithe, poised, and unified action.

This subtlety and grace is to be seen in all the statue's aspects. Instead of the rigid frontality of the African figure we have here an asymmetrical pose, but only slightly asymmetrical: one arm is raised higher than the other, one leg is more bent, and the head is turned to one side. Forward movement is implied, but it is not a vehement, uncontrolled motion. It is a restrained pose held in check by a countermovement, a pose that suggests firm purpose but also self-imposed restraint. What better qualities could grace the king of the gods? Firmness and restraint are reflected also in his face, a serene visage whose protruding beard, straight nose, and large eyes sustain the feeling of steadfastness and self-confidence. (Scholars are not agreed as to whether this statue represents Zeus hurling his thunderbolt or Poseidon poising his trident, but in either case it represents a powerful god.)

One of the things which Greek artists searched for and theorized about was a system of perfect proportions for the human figure, that is, a relationship between the various parts of the body that is more beautiful than any other. Whether or not there exists a set of proportions which is eternally most perfect is a question which philosophers have long debated. Our relativistic age tends to discount such absolute ideals, and the Greeks themselves changed this canon of proportions between the time of Polyclitus in the mid-fifth century B.C. and the era of Praxiteles a century later. What cannot be denied, however, is that in his search the Greek sculptor discovered some arrangements of the human body which are, and have been for many periods in history since then, regarded as particularly pleasing.

The Role of Light in Sculpture

Even more than painting, the art of sculpture is dependent for its effects upon light. A painter paints light and shadow into his picture, after which they never change. On a dark day the picture may appear darker and a tinted light may alter its color scheme, but otherwise the painting is immune to changes of illumination. But a sculptor is concerned with light almost as much as with the wood or bronze he works with, for sculpture in its most basic sense is the arrangements of convex and concave surfaces to form certain patterns of light and shadow. The contrasts between the two may be abrupt and involve sudden changes from one to the other, as in the Mali figure, or subtle and unobtrusive, as in the Zeus.

Nor is the sculptor's light fixed, as is the painter's. He must calculate his effects for a variety of lights. That is, the source of illumination on a statue may change as the sun moves or as artificial illumination changes, and what was lit at one time may be cast in shadow at another. All this the sculptor must consider as he fashions his piece, as well as the fact that the viewer may move around the statue, if it is freestanding, and see it from different angles.

Finally, it is light that gives character to the material—the bronze, wood, marble, or terracotta—of which the statue is made. Accordingly, the artist may polish his statue or leave it rough depending on the effect he wishes to produce. He may contrast indented parts with protruding parts which cast considerable shadow, or he may use broader, smoother surfaces which move gently from lighted areas to darker ones. It is this latter mode that the unknown sculptor of the Zeus employed. He could have achieved some strong contrasts of light and dark if he had wanted them, simply by making the muscles bulge more or by giving his statue a robe with deep folds in it such as appear in many other Greek statues or in the sculpture of Michelangelo (see fig. 43). That he did not do so must mean that gentle contrast is what he wanted. Compared to the African statue, the Zeus has only a few concavities and those are very shallow. Most of the figure consists of convex surfaces that stress its mass and volume, and therefore emphasize the very physical, corporeal aspect of the god. Hard bronze has thus been transformed into what seems like warm, soft flesh, an illusion which is heightened by the artist's thorough knowledge of human anatomy.

What few concavities there are in the Zeus statue are subsidiary to the general convexity, everywhere except around the neck and under the beard where the concavity is deep and pronounced. Here the artist has learned a lesson from nature, who thus set off the human head and made it the physiological and esthetic focus of the human body. Certainly the deep shadow cast by the strongly projecting beard serves to dramatize the separation between the rather simple body and the highly elaborated head. In this respect both the classic Greek and the African sculptor—who lived twenty-three centuries apart—made the most of nature's example.

Today both statues stand in museums, but we must not forget that neither work was regarded merely as a work of art by its maker, but as a useful and necessary object in its community. The Zeus was a votive statue erected to honor that god and enlist his aid in furthering the prosperity and happiness of his worshippers. The ancestral statue functioned even more intricately in the religion of its makers. It was not intended to be a representation of a woman but a residing place of her spirit. After death, it was believed, the spirit of the deceased wandered among the living and had the power to work evil or good upon them. It was imperative, therefore, for the members of a tribe to pacify that spirit and to persuade it to use its power for the benefit of the tribe. It was not a portrait of the dead ancestor, therefore, but rather a physical representation of her power; and its particular form—the arrangement of its volumes and patterns—had been arrived at over the years because those particular proportions and relationships had proved successful in harnessing supernatural power in the past.

Thus the general form of such a statue is traditional with a certain tribe, but within that tradition each artist used his creative imagination and manual skill to achieve a certain amount of individuality for his version of the accepted prototype. The actual use of the statue involved rituals and ceremonies supervised by the tribal priests or shamans. Sometimes the statues were adorned with extraneous materials, oil or color, strings of beads, animal teeth, or sea shells, all of which had magic significance; and the statue was often addressed as though the spirit were actually present in it.

The Materials and Techniques of Sculpture

If the philosophy of a people—their *Weltanschauung* or philosophy of life—plays the major role in determining what the art of that people will look like, there are also many other factors of lesser importance. Among these are the material out of which the art object is made, although, of course, the artist usually chooses that material which will best permit him to express the qualities he desires. However, there are certain effects which one material can produce, other effects which it is incapable of producing, and still other effects which are possible but not characteristic of that material. A statue carved in stone has a definite carved look by virtue of the fact that it is cut into by a chisel propelled by a mallet. It takes considerable pains on the part of the artist to disguise this chiseled look, although this is sometimes done. A statue carved in wood has still another kind of carved look, for wood has more strongly directional grain than stone. It is easiest, therefore, to cut wood either with the grain or against the grain. It takes great effort and extra care to carve curved or diagonal surfaces in wood without splitting the material. The predominantly horizontal and vertical arrangement of the volumes in the African statue lends it a direct, simplified, primitive character which adds considerably to its impact on the beholder. In other parts of Africa, the Ivory Coast, for example, sculpture is more curvilinear and imparts a very different, more elegant and sophisticated effect than that produced by this figure. The act of carving wood affects also the scheme of ornament of the Sudanese statue, hence the prevalence of straight grooves in parallel arrangement and in a variety of crisscross patterns. The straight cuts here augment the uncompromising ruggedness of this statue, and the rough marks of the knife add to the feeling of rude power which the statue exudes.

In making a bronze statue such as the *Zeus from Artemision,* a sculptor generally works in clay, which is soft and malleable as long as it is kept moist. Unlike carved wood or stone, which is always subtracted from the block by the sculptor's chisel, clay is generally built up bit by bit so that the volumes of a modeled statue grow and expand until, when the sculptor stops work, the statue has reached its maximum bulk. Unless the artist purposely obliterates this characteristic, a modeled statue will always retain this character of having expanded outward from within, whereas the surface of a carved statue will normally retain the quality of having been cut into and uncovered from the outside inward. The verb "to model," when used in connection with art, has three distinct meanings, the best known of which signifies the act of posing for an artist or a photographer. In the art of sculpture, to model means to fashion out of some soft substance such as clay or wax, as opposed to carving or using such modern processes as welding. Finally, in the art of painting, to model is to arrange light and dark tones of colors in such a way as to imitate effects of light and shadow and thereby to suggest mass, volume, and consequently the third dimension on a flat, two-dimensional surface. It is interesting to note that, despite their apparent difference, the meanings of the word "modeling" in connection with pictorial and sculptural techniques do have something in common, for as the painter uses his color to suggest light and shadow, so the sculptor shapes his clay, indenting it here, letting it bulge, curve, or project from the surface there, in order to produce the arrangements of light and shadow discussed above.

When the clay statue is finished, plaster is poured around it which, when it dries, makes a mold of the statue. This mold must be made to come apart in numerous pieces so that the statue may be extricated from it without damage. The mold is then reassembled and bronze poured into it to duplicate exactly the clay original. In the interest of saving metal and making the final statue lighter, systems were developed for making the statue only a thin shell instead of a solid chunk of bronze. One way of doing this was to coat the interior surface of the mold with a layer of wax, then to fill the mold with clay or some other material that might later be removed. When this whole complex was heated, the wax could be made to run out, leaving a narrow space between the mold on the outside and the core on the inside. This space was then filled with molten bronze which, when cooled, took the exact shape of the original clay statue and which, when the core was removed, was hollow inside. This process of casting bronze statues, called the *cire perdue* or "lost wax" method, has been used in the West ever since the Renaissance and was probably used by the ancients as well.

Roman Copies

Whenever we think of Greek sculpture we visualize snow-white marble statues. Actually, the ancient Greeks worked frequently in bronze, but the fact that this metal is valuable and reusable has sadly reduced the number of ancient bronzes that have come down to us. Only a few which were buried and thus protected from scavengers had been recovered until recently, when improved methods in deep-sea diving led to the discovery of many ancient bronzes which were lost at sea when the ships that carried them from the foundry to their destinations were sunk for one reason or another. Our misconception about the frequency with which marble was used is aggravated by the fact that most of the statues in museums which we call Greek are actually Roman copies of Greek statues. The *Apollo Belvedere,* the *Borghese Warrior,* the *Dying Gaul,* the *Spearbearer,* and almost all the Venuses except the *Venus de Milo* are Roman copies of Greek originals, most of which were originally made in bronze. The *Discus Thrower* gives us a particularly unreliable idea as to what Greek sculpture was like, because, although we have five Roman copies of this famous ancient statue, none of them has a head, hands, or feet. The versions we see most often have been restored by different sculptors. This accounts for the fact that the head looks down in one version and back toward the discus in another.

Why, we might ask, did the Romans have these statues copied in marble instead of bronze? The answer lies in the fact that in Roman times manual labor, even a skilled artist's, was cheaper than the complicated technological process of casting bronze. And of the few bronze casts which the Romans did have made, the majority have disappeared for the same reason as have the Greek originals. Quite naturally, the Roman copies are inferior to the originals, partly because the copyists were not as talented as the original artists and partly because no imitation can be as fresh and inspired as an original creation. One fairly dependable way of knowing that a marble statue derives from a bronze original is the presence of a tree trunk which gives to the brittle stone statue an added support which the bronze original did not need.

Brief mention must here be made of the justly famous sculpture from the Parthenon and many statues from other temples which are original Greek work but which are often in a sadly weatherworn condition. For these various reasons we have selected for this discussion a statue which, though by an unknown sculptor, is today very close to its original appearance; not quite, though, and here we come to another misconception which has come down to us, and one which has affected the character of sculpture in the West for centuries. Most statues in ancient Greece were painted in natural colors. That is, eyes, face, hair, and costume were touched with paint, a fact which was not known to the sculptors of the Renaissance who thought they were reviving and carrying on the great art of the ancients. Nor was it known to the thousands of sculptors of the Neoclassical persuasion who in the eighteenth and nineteenth centuries decorated our parks, public squares, government buildings, public libraries, schools, and museums in Europe and America.

In the *Zeus from Artemision,* as in most Greek original bronzes, the eyes are open holes which were once filled with stone or mother-of-pearl for the white of the eye and some dark substance for the iris. Beyond any doubt, the chief object of the Greek artist was to give the spectator the illusion of seeing the god striding majestically forward, about to hurl his thunderbolt at some adversary in the climactic moment of some venerable myth. Yet when we apply the word *realistic* to this statue we must remember that the word *realism* is a very relative term. Compared to the Dogon statue we should call the Zeus realistic, but compared to most sculpture from the Hellenistic era, the late fourth and the third centuries, and alongside most Roman statuary, the Zeus would appear highly idealized. The sculptor of the Zeus, like all sculptors of the fifth century, B.C., selected those features of the human form which he felt were most perfect. Not only in the proportions of the body, but in the posture of the god and in the expression of his face, the artist concentrated on what was general, significant, and timeless, and suppressed all that was particular, trivial, and evanescent. It is for this reason that we feel we are looking at a perfect type rather than a specific individual.

Later sculptors reversed this situation, delighting in poses that imply change and display rippling muscles, smiling or grimacing faces, such imperfections as fatty flesh and wrinkles, and such irregularities as big noses or heavy jowls. They tended to depict individuals rather than types, and thus the art of real portraiture began only after the end of the Golden Age and the beginning of the Hellenistic era.

The *Zeus from Artemision* belongs actually to a period that has been called the Transitional or Early Classic period, an era that lies between the Archaic period, when the human figure was still stylized, stiff and without animation, and the Classic or Golden Age, when sculptors combined fidelity to natural appearance with the dignity and the restraint which is the hallmark of classicism.

Nonetheless, the very fact that the fifth-century Greek represented his gods as believable and tangible human beings is quite remarkable. Many peoples in history forbade the representation of divine personages entirely, for example, the Jews, the Moslems, and for 600 years, up to the second century A.D., the Buddhists. Even in the Christian faith at various periods—and among certain sects still today—no representation of holy personages is allowed. If these attitudes show an antiphysical, otherworldly attitude toward divinity, the Greeks' was just the opposite. There was no sharp cleavage between the spiritual life and the physical. Not only prayer and burnt offerings, but athletic events and competitions of playwriting and acting were part of the Greeks' religious rites. The gods, as a matter of fact, were thought of as human beings with more power than those on earth. Otherwise they had the same desires and passions as human beings, and the same weaknesses, as the stories about their jealousies, their infidelities, and their lapses into downright treachery make abundantly clear.

We can answer now the question that began this discussion: What is the virtue of taking the human figure, a thing of considerable beauty in itself, and transforming it into a piece of wood carved with notches and grooves? The answer is that if art is not merely the imitation of nature but an interpretation of it (nature seen through a temperament), both the ancient Greek bronze and the nineteenth-century African carving are interpretations of the human figure. Neither is an absolute copy of the human body. One stresses the human aspect of man. The other relates the human form to a more primal image that suggests natural forms, tree trunks and rock formations, skeletons and cocoons, grasshoppers, seashells, and armorplated crustaceans. It seems to say: Man is not merely a flesh-covered vertebrate skeleton with blood and glandular secretions flowing through it. Man is part of a vast and mysterious universe, and within the human body which can be so graceful and so noble, there is another aspect of man, unknown and uncharted, full of strange forces and conflicts, unfathomed thoughts and uncivilized urges. Are we to depict merely external appearances and ignore all this?

Both statues are meaningful images of man. Each expresses its concept in the organization of three-dimensional volumes and some reference to natural forms. The one, a hollow shell of bronze fashioned into flowing lines and subtly interpenetrating surfaces, exemplifies the classic ideal of rationalism, restraint, and harmony. The other, a chopped and grooved piece of wood, provides our eye with an intriguing visual adventure and projects with remarkable vigor the more mysterious, aggressive, and strangely disturbing aspects of man.

Projects

1. Find an example of African sculpture from the Ivory Coast, preferably a human figure rather than a mask or animal carving. How is the effect it produces on you different from that of the Dogon statue? To what can you attribute this difference? Find words to describe its rhythmic pattern, the character of its ornament, and the interrelation of its various parts. Then try to relate these characteristics of its physical form to the effect it produces on you.
2. Compare the Zeus statue with a standing figure from the Archaic period and one from the Hellenistic era of Greek sculpture. How did the artist treat his marble or bronze in each case with regard to light and shadow? Can you describe the effect produced on you by these differences in treatment?
3. Look at other examples of primitive art such as Indian carvings from Alaska and the northwest coast of North America or sculpture from New Guinea and other Pacific islands. Can you describe some of the features that make for the great differences of style?
4. Select a freestanding statue from ancient Egypt. Enumerate some of the characteristics of its style and compare these with those of the Mali figure and the Zeus. Can you relate these characteristics to the principal religious beliefs of the ancient Egyptians?

Suggested Reading

Boardman, John. *Greek Art.* New York: Frederick A. Praeger, Inc., 1964.

Carpenter, Rhys. *Greek Sculpture.* Chicago: The University of Chicago Press, 1960.

Charbonneaux, Jean. *Greek Bronzes,* trans. Katherine Watson. New York: Viking Press, Inc., 1962.

Christensen, Erwin O. *Primitive Art.* New York: Thomas Y. Crowell Co., 1955.

Elisofon, Eliot. *The Sculpture of Africa.* New York: Frederick A. Praeger, Inc., 1958.

Fagg, William, and Margaret Plass. *African Sculpture.* *New York: E. P. Dutton & Co., 1964.

Heyden, A. A. M. van der, and H. H. Scullard. *Atlas of the Classical World.* Camden, New Jersey: Thomas Nelson & Sons, 1959.

Lamb, Winifred. *Ancient Greek and Roman Bronzes.* Chicago: Argonaut, Inc., 1966.

Lange, Kurt, and Max Hirmer. *Egypt.* New York: Phaidon Art Books, 1956.

Leuzinger, Elsy. *Africa: The Art of the Negro People.* New York: McGraw-Hill Book Co., 1960.

Linton, Ralph, and Paul S. Wingert. *The Arts of the South Seas.* New York: Museum of Modern Art, 1946.

Lommel, Andreas. *Prehistoric and Primitive Man.* Landmarks of Art Series. New York: McGraw-Hill Book Co., 1966.

Lullies, Reinhard. *Greek Sculpture.* New York: Harry N. Abrams, Inc., 1957.

New York Museum of Primitive Art. *Sculpture from Africa.** Greenwich, Connecticut: New York Graphic Society, Ltd., 1962.

New York Museum of Primitive Art. *Sculpture from Three African Tribes.** Greenwich, Conn.: New York Graphic Society, Ltd., 1959.

Richter, G. M. A. *Sculpture and Sculptors of the Greeks.* New Haven, Connecticut: Yale University Press, 1950.

Segy, Ladislas. *African Sculpture.** New York: Dover Publications, Inc., 1958.

Smith, William S. *The Art and Architecture of Ancient Egypt.* Baltimore: Penguin Books, Inc., 1958.

Strong, Donald E. *The Classical World.* Landmarks of Art Series. New York: McGraw-Hill Book Co., 1965.

Consult also the general bibliography at the end of this book for the titles of art histories, encyclopedias of art, and books of a general nature which are useful in connection with more than one chapter of this book.

*Available in a paperback edition.

2 | Socrates in Stone
The Parthenon

After the Holy Bible the most powerful force that has shaped Western civilization is the culture of ancient Greece. The reason for this influence is partly circumstantial in that Greek culture was adopted by the Romans who disseminated it in their conquest of the world; and it is partly intrinsic in that of all ancient peoples the Greeks were most humane in the basic sense of that word. "Man is the measure of all things"; in this short sentence Protagoras summed up the Greek ideal, which we recognize as ours today. In their philosophy, in their government, in everything they did and thought, the integrity of the human being was central. Socrates' unflagging search for truth, for self-knowledge, and for action governed by reason is still the ideal of our civilization today.

But granted that the philosophy of a people can be expressed in their sculpture and in their painting, can we also say that so abstract an art as architecture can reflect the ideals and mentality of a people? Can the motto "Know thyself," which was inscribed on a stone in the sacred precincts of Apollo at Delphi, be translated into a stone column or a wooden beam? The answer is easy if we think retrospectively. We have the philosophy of the Greeks as written down by their poets, dramatists, and philosophers; and we know their architecture from fairly well-preserved ruins; it is easy to look at each and predicate the spiritual kinship of the two. But let us try it *a posteriori;* let us pretend that we know nothing about the builders of the Parthenon except the Parthenon. What sort of people can we make them out to have been?

Compare the photograph of the Parthenon (fig. 5) with the exterior of any other building in this book (figs. 12, 14, 15, or 37). The briefest glance will tell us that the Parthenon is a simpler building—basically a rectangular box surmounted by a triangular prism. The simplicity of the structure evokes in us a feeling of repose (certainly a lack of turmoil), clarity (one feels that the back of the building is just like the front, one of the sides just like the other), and logic (what can be more logical than rows of vertical columns holding up a horizontal roof?). Simplicity, clarity, and logic—if there is any way of translating them into stone—are certainly expressed by this building. It is as close as any architecture can get to what we call the classic spirit, a spirit to which Western civilization returned again and again in its history, a spirit whose absolute antithesis is expressed by the Gothic cathedral (fig. 37) with its exaggerated verticality, its obsessive desire to reach into the sky, and the profusion and confusion of its sculptured decoration. As we begin to examine the Parthenon section by section, can we say that chiseled stone is able to express the spirit of the ancient Greeks?

The Greek temple was not really a building as we understand it—an enclosed space meant to be used by a group of people. It was more a sculptured shrine that sheltered the statue of a god or goddess. Unlike the Christian church, it needed no large interior to accommodate a congregation or subsidiary spaces for altars, chapels, baptisteries, vestries, and so on. A single rectangular room sufficed, with a large door for entrance and illumination at one end, and at the other, the cult statue. In some temples—the Parthenon, for instance—there was a smaller room whose purpose was probably to house precious ceremonial objects, but these two rooms were not connected. They stood back to back, each with its own entrance, an arrangement that contributed greatly to the symmetry and clarity of the temple. (See plan in fig. 7.)

The Greek Orders

In his architecture the ancient Greek solved his problems in the simplest and most direct fashion. He let the box shape of the inner room or rooms, the cella, dominate its design and repeated the rectangularity by surrounding the cella with a continuous line of columns called the peristyle. The vertical accents of these repeated columns (colonnades) against the horizontals of the roof line and the three-stepped platform emphasize the rectangularity of the whole. Covering the entire structure was a gently sloping triangular or gabled roof.

The Greeks evolved three systems of architectural design, which we call the classical orders. The Doric order, the simplest and the most used, was developed on the Greek mainland and in the colonies in Sicily and southern Italy. The Ionic, whose hallmark is the scroll-shaped capital, was a favorite in the Aegean Islands and Asia Minor (now western Turkey). Most elaborate of all was the Corinthian order, whose leaf-covered, basket-shaped capital became a favorite in Hellenistic and Roman times.

The difference between these orders involves more than the capitals of their columns, however. The three orders differ in proportion, in the relationship of the various parts, and even in the choice and size of carved

Figure 3 I Doric, Ionic, and Corinthian Fluting

detail such as moldings and cornices. The final result is a different spirit in each of the three orders. The simple Doric connotes strength and stability; the more slender Ionic, grace and elegance; and the florid Corinthian, opulence and pomp.

The Ionic column is slenderer than the Doric (its height is nine times its lower diameter instead of seven times as in the Doric); and it rests on a base that adds to the impression of height. The flutes or grooves in the shaft of the Ionic and Corinthian column are deeper, more semicircular than Doric flutes, and the ridges between the flutes are flat. The result is that when sunlight strikes these columns the contrast between the shaded flutes and the brightly-lit ridges is sharper than in the Doric column where the flutes are only arcs of circles and the spaces in-between pointed ridges (see fig. 3). The Ionic and the Corinthian columns seem even taller because each of them has more flutes, usually twenty-four, whereas the Doric generally has twenty.

Since the three classical orders continued to be used in Europe and America right down to the present, let us examine their various parts (see fig. 4). The classical column consists of a shaft which may or may not sit on a base and which is crowned by a capital. Above rests the entablature, a section made of three elements: the architrave which lies like a beam across the columns; the frieze which is usually decorated; and the cornice which is a projecting and often richly carved molding. The triangular area which is formed by the gabled roof in the front and back of the temple is called the pediment. In the Doric order, which most concerns us here, the column stands directly on the floor without a base. Its capital consists of two major elements, a bowl-shaped part and a flat block. The Doric entablature is made of the architrave (a broad undecorated area), the frieze which consists of triglyphs (vertical rectangles of stone marked with vertical grooves) and metopes (square stone slabs decorated with sculptured reliefs), and the projecting and decorated cornice.

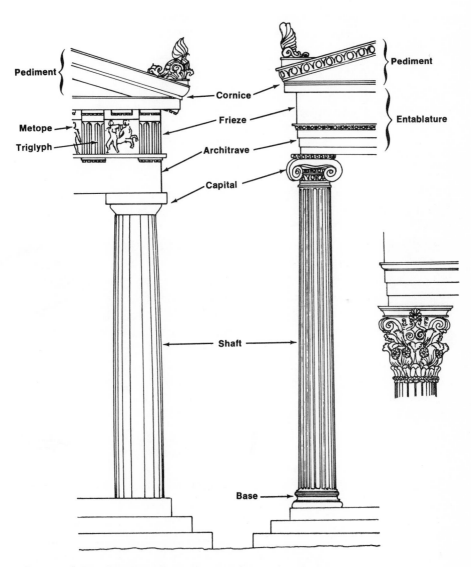

Figure 4 | The Greek Doric, Ionic, and Corinthian Orders

The Parthenon: Exterior

A more spectacular site for a temple could hardly be imagined than the abrupt table of rock that rises dramatically above the skyline of Athens. This is the Acropolis, in early times a fortified citadel and later the city of the gods. A winding path and steps cut into the rock lead upward to the Propylaea, the gateway to the sacred precincts. Above us on the right as we mount the steps stands the tiny Ionic temple of the Wingless Victory (Nike Apteros). From the platform on which it stands one can look over hills full of other temples and shrines to the sparkling Mediterranean on the eastern horizon. From the northern side of the rocky plateau we look down on the ruins of the agora, once the commercial center of Athens. On this northern side of the Acropolis stands the Ionic temple we call the Erechtheum with its famous Porch of the Maidens whose entablature rests on the heads of six graceful female statues.

Across from the Erechtheum, on the highest level of the Acropolis, stands the Parthenon, the largest of the buildings here and the most famous of the Greek temples. As we approach it today, ruined as it is, we are struck first by its simplicity of line, basically a rectangular building with a gently sloping A-roof. As the sun strikes its fluted columns, its projecting cornices, and its other carved surfaces, casting shadows of various degrees of darkness, we realize that this building was conceived sculpturally, as a three-dimensional composition of masses and voids. If we had seen it when it still had its roof and the solid walls of the cella, we would have been struck by the alternating rhythm of the solid columns, the empty spaces between and around them, and the deep shade of the ambulatory or walkway between the columns and the cella walls. There were no windows to complicate this relationship. One door in front and one in back marked the cardinal points of the building's orientation. The columns of its peristyle are about thirty-four feet high, the entablature above them eleven feet high, and at the front and rear of the temple the triangular pediments rise an additional fifteen feet. These pediments were once filled with statues which at the east end depicted the birth of Athena and on the western end represented the contest between Athena and Poseidon for possession of Attica, the region of Athens and environs.

The Doric frieze, as we have noted, consisted of alternating triglyphs and sculptured metopes. In the Parthenon the metopes represented scenes

Figure 5 | ICTINUS AND CALLICRATES. The Parthenon, view from the west. 447–432 B.C. Acropolis, Athens. Marble, 228′ long, 101′ wide, 58 ½′ high above platform. Sculpture by Phidias

of struggle: contests between gods and giants, Greeks and Amazons, Centaurs and Lapiths (legendary Stone Age people), and episodes from the Trojan War. All this sculpture was carved by or executed under the direction of Phidias, the greatest of the Greek sculptors. We must not forget that all of this sculpture, though carved in fine marble, was painted to resemble nature and that other decorative parts of the building were brightly colored with red, blue, green, black, and gold paint. The severity of the roofline was broken by carved marble ornaments of plant and animal forms at the apex and sides of the pediment.

The Parthenon: Interior

The platform upon which the Parthenon sits consists of three steps, each of which is one foot four inches high and over two feet wide, too large to be climbed comfortably. Normal sized stairs were provided immediately before the front and back doors. Mounting these steps we come to the peristyle or continuous colonnade that surrounds the temple and forms an ambulatory nine feet wide on the sides and eleven feet wide front and back (see fig. 6). Inside the peristyle, at both front and back, a range of six columns forms a porch or portico. From inside this porch we could in ancient times have looked through the front door into the temple's gloomy interior; for there was no illumination other than the daylight that came

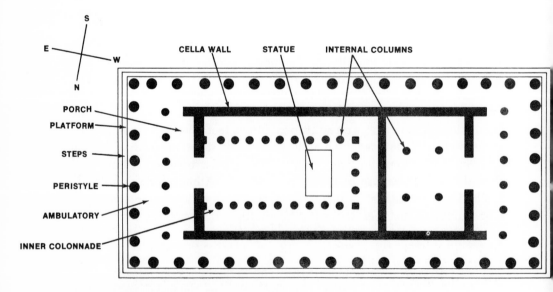

Figure 6 | Plan of the Parthenon

Figure 7 | The Parthenon, reconstruction of the interior

through the large doors (13¾ feet wide and 32 feet high) and the dim glow of candles or oil lamps. In the easternmost of the two rooms a gigantic statue of Athena Parthenos (Athena the Virgin), one of Phidias' most famous works, rose forty feet into the air. The goddess was represented standing, armed with spear, helmet, shield, and aegis (a magic breastplate decorated with snakes), and holding a winged statue of Victory in her right hand. Her face, hands, and feet were made of ivory; her eyes were inlaid with precious stones; and her drapery, armor, and accessories were carved in wood but overlaid with plates of gold which could be removed in times of danger. We know this only from the descriptions of ancient writers, for the statue with all its precious materials disappeared in ancient times. We wonder how many other statues in ancient Greece, less famous than the Athena Parthenos, were made of such varied materials.

The ceiling above Athena's head was undoubtedly made of wood, its beams resting on the top of the cella walls and the two rows of Doric columns inside this room. Today nothing remains of the roof, ceiling, beams, or columns. Marks on the floor, however, show that these inner columns ran down the sides of the room (forming a navelike central space and two side aisles) and across the rear of the room in back of the statue. These columns were actually two levels of columns, the first supporting a gallery, a kind of balcony, and the second level supporting the beams. No doubt there were more statues as well as trophies and other furniture in the room.

The room at the west end of the Parthenon was used as a treasury or storeroom for objects of value used in the cult's ritual. Only about half as large as the shrine room, it had four single Ionic columns to hold up its ceiling. It is quite obvious from this description that more care was given to the exterior than the interior of the temple. Even if we recall that the Greek temple was not a church as we know it but a shrine that housed a cult statue, and that religious rites in Greece were performed out of doors—in the theaters, on the athletic fields, and at outdoor altars—we must still admit that the interior of the Parthenon must have been dark and unimpressive, cavernous, and cluttered spatially. The gigantic statue, the top of whose helmet nearly touched the ceiling, must have dwarfed the colonnades. We can only surmise that the rigidity of religious traditions prevented the architects Ictinus and Callicrates and the sculptor Phidias from exercising the same sensitivity on the interior that they displayed on the outside of the building.

Indicative of the Greeks' sensitivity to esthetic effects is the fact that only the nonstructural members of the building—cornices, friezes, and sculptured decoration—were painted. Structural elements like the columns and the architrave were left in the color of the stone, a rich, cream-colored marble (which has turned reddish tan because of oxidation through the ages). There were also various vegetal decorations on the roof carved in marble: three large nine-foot ones over the gable and over the ends of the triangular pediments in addition to smaller ones all along the roof at the sides. There was one other place where sculpture decorated the Parthenon. This was a continuous frieze (a frieze in the broadest sense is a horizontal band of decoration) at the top of the cella wall in the ambulatory. About 3½ feet in height and very shallow in its relief (only about 1½ inches), it represented the procession of townspeople gathering and moving slowly up to Athena's temple on the goddess' birthday. Once 525 feet long, it depicts horses, chariots, men with olive branches (Athena's symbol), musicians, youths, sacrificial animals, magistrates, and finally, the gods, seated and waiting to receive the worshippers. In contrast to the mythological subjects of the other sculpture, this Panathenaic frieze includes a contemporary event and living people. Part of this frieze remains on the temple today. Other sections of it are in the British Museum, the Louvre, and the Athens Museum.

There are three places, therefore, where sculpture adorns the Parthenon: in the pediments, on the metopes, and on the ambulatory frieze. It is significant, in view of what we have said about the Greeks' sensitivity to visual effects, that each of the three is done in a different degree of relief. The pediment figures are actually carved in the round (though conceived to be seen from one side only) and then attached to the pediment wall. The relief of the metopes is high, but parts of the figures merge with the marble slab which forms their "background." Finally, the Panathenaic frieze is, as has been noted, in very shallow relief. The differences are attuned to the illumination that falls on the sculpture and to its prominence on the building. Set in the deep space of the pediment and lit by strong light, the topmost sculpture is the most prominently visible and most concentrated in its site. The metopes, set in the shelter of the crowning cornice, are also dispersed around the four sides of the temple, episodic in effect rather than concentrated and unified. The only light that the ambulatory frieze receives is that which reflects from the floor and cella walls—indirect light—and the subtle surfaces of the shallow relief are calculated to make the most of this pale illumination.

The Parthenon: Construction

The Greek temple, though it is remarkable for the care and sensitivity with which it was built, was not a complicated building in plan and structure. Walls were made of carefully cut stones fitted together without the use of mortar. Instead, each stone was fastened to those below it with iron dowels and to the ones next to it with iron clamps. Holes or grooves were cut into the stones, the dowels or clamps inserted, and molten lead poured around them to seal them tightly. Each course of stone was laid horizontally upon the one below it with meticulous care. The outer faces of the stones were left rough until they were in place. Then the walls were smoothed and rubbed down to a fine polish by slaves.

Columns were generally constructed of ten or twelve superimposed drums. Projecting knobs were left on these drums at the quarry so that they could be handled with slings, ropes, and crowbars. At the building site the flat faces of the drums were cut smooth and a shallow hole sunk at the center of each face. Wooden pegs, inserted into these holes, provided a simple method of centering one drum on another.

After the roughly cut drums had been assembled, the column was cut smooth with allowance for two deviations from a simple cylindrical form. First of all, the column was tapered so that it was wider at the bottom than at the top. Secondly, the apparently straight lines of the column's sides were given a slight outward curvature which we call the entasis of the column. If left straight, the sides of the column would, through an optical illusion, appear slightly concave. A convex silhouette of the shaft served to make the sides of the column look straight. The entasis of columns in early Doric temples is quite noticeable and somewhat unpleasant. In the Parthenon the curvature is subtle, deviating from a straight line by only $^{11}/_{16}$ of an inch in the 34-foot columns. The result is a graceful form whose role in the framework of the building is to make it elastic and organic, more like a living, growing thing than an inert mass of stone.

The problem of carving the final form of such a column must have been considerable. A plumb line—a string with a weight on it—would, of course, define the purely vertical direction, from which the taper of the column and the curvature of the entasis had to be calculated. Undoubtedly some system of templates had to be devised to allow whole teams of stonecutters to shape the column and after the smooth surface was achieved, to carve the twenty shallow flutes into it.

The columns of the peristyle were connected, as has been mentioned, by the stones of the architrave. The top of the architrave, at the level of the frieze, was connected to the cella walls by stone slabs whose undersurface was carved and painted to form an attractive ceiling over the ambulatory. The ceiling which covered the cella and which rested on the two rows of interior columns was made of wood. Between this ceiling and the sloping rafters which held the roof tiles (the Parthenon had marble shingles) was a network of beams and struts about which we are uncertain, since they were made of wood and have long since disappeared.

The Parthenon: Refinements

For centuries men have marveled at the beauty of the Parthenon, attributing its perfection to the existence of a mathematical formula, a module or repeated unit of measure, and any number of reasons. Whatever the secret is, it certainly lies in the fact that the Parthenon incorporates all the finest qualities of earlier Doric temples. Its architects selected all those things which they felt most successful in previous buildings, those proportions and that combination of details which they thought looked most harmonious together.

About one thing there is no doubt: the builders of the Parthenon spared no trouble to achieve these effects. Archeologists who have measured the various parts of the Parthenon, as well as other Greek temples, have found that the architects often departed ever so slightly from absolute geometric forms. It is safe to say, as a matter of fact, that scarcely any of the straight lines in the Parthenon is actually straight. The best known of these refinements is the entasis of the columns just discussed. But if we consider the pediment we will find that its horizontal base—the cornice, that is—is not a straight line but is higher in the middle than at each end. The sides of the triangle are also curved. There seems to be a logical explanation for this: a straight line placed in certain relationships with lines diagonal to it appears to us slightly curved unless "corrected" by being curved in the opposite direction.

Since the cornice curves, the frieze and architrave below it must follow suit, as must the platform upon which the columns sit and the three steps that lead up to it. All of these "horizontals," then, are slightly higher at their centers than at their ends. The question arises as to how the Parthenon's architects got whole teams of stonemasons to cut and lay stones so that the platform at the front of the temple, which measures 101 feet, is $2\frac{3}{8}$ inches higher at the center than at the ends, and the sides, which measure 228 feet, rise $4\frac{1}{4}$ inches. Archeologists believe that the system involved some wooden blocks of graduated size, set at intervals beneath a taut string.

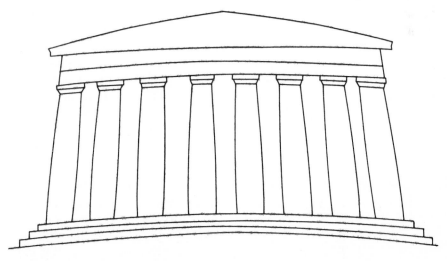

Figure 8 | Schematic drawing of some refinements in the Parthenon

As if it were not difficult enough to set forty-six columns on this sloping platform (only the tops and bottoms were beveled; the joints of the drums are perpendicular to their axes), the columns themselves are not strictly vertical. All the columns of the Parthenon slant inward about $2^1/_2$ inches. That is, the columns in the front lean toward those in the back and those on the north lean toward those on the south, except for the corner columns. They, of course, lean diagonally so that if they were projected into the air, they would meet at a point a mile or so above the earth. The walls of the cella also lean inward and certain other elements, the entablatures, for example, incline outward.

Some of these refinements are difficult to see. Indeed, their whole purpose is to be unnoticeable when one looks at the building from normal angles. But if one sights along the edge of the steps, for example, one can easily see their curvature. One of the refinements that is quite apparent to the naked eye, though one is not aware of it until it is pointed out, is that the columns that surround the Parthenon are not equidistant from each other; each corner column is over two feet closer to its neighbor than are the other columns. Each is also greater in diameter than the rest. The theory behind this deviation is that the corner columns are seen against the sky, and therefore would seem thinner and farther apart were these dimensions not corrected.

Another such deviation that is quite apparent when it is pointed out is the spacing of the triglyphs and metopes in the frieze. It is believed that the triglyph originated as the end of a wooden beam in days before temples were built of stone, and that metopes were originally the spaces between the beams which were filled up with decorated plaques to keep the weather out. At any rate, in stone Doric temples, one triglyph appears above each column and another halfway in-between. If this system were rigorously followed to the corners there would be half a metope left over. Since the corner in all architecture is a crucial point both structurally and esthetically, the Greek architect felt it much more satisfying to move all the triglyphs except the central ones over very slightly at an accelerated rate so that the corner of the building would end with a strong accent, a triglyph.

The Parthenon was used for many centuries after the decline of Athens. Restored and redecorated by the Romans, it was transformed into a Byzantine church, a Catholic cathedral, and, after the Moslem conquest, a mosque. It was still in good condition in 1687, when it was used as a powder magazine by the Turks in a war against the Venetians. A direct hit by a Venetian cannon resulted in an explosion that blew out the center of the cella wall and fourteen columns on the north side. The latter have since been reassembled, but much of the marble from all parts of the temple, especially the stones of the cella wall, was carried away later for other building projects.

Between 1803 and 1812 the British envoy to Constantinople, Lord Elgin, got the permission of the Turkish government, which then ruled Greece, to remove the sculpture from the Parthenon and other temples and ship them to London. Now known as the Elgin Marbles, they have influenced the course of Western art ever since.

Projects

1. Find four examples of ancient Egyptian post and lintel construction. What differences and what similarities do you find between these and the Greek orders with respect to (1) general form, (2) proportions, and (3) a sense of logic in decoration?
2. What relationship can you establish between the architecture of the Greeks and that of the ancient Babylonians, Persians, and Minoans? Cite specific examples and give the dates of each.
3. Compare the Parthenon with one of the Doric temples from southern Italy, for example, one of the temples at Paestum. Can you see any evidence of "refinements"? How do the proportions and the refinement of the details compare?
4. Look for columns, entablatures, and pediments in the architecture around you. In what ways are they different from the Greek in their function and in their forms?

Suggested Reading

Berve, Helmut, and Gottfried Gruben. *Greek Temples, Theaters and Shrines.* New York: Harry N. Abrams, Inc., 1963.
Boardman, John et al. *Greek Art and Architecture.* New York: Harry N. Abrams, Inc., 1967.
Dinsmoor, William B. *The Architecture of Ancient Greece.* London: B. T. Batsford, Ltd., 1950.
Lawrence, Arnold W. *Greek Architecture.* Baltimore: Penguin Books, Inc., 1957.
Robertson, Donald S. *Handbook of Greek and Roman Architecture.* *New York: Cambridge University Press, 1943.
Scranton, Robert L. *Greek Architecture.* *New York: George Braziller, Inc., 1962.

*Available in a paperback edition.

3 | The Conqueror Builds
The Pont du Gard and the Colosseum

We must not get the impression that the Greeks built nothing but temples. They lived in houses, shopped in markets, and stored things in warehouses just as we do. Their rulers lived in palaces and wealthy people had town houses, country estates, and seaside villas. But the very fact that only their temples have come down to us in a fair state of preservation proves that the Greeks thought so much of their religious shrines that they built them of permanent materials and lavished on them their highest artistic abilities. The Romans on the other hand were satisfied in their temples with mere adaptations of Greek and Etruscan prototypes. It was a more worldly and utilitarian kind of architecture that challenged their most creative powers—theaters and amphitheaters, forums (large complexes of civic buildings), spacious public baths, palaces, apartment houses, private villas, roads, bridges, aqueducts, and sewers (if we may call these architecture). Many of these involved sophisticated engineering, and Roman architects devised a host of new building devices, techniques, and systems to realize these vast projects. The most important of these devices, which was not invented by the Romans but was first used by them to the fullest of its potential, is the arch.

The Semicircular Arch

As the Romans used it, the arch was a semicircle made up of trapezoidal or wedge-shaped stones (fig. 9). During construction the arch had to be supported by a wooden structure called the centering until the topmost stone, the keystone, as we call it, was in place. Then the centering could be removed and used for the next arch. Sometimes a small projection called an impost was allowed to protrude on the inner surface of the arch, just where the surface begins to curve, a shelf upon which the centering could rest. Generally mortar was used between the stones, although the

Romans also built arches whose stability was insured simply by the forces at work within the arch: the downward pull of gravity caused the wedge-shaped stones to press against one another. Part of the downward pull of gravity was therefore transformed into a sideward pressure called thrust. As long as the sides of the arch were held in, the arch could support great weights and make possible buildings several stories high, structures which would be impossible in a post and lintel construction. The weight-bearing ability of the arch is limited only by (1) the compressive strength of the stone and (2) the absorption of the thrust on each side.

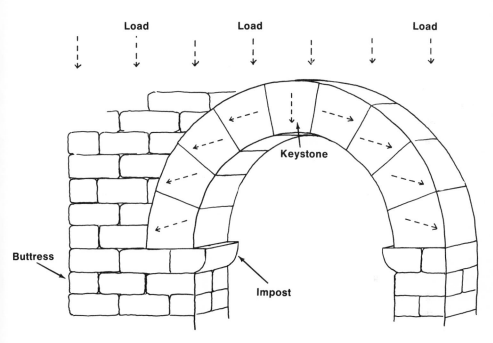

Figure 9| The dynamics of the semicircular arch

There are two ways in which this thrust may be absorbed. A thick section of masonry may serve as a buttress, or another arch of the same size and weight may be used to neutralize the thrust. Long series of arches, called arcades, were frequently used, but eventually, at the end of such an arcade, a solid buttress was required. The chief advantage of the arch over the post and lintel lies in the fact that stone has great compressive strength but a low degree of tensile strength. At its center a lintel is subject to both compressive forces on its upper surface and tensile forces on its lower surface (fig. 10). That is, if too much weight is put on a lintel it tends to push together at the top and pull apart at the bottom until the stone cracks under the strain. The same thing will happen if a stone lintel is made to span too great a distance between vertical supports.

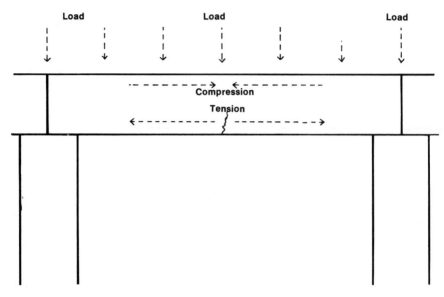

Figure 10   The dynamics of the post and lintel

The arch has several other advantages over the post and lintel besides its greater weight-bearing capacity. Whereas the lintel, if not the posts, must be quarried in one piece, transported and set up with great effort and manpower, arches may be assembled on the spot with stones or bricks small enough to be handled and hoisted into place by one or two men. But more significant for the development of architecture is the fact that a lintel can stretch only so far between two posts, depending on the quality of the stone and the weight it has to bear. A large space could never be spanned in ancient Egypt, Mesopotamia, Persia, or Greece without interrupting the unity of that space with a forest of columns. We can hardly imagine a bridge across a deep river built of posts and lintels! An arch, on the other hand, can span anything from a few feet to a hundred or more feet in width, as long as it is solidly buttressed. The Romans soon realized this great potential and used the principle of the arch to cover vast spaces that were unbroken by vertical interruption. In doing so they began a new era in architecture, one that dominated building until steel was introduced into architecture in modern times.

The Pont du Gard

To judge from the trouble the Romans took to obtain clear mountain water, this commodity must have been very important to them. To conduct this water from its source to the city required numerous aqueducts—covered troughs which ran along mostly at ground level, sometimes underground, and sometimes, as rarely as possible of course, up in the air, supported on a bridge-like construction of arches. The reason that the water had to be kept at a constant level is that, unlike water in pipes, water in a trough cannot run uphill, and in Roman times it was more economical to build these elevated portions of the aqueducts than to manufacture and service pipes made of metal or terra-cotta, although such pipes were used in the plumbing systems of public baths and the private homes of the wealthy. At one time Rome was supplied with thirteen aqueducts totalling nearly 300 miles. But only about thirty of these miles were above the ground. The ruins of many aqueducts may still be seen, not only on the outskirts of the modern city of Rome but in many parts of Europe and North Africa that were once a part of the Roman Empire.

The most spectacular of these suspended portions of an aqueduct is the so-called Pont du Gard just outside of Nîmes, one of ancient Rome's most important cities in southern France. There, over a little stream which becomes a raging torrent every spring, the trough runs 161 feet above the river's bed. This trough, which is big enough for an average person to walk through without bumping his head, rests on three levels of arches. The arches of the first two levels increase in size from fifty to eighty feet in diameter as they approach the center. The central arch is larger so as to facilitate the river's flow. These arches rest exactly on top of each other, their weight transmitted directly to the ground, their thrust passed from one to the other and absorbed finally by the hills which parallel the river. The top level of arches are only fourteen feet in diameter, probably to give a more continuous support to the long trough which measures 902 feet from hill to hill. As might be expected, the lowest of the arches are thicker or deeper than the rest to make the structure as stable as possible. What is not expected, and hardly believable, is that the arches were assembled without mortar! That is, the individual stones were cut so carefully that their own weight and thrust has held them in place for nearly twenty centuries (although some restoration has been necessary in modern times). The road which crosses the river at the level of the lowest arches is not ancient but was built in the eighteenth century.

Roman ingenuity in cutting construction costs is evident in the unusual way the arches were built up. Each of the arches of the first two levels was constructed in layers like plywood. That is, each of the arches that span the river, for example, is really four arches that touch each other face to face. Such a method meant that a narrow section of centering could be used to build one arch and then be moved over for each additional layer of the arch. The stones that protrude from the sides of the Pont du Gard (barely visible in fig. 11) are evidence of another cost-saving trick. The wooden scaffolding used for hoisting up the huge stones could rest on these shelves instead of having to reach up from below. The projecting shelves on the inner surfaces of the arches, the imposts upon which the centering was built, are clearly discernible in figure 11.

Figure 11 | The Pont du Gard, Nîmes, France. c. 15 A.D. Limestone, 161′ high, 902′ long

The Vault and the Dome

Of all the people in the ancient world the Romans were most like Americans. Besides placing great emphasis on material success, physical comfort, and the pursuit of happiness here on earth, they, like us, rated efficiency over beauty, ostentation over sobriety, and economy over integrity in architectural matters. Where, for example, the Greeks made the Parthenon entirely of marble, the Romans poured concrete into wooden or brick molds and then covered the result with thin sheets of fine stone or, in places where one could not detect the substitution, with stucco painted to look like fine stone. The three Greek orders, each with its distinctive forms, system of proportions, and subtle relationship of parts, were casually transformed by the Romans and indiscriminately mixed in their buildings. In multistoried structures, for example, the Doric was used on the ground story, the Ionic on the second, and the Corinthian on the third. Columns were generally left unfluted or, occasionally, fluted part of the way down and left plain or treated differently the rest of the way. But what the Romans lacked in sensitivity they more than made up for in grandeur.

Besides allowing the Romans to build such spectacular structures as aqueducts and bridges, the arch permitted large windows in walls whose weight might have crushed a post and lintel opening. Thus three- and four-story buildings could be raised, because as long as the arch was buttressed sufficiently, it was a stable construction.

The arch also had two important offspring. If extended along its axis, it became a long, tunnel-shaped construction called a vault. A simple, semicircular vault is called a tunnel vault or, more often, a barrel vault. If rotated around a vertical axis for 360 degrees, the arch describes a hemisphere which in architecture is called a dome. Both these devices, the vault and the dome, were much used by the Romans and continued to be used throughout the history of architecture right into the twentieth century. As in everything else, the Romans worked out efficient and economical systems for building their ambitious architectural projects, systems that involved brick, mortar, and concrete.

Brick had been used long before Roman times, especially in the Mesopotamian region where stone was scarce. But scarcity of stone is not the only factor that made brick desirable. Clay is a plentiful substance in many parts of the world and, when shaped and left to dry in the sun, affords a marvelously cheap building material. Such sunbaked brick has the disadvantage of not being durable and was not used for important structures. For these, kiln-baked brick, very much like ours in substance but quite different from ours in shape, was used. Roman bricks were thinner and longer and came in various shapes and sizes depending on the end for which they were destined. Most often they were triangular in shape.

Sometime before the first century the use of mortar began to make a great difference in wall building. Instead of being held together by clamps or a mortar made of liquified clay—or just by gravity and friction—a wall was now a monolithic whole, bound together by a substance that was sometimes harder than the stone or brick it connected. Roman mortar was made of lime, sand, water, and as a cementing agent, a volcanic ash called *pozzolana* which was plentiful in the environs of Pozzuoli, a town near Naples.

Concrete, on the other hand, consisted of the same lime, *pozzolana*, and water mixture with a rougher aggregate: gravel or crushed stone, chips from the cutting of fine stone, pebbles, or any fragments of a hard material that happened to be available. The Romans quickly recognized in concrete a highly efficient and economical material. Unlike stone, which had to be quarried, cut into proper shape and then transported from the quarry to the building site, concrete was mixed right on the spot. And where skilled stonecutters and masons were required for stone construction, unskilled laborers could be taught to pour concrete. Waste materials, chips, and fragments of stone and brick could be utilized in the mixture, and finally, concrete was a plastic material and could be formed into any desired shape by being poured into molds made of wooden boards or brick.

Unlike us, the Romans did not build walls of solid brick but used brick more as a skin to hold in the concrete. The inner and outer faces of a wall were built up in courses of triangular bricks so that one flat edge of each brick paralleled the outer surface of the wall and its point faced in. Concrete was then poured into the space between the two brick courses, the concrete hardened around the brick's points, and the wall thus became one solid mass of brick facing with a concrete core. Such walls were almost always covered, either with stucco or thin sheets of a fine stone such as marble.

Stucco is a plaster made of lime, sand, water, and a fine-grained aggregate such as marble dust. It could be given a high polish when dry, decorated with paint, or even worked as sculpture.

To economize on scaffolding and centering the Romans often built vaults by first constructing arches of brick and mortar, so spaced that long, flat bricks could be laid across from one to the next and thus form a thin brick shell that required only light centering. Once self-supporting, this skeleton of brick and mortar was, like the shell of an egg, able to withstand great pressure as long as that pressure was evenly distributed. Concrete was then poured over the brick shell and the entire vault made into one vast monolithic unit. Meanwhile the centering had been moved on to the next section of the vault and the process continued. Sometimes the aggregate in the concrete used for vaults was a lightweight volcanic stone called tufa which reduced considerably the weight of the vaults. Domes were often similarly constructed.

One may wonder if a vault that has been cast, as it were, into one monolithic whole still needs buttressing. The answer is that it does, for an unbuttressed vault, even though it is one single mass of brick and concrete, would be like a lintel, in that concrete, like stone, is lacking in tensil strength. Any slight flaw in an unbuttressed vault would commence its collapse. The result is that Roman walls are always immensely thick, since they function as both supports and buttresses. It might be pointed out here that brick and concrete construction was practiced only in parts of the empire that had a good cementing agent available. The great structures in Nîmes and Arles, for example, are built of cut stone. On the other hand great masses of Roman brick and concrete masonry may still be seen in many parts of Europe today, testaments to the durability of this combination.

The Colosseum

Beyond a doubt the most impressive ruin, the one that best exemplifies for us "the grandeur that was Rome," to use Poe's phrase, is the Colosseum, or the Flavian Amphitheater, as it is sometimes called. Gigantic in size, amazing in its structural complexity, and still relatively well preserved, it receives added glamour and notoriety from the bizarre and sometimes unspeakably cruel spectacles that its walls once witnessed. Built in the first century of our era, it stands on a site where once stood a colossal bronze statue of Nero 120 feet high, and hence its name. Scholars disagree on its seating capacity, their estimates ranging from 50,000 to 100,000 including standees. Its arena measured 290 by 180 feet and featured a variety of spectacles including fights between gladiators, between men and animals, and among animals alone. The latter included lions, leopards, bears, bison, boars, deer, even rhinoceri. Combats between two men were most popular and involved a variety of weapons including, besides swords and spears, a heavy net which one man tried to throw over his armed opponent. An idea of what such combats may have looked like may be gathered from the imaginative reconstruction of such a scene in the painting reproduced in figure 52.

The crowd's demands for novelty must have tried the imagination of the arena's managers. Among the grosser spectacles were battles among dwarfs or between dwarfs and women. The arena could be transformed

into a forest through which wild animals were stalked by hunters. Despite
its wooden floor the arena could be flooded for the enactment of mock
naval battles. In one such event 300 men took part. Beneath the wooden
floor were passages, storage and dressing rooms, and pens for the wild
animals. A system of machines and elevators provided surprise entrances
and exits that must have delighted the mob. As a whole the building
measured 620 by 513 feet and consisted basically of a honeycomb of
vaulted passageways which served the double function of supporting the
spectators' seats and allowing easy access from the street to the seats. As
in any good stadium or theater, these seats were arranged so that all
spectators could see the arena. Most of the Colosseum's seats rise at an
angle of 37°. At intervals, of course, there were entrances, stairways up or
down, and aisles.

The Colosseum: Exterior

The outer wall, part of which is missing today, was 160 feet high and
consisted of three levels of arched openings which look like arches but are
actually the ends of vaults. There are 80 of these openings on each level.
The ones on the street level served as entrances, and those on the other
two stories, with their balustrades, formed places from which spectators
could look out over the city. They also provided a source of light for the
corridors and stairways inside. Each of these openings was flanked by
three-quarter columns. That is, the columns were not freestanding, but
were carved out of the stone wall itself. Such columns are generally called
engaged columns, or, depending on the degree of their projection from the
wall, half-columns or three-quarter columns. Other than thickening the
wall very slightly, these columns served no practical purpose in supporting the building. But visually they function by seeming to support it, and,
combined with the uninterrupted entablature which encircles the building and separates one level from the next, they divide the wall into units
whose repetition around the curved wall give the whole a marvelous
rhythm. Columns, entablatures, and other carved ornaments combine
with the dark voids of the arched openings to give the façade a constantly
changing pattern of light and dark as the sun moves across its surface.
  The engaged columns on the ground level, which once rested directly
on a platform that has now been swallowed by the modern city, are of the
Tuscan order, a Roman version of the Greek Doric order. The columns on

Figure 12 | The Colosseum, Rome. 72-80 A.D. Brick, concrete, limestone, and
marble, 620´ long, 513´ wide, 160´ high

the second and third stories which sit on pedestals (a favorite device of Roman architects to make columns more impressive) are of the Ionic and Corinthian orders respectively. There is a logical progression, therefore, from a simple and solid first level to a lighter and more ornate third story. Even the cornice that crowns this third story is the most complicated of the three. And to sustain this impression of graduated lightness, the third story is set back two feet. The fourth story, which was added at a later date, is blank except for a few rectangular openings. Instead of columns it has shallow pilasters—flattened out engaged columns—whose capitals are of the Composite order, a Roman blend of Ionic and Corinthian. Despite the fact that this level is higher than any of the other three, and its crowning cornice is the most complicated as well as the farthest projecting of the three, it appears lighter than the others. It actually is thinner in construction, but we could not possibly know that by merely looking at it. The visual reasons for its lightness are the flatness of its surface and the lack of large, shadow-filled openings. The corbels or stone shelves which project all around on this level once supported the bases of long poles from which were stretched ropes and canvas to shade parts of the stadium.

The Colosseum: Interior

It was on the inside of the Colosseum that the Romans showed their genius for solving practical problems in architecture. The main problem, of course, involved raising seats so that every spectator could see the arena. The Greeks had built semicircular theaters for their dramatic performances into a hillside. Obviously such theaters could not be built where there was no suitable hill, a problem which the Romans solved by raising their seats on vaulted tunnels. These passages were of two kinds, those that ran concentric to the arena and those which radiated outward from the arena and therefore crossed the concentric corridors. As one entered the Colosseum, one passed through three sections of barrel vault (a, b, c in fig. 13) across two of the concentric passages (d and e). Since every spectator had to pass through these outer corridors, they were unobstructed by stairways and their vaults were higher than those of the radial corridor, probably to reduce the reverberation of noise. If one continued walking toward the arena one entered a wedge-shaped passageway whose ceiling was a barrel vault of ever-diminishing diameter (f). Here a number of stairways and landings led to the second level. If, however, one continued toward the arena, one crossed another concentric corridor (g) and then entered a funnel-shaped passage whose barrel vault decreased in height to provide a sloping floor for the stepped seats above it

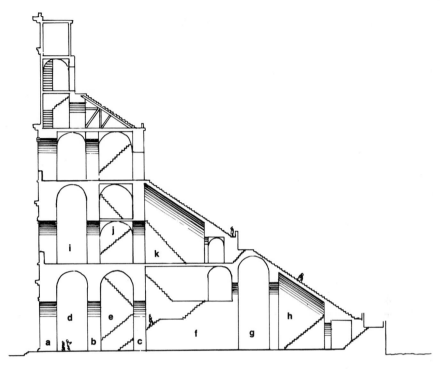

Figure 13 | Section through the Colosseum

(h). After crossing a fourth concentric corridor one mounted a short staircase to reach the railing at the arena's edge.

If one chose, instead, to take the stairs to the second level, one emerged in one of the two concentric corridors which stood immediately above the two below. The outer one of these was the same height as the one below it (i), but the inner one (j) was split into two levels to provide a landing between the flights of steps that led to the third story. If one's seat was on the second floor, one could enter another funnel-shaped passageway (k) whose slanted ceiling supported the second tier of seats, or one could mount to the third floor and descend to one's seat. We are not certain about how the upper levels of the Colosseum were arranged, since the deterioration there is most severe and the seats in these levels, the cheapest in the house, probably rested on wooden frameworks. The construction of the Colosseum is actually much more complicated than this brief description would indicate. The stairways, for example, were not placed in every radial passage but only at necessary intervals.

The photograph in figure 14 shows a section of the Colosseum where the outer wall has disappeared leaving only the first two levels, with their funnel-shaped vaults, still visible. The wooden floor of the arena is also missing so that the passageways and chambers which once were below the arena are now visible at the lower left. The distant hill is the Caelian, one of the seven hills of Rome. Basically, then, the Colosseum is an elliptical building consisting of a network of intersecting barrel-vaulted passageways. Eighty of these passageways are radial and lead toward the arena. Other passageways (different numbers on the different levels) are concentric and allow easy communication around the arena. Where the concentric corridors and the radial corridors intersect, vertical piers of masonry are formed. In other areas the radial corridors form funnel-shaped vaults and become the direct supports of the seats above them.

The actual core of the building is made of brick-faced concrete. Many of

Figure 14 | The Colosseum, interior

the walls were plastered with stucco and undoubtedly decorated with painted or sculptured ornament, applied pilasters, entablatures, and other moldings. The wall of the façade and important inner ones (especially on the lower levels where the most important people sat) were made of travertine, a fine quality of limestone, held together by clamps of iron set in lead. The pockmarked surface of the Colosseum today is due to the reclaiming of these clamps by people through the ages. All vaulting was of concrete and brick except the outer arches which were made of cut travertine. The vaults of the high corridors were built with brick ribs. Marble was used only for columns and other ornament and for the seats in the lower section of the stands where the emperor, senators, and other leading citizens sat. Everywhere in the structure one feels the practical temper of the Roman mind in reconciling problems of structure, utility, and beauty. The arched openings around the first three levels are an example of this. Structurally their supports, all superimposed, form a solid skeleton for the building as well as a buttress against its outward thrust. This skeleton is emphasized visually by the vertical half-columns and the horizontal entablatures between levels. The arched openings not only buttress one another and lighten the thick exterior wall, but also admit light into what, in the days before electricity, would have been an uncomfortably gloomy series of stairs and corridors. Esthetically these arched openings offered picturesque views of the street below and the city beyond and thus made the outer corridors pleasant foyers where a spectator could stretch his legs between events, meet friends, and eat or drink in a well-lighted, well-ventilated, high-ceilinged, and literally endless space.

When the Colosseum was inaugurated in 80 A.D., a series of spectacles began which lasted four hundred days and involved the slaying of five thousand wild animals. The number of human casualties is not recorded. Begun by the emperor Vespasian and completed by his son Titus, it was decorated and altered by subsequent emperors. The fourth story was added by Alexander Severus in 223. According to tradition, hundreds of Christians met their deaths here, among them St. Ignatius of Antioch (107 A.D.), Sts. Abdon and Sennen (251), and Sts. Vitus, Crescentia, and Modestus during the last great wave of persecution in 303. The last combat in the Colosseum was held in 523. During the Middle Ages it was used as a fortress by a variety of people. Later, part of it was used as a hospital, part of it for factories, and always it served as a quarry for those who needed stone. Most of the Renaissance palaces and churches in Rome incorporate stone that came from the Colosseum. It was not until the early nineteenth century that attempts were made to preserve rather than demolish this historic structure.

Projects

1. Study in greater detail the construction methods of the Romans, their systems of laying bricks, pouring concrete, and erecting vaults and domes.
2. Find several examples of barrel vaults in periods of history other than the Roman. Judging from the photographs of these vaults, explain how the builders solved the problems of support and illumination. Discuss your selections in chronological order.
3. Compare the plan of a typical Greek theater (e.g., the theater at Epidaurus) with a Roman theater (e.g., the Roman theater in Orange, France). Compare both their plans and their structural systems.
4. Investigate the form and structural system of the Roman house, for example, the House of Pansa or the House of the Vettii in Pompeii.

Suggested Reading

Brown, Frank. *Roman Architecture.* New York: George Braziller, Inc., 1961.

Kähler, Heinz. *The Art of Rome and Her Empire.* New York: Crown Publishers, Inc., 1963.

McDonald, William L. *Architecture of the Roman Empire.* New Haven, Connecticut: Yale University Press, 1965.

Wheeler, Mortimer. *Roman Art and Architecture.* New York: Frederick A. Praeger, Inc., 1964.

*Available in a paperback edition.

4 | The Master Builders
The Pantheon and the Baths of Caracalla

Less spectacular than the Colosseum but in other ways a quite remarkable building is the Pantheon in Rome (fig. 15) which is still standing and may be said to be still in use today. As its name indicates, the Pantheon was a temple dedicated to all the gods. Somewhat hemmed in by the modern city and sitting partially below the level of the city streets, the Pantheon was once raised on a platform and flanked by colonnades and other buildings. Its very characteristic three-part exterior form—a pedimented portico, a transitional vestibule, and a cylindrical rotunda—was therefore not so apparent in ancient times as it is today, a fact ignored by Renaissance and later English architects who made use of this form. Nor was its original setting taken into account by Thomas Jefferson, who used the Pantheon as a model for the Rotunda at the University of Virginia and his own home, Monticello.

The Pantheon: Exterior

Today the Pantheon stands alone on an island which one may walk around and find that it is not an attractive exterior. The circular brick wall of the building which was once sheathed in stone and stucco is divided into three levels by two continuous cornices and is terminated at the top by a third. There are no openings in this wall except some tiny windows on the third level whose purpose will be discussed when we describe the building's structural system. The transition between the triangular porch roof and the rectangular area behind it is softened by a second "pediment," a sort of echo of the first, which projects from the façade of the vestibule. The corners of this second pediment coincide with the molding that continues around the building and helps tie the rectangular vestibule to the round rotunda. The dome is not hemispherical on the exterior but saucer-shaped, so that it is not visible from the outside unless one moves some distance from the building.

Compared to the porches of Greek temples, the front porticos of Roman temples were quite deep, sometimes nearly half the length of the building. In the Pantheon, the porch forms a rectangle nearly half as deep as it is

wide (108 by 45 feet). It is a sort of temple without walls all by itself. The
sixteen columns of the porch divide its space into a wide central "nave,"
which was once covered with a bronze barrel vault, and two smaller
"aisles" which end in semicircular niches (recessed spaces in a wall) that
once held statues of two emperors. (See fig. 16, a, b, and c.)

As one enters the porch one becomes aware of its gigantic dimensions,
an impression that must have been even more striking when the level of
the square in front of it was four feet lower than it is today. As it is today,
one mounts two rather shallow steps and passes between two of the eight
columns which tower 46½ feet above the floor. Each of these has an
unfluted shaft of gray granite that is monolithic, made of one single piece
of stone. The ornate Corinthian capital above it is 8 feet high and is of
Pentelic marble which once was white. The eight columns inside the
porch have shafts of red granite. Each of these columns has a diameter of
nearly 5 feet at its base and weighs 60 tons.

Figure 15 | The Pantheon, Rome. 118-125 A.D. Brick, concrete, and stone.
| Portico: 108´ wide, dome: 142½´ wide and 142½´ high

The entablature, which rises 11 feet above the columns, consists of an architrave divided into three horizontal bands (as was usual in the Corinthian order), a frieze which carries an inscription, and a cornice whose chief ornamentation consists of dentils, repeated rectangular shapes that resemble teeth. The dentil motif is carried into the pediment, across the rectangular vestibule area, and around the exterior wall of the rotunda at each of the levels, another attempt to tie the three dissimilar units together.

There was sculptural ornamentation in the pediment (a battle of the gods and giants), on the vestibule (a quadriga or four-horse chariot carrying Victory), and elsewhere, but all these were of bronze and have therefore disappeared. The inscription on the frieze attributes the building to the emperor Agrippa who actually built an older structure which this replaces. The present building was erected by Hadrian between 118 and 125 A.D. When it was new the Pantheon was faced on the outside with polished Pentelic marble on the lower level and with colored stucco above. Its dome was covered with gilded bronze plates which were taken to Constantinople in 655 and replaced with lead. The roof of the porch was once carried on a framework of bronze beams which were removed in 1632 to be melted down for cannons for the fortress Castel Sant' Angelo (originally the gigantic tomb of the emperor Hadrian). Some of this bronze still exists today in the twisted columns of Bernini's huge canopy over the main altar in St. Peter's.

The Pantheon: Interior

The entrance to the rotunda comes, as has been said, at the end of the central space of the porch (a in figs. 16 and 17). Just before we enter the domed area this space drops down to a lower level. The resultant effect of this lowering of the ceiling just before the entrance was undoubtedly part of an esthetic plan. We must remember that in ancient times the exterior of the rotunda was masked by adjoining colonnades and buildings. All one could see clearly was the rectangular porch which led, one would expect, to the usual rectangular cella. It must have been more of a surprise then to step from the porch into the rotunda than it is today, when we see beforehand what we are entering. Surprise is perhaps the wrong word. Even those who had visited the Pantheon many times must have felt a thrill when they stepped from the shaded, tightly enclosed tunnel into the soaring, circular, and hemispherically domed space 142 1/2 feet in diameter. Still today it is one of the most memorable architectural experiences in the world.

Axial Orientation

In a rectangular building, the Parthenon for example, we feel an axis running down the center of the building from the front to the back and parallel to the rectangle's two long sides. In a square building this horizontal pull is less pronounced, but we still feel an axis running from the front door to the opposite wall, again parallel to the building's other two walls. In a circular building this horizontal pull is overcome by our response to a vertical axis around which the circular space seems to rotate. In the Pantheon we feel such a vertical pull from the center of the circular floor to the apex of the dome which, in this case, is open to the sky; for in the top of this gigantic dome is a circular opening 27 feet in diameter. Since this oculus, as it is called, is the principal source of illumination (not much light comes through the entrance from the shaded porch outside), the illumination of the building reinforces the vertical axis of the Pantheon.

But it would be wrong to think that the Pantheon has no horizontal articulation at all. What might be a monotonous, barrellike cylindrical

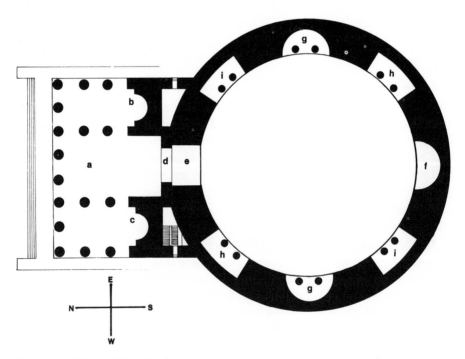

Figure 16 | Plan of the Pantheon

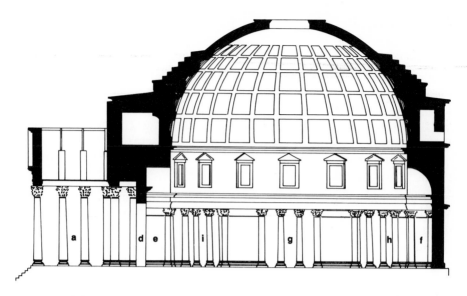

Figure 17 | Section through the Pantheon

space below the dome is broken in eight places. The entrance doorway is, of course, the most important of these breaks. Opposite the entrance is the second most important break in the wall—a recessed space which is sometimes referred to as a niche but which, because it is large enough to enter and walk around in, we shall call an alcove (f in figs. 16 and 17). This alcove is semicircular in plan and is covered by a half dome, a smaller echo of the vast hemisphere above it. The fact that this alcove, like the entrance door, is surmounted by an arch sets up a relationship between it and the front door, a relationship which establishes a sec-ondary axis, a north-south orientation. Two more semicircular alcoves, but this time without the surmounting arch, make a tertiary axis from east to west (g-g). Four more alcoves mark subsidiary axes in northeast to southwest and southeast to northwest directions (h-h and i-i in figs. 16 and 17). Instead of being semicircular in plan, they are rectangular (actually trapezoidal) in plan. The result, therefore, is a division and subdivision of axiality, as well as the establishment of a rhythmic pattern, alternating semicircular and rectangular spaces that give the circular wall a varied pattern of light and dark. From a practical standpoint, the alcoves (there were seven of them, the eighth opening being the entrance door) served to house altars, probably of the seven planetary gods.

The integrity of the circular wall is preserved, nevertheless, by the continuous entablature which is interrupted only by the entrance and the opposite alcove. It is affirmed also by the two columns which stand in front of each alcove except the one opposite the entrance (see fig. 18). At the edge of each alcove Corinthian pilasters echo the shapes of the two columns that stand between them, and make an intriguing transition from the three dimensions of the alcove to the two-dimensional character of the wall. They also set up a varied rhythmic pattern: pilaster, column, column, pilaster, wall, pilaster, column, column, etc.; this rhythm is interrupted only by the entrance and the opposite alcove, both of which have pilasters but no columns.

From underneath, the Pantheon's dome reveals a network of intersecting ribs, some radial and some concentric. Structurally they are an efficient way of making a skeleton upon which the dome was built, and esthetically they articulate the surface, provide pleasing effects of light and shadow, and form a pattern of diminishing squares that enhances the effect of perspective, leading the eye upward to the climactic opening at the center of the dome. One may wonder at the idea of leaving a building open to the sky like this, but alternatives were impossible without a complete change in the building's design. The tremendous weight and thrust of the dome on the walls of the Pantheon precluded having windows anywhere else. We must remember, too, the mild climate of Mediterranean lands, where people live out of doors much more than we do, where a house is frequently built around an open courtyard, and where peasants in many rural areas have no glass in the windows of their houses even today. When it rains—and Italy is a dry country on the whole—it rains in the Pantheon, and this seems not to have hurt the building much through the centuries. One advantage which this oculus has over other kinds of windows is that this single, central source of light adds to the remarkable feeling of unity and centrality of the enclosed space. This space, incidentally, is as high as it is wide, for the diameter of the dome equals the height of the dome from the floor—142$\frac{1}{2}$ feet.

No description of the Pantheon's interior is complete without the mention of its richness of color. Where the Greek ideal was to build temples of solid marble, the Romans, as we have seen, used less expensive materials like brick and concrete which they then covered with a veneer of thin slabs of fine stone. A wealth of rich colors and textural contrast was achieved on the internal walls of the Pantheon. Porphyry, a handsome purple stone, was used in many of the panels, especially the striking round ones. Other panels, as well as the columns and pilasters of the alcoves, are of a yellow stone called *giallo antico.* The columns on the altars are of purple-veined Phrygian marble, and other details here and there are of golden or white Parian marble. Carved moldings of acanthus leaves and egg-and-dart patterns add to the richness of the interior. The

Figure 18 | *The Interior of the Pantheon,* as depicted in an oil painting by Giovanni Paolo Pannini. c. 1750. Kress Collection, National Gallery of Art, Washington D.C.

recessed squares or coffers between the ribs of the dome, which lighten the weight of the concrete dome, were also treated decoratively. We don't know exactly how they were treated but we believe they were gilt or otherwise painted and decorated with an ornament at their centers, probably rosettes—flowerlike ornaments with radiating petals—made of bronze.

The Pantheon: Construction

The more one studies the construction of the Pantheon, the more one marvels at the Romans' ability to conceive grandiose designs and then invent ways and means to achieve them. Not only does the Pantheon enclose the largest space unbroken by vertical supports ever devised by man up to that time; not only is its dome larger than many later domes, such as Brunelleschi's on the Florence Cathedral or Michelangelo's on St. Peter's; and not only is the Pantheon still standing and virtually in its original condition; but it is a brilliant piece of logic in wedding utilitarian needs to structural demands.

One reads sometimes that the walls of the Pantheon are twenty feet thick to support the colossal weight of its brick and concrete dome. Actually what happens is much subtler. The dome, which is thinnest at its summit (about four feet thick) thickens as it approaches the wall which supports it in order to absorb some of its own thrust. On the exterior of the dome this thickening takes the form of concentric steps, a device used by many domes ever since (for example, the dome on the Jefferson Memorial in Washington). The thrust of the dome is absorbed by the wall it sits upon, but this wall does not have to be solid throughout, as long as it satisfies its role as a buttress. Thus the upper part of the wall contains a passageway which is illuminated by the very small windows we noticed on the outside, and on the ground level, the wall is made thinner by the seven alcoves and the entrance. To compensate for this weakening of the wall, there are arches buried in the masonry and invisible to the observer (although some of them are visible on the bare exterior today). These arches (see fig. 19) divert the thrust of the dome from the alcoves to the eight areas between. It is here that the wall is twenty feet thick, so that it might be said that the dome of the Pantheon actually rests on a network of hidden arches that conduct its weight and thrust to eight huge piers. Even these piers are not completely solid but have hollow spaces with hidden arches above them to deflect the weight of the wall.

Here we see a different architectural philosophy from that of the Greeks. Unlike the Parthenon, whose structural principle of horizontal elements and vertical support is immediately apparent as we look at it, the Pantheon's structure is intentionally contrived and full of illusion. There are forces operating here that we know nothing of. The lightness we feel when we look at the interior is deceptive, as is the veneer of polished stone which hides the rough brick walls like a cosmetic. Visually the gigantic dome seems to be supported, in large part, by the twelve slender Corinthian columns in the alcoves. We do not see the three small arches that connect the tops of those columns and pilasters or, more importantly, the doubled arch that spans the entire alcove and takes the weight off it (see fig. 19). It is not until the Renaissance, when Brunelleschi buried a chain of wooden beams around the base of his dome for Florence Cathedral, and Michelangelo used a real chain in the dome of St. Peter's, that we meet again such artful juggling of visual and structural elements.

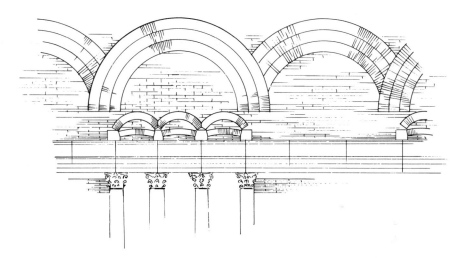

Figure 19 | Hidden arches in the walls of the Pantheon

In 608 the Pantheon was transformed into a church by Pope Boniface IV and called Our Lady of the Martyrs (Santa Maria ad Martyres), because the bodies of the martyrs in the catacombs were exhumed and reburied here. In 1101 the building was used as a fortress. In 1623 Pope Urban VIII had the bronze portions of the building melted down for the above mentioned columns and cannons, and another pope, Benedict XIV in the mid-eighteenth century, stripped away the colored marbles on the second level of the interior to decorate his own palace. Many of Italy's great are buried inside the Pantheon, for example the painter Raphael, the composer Bellini, and several Italian kings.

The Baths of Caracalla

Round domed buildings were also used for hot or steam baths in the bathing establishments of imperial Rome. As such they were part of a large complex of many buildings which were set in a landscaped area of several acres. Actually, the public bath was more than the name implies; it was a combination of athletic club, country club, and civic center where Romans could bathe, take exercise, watch athletic events, read books, hear lectures, or just pass the afternoon (the baths opened at one o'clock and closed at sunset) chatting, arranging business deals, or lining up votes for the next political contest. Nevertheless, bathing was the principal activity in the *thermae* and involved fixed procedures almost like parts of a ritual. It has been estimated that the average Roman used 300 gallons of water per day. New York's per capita consumption today is just under 150 gallons.

Public baths were intended primarily for men; women used either public baths of their own or a segregated section of the men's establishments. In the fourth century A.D. there were eleven public baths in the city of Rome, though all citizens of means had baths in their own houses. Even the remotest frontier town in the far-flung empire had its baths. Roman Paris, for example, had several, one in the forum which stood near the present Luxembourg Gardens, one near the Sorbonne, and one which today still has its vaulted ceiling and is part of the Cluny Museum. From the Rhine to the Sahara, from Spain to the Persian Gulf, Roman colonials built themselves baths. Even army camps in faraway England had them, as the city of Bath's name demonstrates.

The Baths of Caracalla, which were built between 211 and 217 A.D., exist today in the form of ruined walls, piers, vaults, and arches, portions of which form an outdoor theater today for the performances of opera in the summertime. Scholars do not agree on the precise shape and use of every room, but an approximate reconstruction has become generally acceptable.

The baths stood on a flat platform or terrace over one-fifth of a mile long on each side. This platform stood about twenty feet above the surrounding land and was held in by walls which were buttressed with barrel vaults. The resulting vaulted chambers probably housed shops and other utilitarian areas, perhaps even tunnels that allowed vehicles to enter underground and deliver fuel for the furnaces. As we can see from the plan in figure 20, an axis runs through the complex from the entrance on the north to the stadium and water reservoirs on the south, dividing these vast grounds into strictly balanced units like some enormous rectangular butterfly. Its very symmetry, achieved by duplicating every building and courtyard on each side of the axis, was meant to impress the visitor. The same principle of symmetry on a large scale has been used in various times in history down to our own day, especially in the arrangement of government buildings, libraries, museums, and for the same reason: to overwhelm the visitor and impress him with the wealth and power of the city, state, or nation which constructed it.

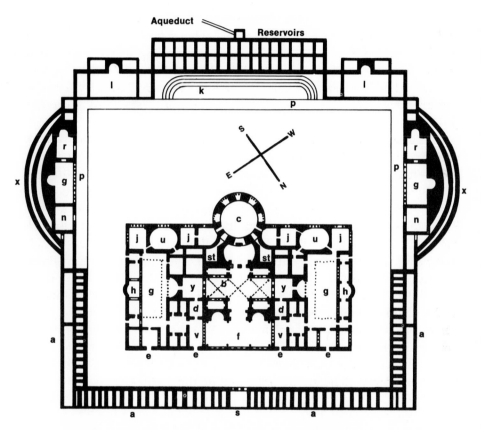

Figure 20 | Reconstructed plan of the Baths of Caracalla, Rome. 211–217 A.D. The central block of buildings is 750′ wide, 380′ long

The form and arrangement of the buildings were not determined by esthetic considerations alone but by the particular demands of Roman bathing customs as well. Although the routine varied at different periods, the bathing ritual consisted of three main steps: exercise to induce sweating, bathing in hot water, and finally immersion in a cold pool.

Accordingly, the main complex of buildings was arranged to facilitate this sequence. After ascending the stairway (s) to the landscaped precincts of the baths, the visitor faced the gigantic central block of buildings which measured 750 feet along the front. Four entrances (e) led into vestibules (v) and dressing rooms (d) where he could disrobe. After exercising in one of the *palestrae* or gymnasiums (g), one of several game rooms (j), or on outdoor courts, he entered the *calidarium* or hot bath (c), one of the steam baths (st), then the *tepidarium* where the temperature was moderate, and finally he took a plunge in the *frigidarium* (f), the pool of cold water. At various stages in this sequence he was rubbed down with soda and fine sand (soap was still unknown), was scraped with a wooden or metal instrument called a *strigil*, and was annointed with perfumed oils. Masseurs, barbers, depilators, and other attendants were provided by the establishment, although wealthy patrons often brought their own slaves along.

The specific use of many of the rooms is not certain, but we know that there were offices, storage spaces, toilets, and waiting rooms. There were also lounges (u) and landscaped courtyards (y), lecture rooms (h), and *nympheums,* indoor gardens with fountains and statuary (n) for the visitor's relaxation and delight. He might walk outdoors down garden paths, under shaded arcades (a), or along elevated promenades (p) to visit libraries (l) and study rooms (r), watch athletic events from the stadium, or walk into the *exedrae* (x) from whose curved terraces he could enjoy the panorama of the surrounding countryside or the distant city.

But the favorite place to pass the hours was the great hall (b) which was located at the heart of the complex, and which was the largest, most elaborately decorated, and for the history of art, the most influential building in the baths. As the largest space ever enclosed by man, this vaulted basilica became the model for many churches in the Renaissance and for large gathering places such as railroad terminals in the nineteenth and twentieth centuries. The Roman basilica in its broadest sense was a large hall of justice and commercial exchange located in the forum. The ordinary basilica was covered with a roof carried on wooden beams and consisted of a large central space and two or more flanking aisles. Since the central space rose higher than the side aisles, windows called clearstory windows or clearstories could be built into the space between the central roof and the aisle roofs. In the Baths of Caracalla the vaulted basilica was preferred over its timber-roofed counterpart, because its vaults could span a greater space than the timber roof, and also because their magnificent sweep and height lent a note of grandeur which was highly desirable in the imperial baths.

Vaults and Piers

A vault in architecture refers to a curved ceiling generally built of masonry. A barrel vault (sometimes called a tunnel vault) is a semicircular vault (fig. 21). A barrel vault, in other words, is a semicircular arch extended along its axis and, like an arch, it exerts sideward thrust as well as downward weight. A stone vault must therefore have a thick support in order to remain stable. Not only that, but this support must be continuous along its entire length. Any opening in the wall that supports a barrel vault must be kept small and must be strongly reinforced by one or more relieving arches. Windows in the surface of the actual vault itself are hazardous too, for every section of a barrel vault is, theoretically, an arch and must be supported and buttressed. Barrel-vaulted buildings are therefore quite dark, and the problem of making large doors leading into adjoining spaces is fraught with danger.

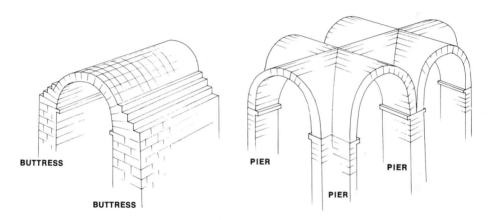

Figure 21 | Barrel vault and groined vault

If, however, a barrel vault is intersected at right angles by another barrel vault of the same radius, several interesting things happen. Their crowns will obviously meet at a single point, and their curved surfaces will intersect to form four angular edges which run downward from the crown to form a square (figs. 21 and 22). These angular edges are called groins and the vault is called a groined vault (sometimes, cross vault). The significant thing that happens, however, is that the sides of the original vault are opened up to allow space for windows or doors, because the wall

Figure 22 | Reconstruction of the basilica in the Baths of Carcacalla. Brick, concrete, and marble, 183' long 79' wide, 108' high

which once held up and buttressed the vault has now been replaced by the four sections of wall just below the four groins. These sections of wall are called piers. The thrust of a groined vault, in other words, converges on the groins and is conducted down to the four corners of the vault; there it is absorbed by the four piers which, if the vault is large, must be buttressed to insure the stability of the structure.

The reconstructed drawing (fig. 22) shows the vaulting system of the basilica in the Baths of Caracalla: one long vault that runs east and west from one end of the building to the other, and three short vaults that intersect it at right angles and provide clearstory windows on the north and south. These groined vaults rose 108 feet above the floor, measured nearly 80 feet across, and rested on eight massive piers. Always clever in disguising the structural devices of their buildings, the Roman architects faced these eight piers with graceful monolithic Corinthian columns 38½ feet high, so it appeared as if they, rather than the tons of masonry behind them, were holding up the vaults. As in the dome of the Pantheon, the vaults here had coffers—indentations in the concrete—of square, hexagonal, and various polygonal shapes. These coffers were decorated with stucco, paint, and perhaps with metal ornaments as well. The walls, which opened here and there into balconies, alcoves, and vestibules, were also of brick and concrete, but their inner surfaces were veneered, as in the Pantheon, with white and colored stone, richly patterned and polished to a high finish. The floor, besides its geometric pattern of colored marble blocks, had mosaic panels that depicted gladiators, athletes, and scenes from mythology. Many statues, some of them copies of famous Greek works, adorned the great hall as well as other buildings and the

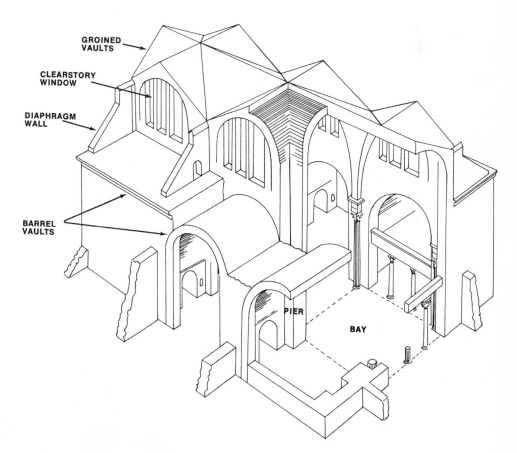

Figure 23 | Structural system of the Roman vaulted basilica

grounds of the baths, sometimes as parts of fountains whose jets of water, splashing into pools or basins, cooled the air and delighted the eye. Many of the Greek and Roman statues in the Vatican and other museums throughout the world were excavated here, among them the *Torso of Belvedere, the Farnese Hercules,* and the group called the *Farnese Bull.*

Since the radii of the intersecting parts of a groined vault are equal, the space immediately below that intersection, which is called a bay, is square. The central space in the basilica in the Baths of Caracalla consists of three bays, each of which is roughly eighty feet square. As we can see from figures 22 and 23, each of these bays leads out to the sides to form six subsidiary spaces. The walls between these spaces and the barrel vaults which cover them serve an important function in buttressing the groined vaults. Above the aisle roofs, moreover, eight triangular walls called diaphragm walls form additional buttresses between the clearstory windows.

Figure 23 is a schematic drawing which illustrates the structural system of a vaulted basilica such as Caracalla's. Tile roofs covered the groined vaults so that rainwater would run off quickly and not penetrate the masonry. Illumination was provided by the large semicircular clearstories on the upper level.

The aerial photograph in figure 24 shows the ruins of the Baths of Caracalla from the southwest. Plainly discernible is the circular *calidarium* whose dome and most of whose walls have disappeared. Beyond it the basilica of the baths once stood. Today nothing remains except the three barrel-vaulted spaces on its north side and a few other remains of walls and vaults. The diaphragm walls and the beginnings of the groined vaults are clearly discernible above the barrel vaults. To the north of the basilica once lay the *frigidarium* or open air pool, and to the east and west stand the walls of various other rooms of the baths and the open air gymnasiums.

After the wane of Roman power, in the fifth century, the Baths of Caracalla fell into disuse, partly because of a decline in population, partly because the early Christians disapproved of bathing for pleasure, and finally because the Visigoths destroyed the aqueduct when they sacked the Sacred City in 537. In subsequent centuries, the baths, like other Roman ruins, served as living quarters for the poor and as quarries for the rich. It is a saying that what the barbarians did not destroy, the Barberini did, the latter being one of the prominent families in Renaissance Rome. In 1563 Michelangelo was asked to transform the basilica in the Baths of Diocletian into a church, and so it is only in the church of Santa Maria degli Angeli that we can see and feel even an approximation of the grandeur and magnificence of a Roman vaulted basilica such as Caracalla's.

Figure 24 | The ruins of the Baths of Caracalla, aerial view

A Comparison

If we glance quickly from the Parthenon to the four Roman buildings we have discussed, we will see that the former consists entirely of straight lines and that the latter are dominated by curves. Relationships which are mostly simple horizontals and verticals in the Greek temple become, in the Roman buildings, complex arrangements of semicircular arches and vaults, domes and half-domed niches, curves in plan and curves in elevation, all set against a framework of vertical columns and horizontal entablatures. The spatial effect of this complication results in a varied rhythmic interplay of solids and voids, of curved and flat surfaces, of space opening up in various directions—under arches, through screens of columns, and into a variety of domed and vaulted areas.

Since many ancient peoples in Egypt, Mesopotamia, and Persia—and even the Greeks—knew the principle of the arch, we can assume that the Greeks rejected it because it was somehow not esthetically satisfying to them. There must have been something about the right angle that better expressed the Greek ethos than the semicircle. Conversely, the post and lintel, though admired enough by the Romans to be used in a decorative way, would not let them carry out their ambitious projects. As it is, the Romans' architectural achievements with the arch were not surpassed (except in its adaptation in the Gothic cathedrals) until the development of structural steel in the twentieth century. And even today, one of the favorite building materials is concrete, which is mixed and poured into wooden molds very much as it was in the Pantheon 1900 years ago.

Basically the Greek temple is conceived in terms of many distinct parts—stepped platform, columns, entablature, pediment—and each part is subdivided into sharply distinct elements—architrave, frieze, and cornice in the entablature, for example. Each of these parts is self-contained, sharply demarcated, and related to others in a sensitive and subtle way. We perceive each of these units separately and also as part of the whole. The components of a Roman building, on the other hand, seem to flow one into the other. We perceive the building as a sculptural whole. Volumes and voids, lines and colors all interpenetrate. And, indeed, the Roman building is a sculptured whole in a literal sense, because the brick, mortar, stone veneer, and decoration have been cemented together to form a single, monolithic sculptured mass; and although the entablatures and columns divide the walls into separate sections, they also tie the interior together and form a skeleton that unifies the whole visually. Thus decoration, besides serving to impress the viewer with its opulence, also serves to articulate the interior, clarify its form, and lead the eye in its path in and out of spaces and from unit to unit.

Greek decoration, being restricted to nonsupporting elements, emphasized the structural members by contrast. Roman decoration, on the contrary, was a camouflage which appeared to be structural when it was not. The 38-foot columns in the basilica of the Baths of Caracalla make us forget the massive piers that are really holding up the vaults; and the equally large but seemingly tiny columns in the alcoves of the Pantheon give no hint of the army of small arches hidden in the wall above them. Roman decoration, in a word, was a cosmetic that presented a glamorous exterior to the eye while hiding the ingenious structural system from the gaze of the spectator.

Above all, Roman decoration was meant to impress. If money was plentiful, then the building was sheathed in sparkling marbles, porphyry, serpentine, and other rare, often imported stones; columns were monolithic and carved ornament and mosaics plentiful. If funds were low, then painted stucco would do. Portions of wall were sometimes painted to look like stone, and columns were constructed of brick, covered with stucco, and painted to look like marble. What could one find that better symbolizes the difference in the two civilizations: the one, idealistic in philosophy and modest in its material aspirations; the other materialistic and practical in outlook, ostentatious—and often vulgar—in its taste, but magnificent in its visions, and ruthless in achieving them?

Great admirers of things Greek, the Romans adopted the classic orders, although they proceeded to use them in ways that were totally un-Greek. They added a base to the Doric column, sometimes omitted the flutes or occasionally fluted a column only halfway down, leaving the lower half smooth or fluted in a different way. The Doric order was too austere for the Romans who preferred the more ornate Corinthian and invented two hybrids of it: the Tuscan, which resembled the Doric with an unfluted shaft set on a base, and the Composite, whose capital was a blend of Ionic and Corinthian. This lack of system with which the Romans used Greek details is not so much due to a dislike for system, for the Romans were highly systematic, but rather to a lack of sensitivity to subtle esthetic relationships. The Roman preferred theatrical effects. Columns, for example, were often set on pedestals to show them off. Sometimes a section of the entablature was set, all by itself, above the capital to remind one of the Greek order, but with a complete lack of structural logic (see fig. 22). The three orders were often superimposed on each other: Doric on the first story, Ionic on the second, and Corinthian on the third, as in the Colosseum. These practices were revived by Italian architects in the Renaissance and passed on to the western world in general. So was the use of an arch enclosed by columns and entablature (see Colosseum again), a combination which would have been incomprehensible to a Greek of the Golden Age, since each element by itself is a satisfactory structural device.

Yet if the Roman's use of decoration was divorced from structure, if his use of the Greek architectural vocabulary was illogical, and if he lacked the sensitivity to visual harmony which characterizes Greek architecture, he succeeded in giving his structures magnificent scale. The various details were related to each other in such a way that they articulated the enclosed space and gave it coherence. Here we come to the main difference between Greek and Roman architecture. The glory of the Parthenon lies in its vibrant, sculptural, rhythmically unified exterior, not in its inner space which was dark, cluttered, and heavy in feeling. Most Roman buildings, on the other hand, were rather uninteresting on the outside—drab brick with perhaps some colored tiles or stucco for decoration. But the interiors sang with color and rang with a dynamic counterpoint of solid and empty spaces. True, the balmy climate of the Aegean land permitted its inhabitants to live out of doors, worship at outdoor altars, and build a roofed interior merely to shelter the statue. The cooler climate of central Italy undoubtedly impelled the Romans to build ever more spacious interiors; but the architectural results are more than concessions to climate. In its complexity, its spatial vitality, and its chromatic and textural richness, a Roman building is a fitting and most eloquent expression of a nation which ruled the world for 400 years.

Projects

1. Examine photographs of the interiors of St. Sernin in Toulouse, the Cathedral of Amiens, and St. Peter's in Rome. How do their vaulting systems compare with what you have seen here? Note any similarities and any differences.
2. Find photographs and diagrams of domes in other parts of the world, particularly those of Hagia Sophia (Santa Sophia) in Istanbul, Florence Cathedral, St. Peter's in Rome, St. Paul's in London, and the Capitol in Washington, D.C. How does each differ in shape and in its relationship to the rest of the building?
3. Investigate the general form and the internal decoration of Hagia Sophia (Santa Sophia) in Istanbul. In what ways is it similar to the basilica in the Baths of Caracalla? In what ways is it different?
4. Examine one building in your vicinity. Draw a floor plan of it, labeling each of the rooms and indicating doors with a "d," windows with "w," and stairways with "s." Use figure 6 as a guide for your drawing.

Suggested Reading

Busch, Harald, and Bernd Lohse, eds. *Romanesque Europe,* trans, Peter Gorge. New York: Macmillan Co., 1963.

Hanfmann, G. M. *Roman Art.* Greenwich, Conn.: New York Graphic Society. 1964.

Kähler, Heinz. *Hagia Sophia.* New York: Frederick A. Praeger, Inc., 1967.

Smith, E. Baldwin. *Architectural Symbolism of Imperial Rome and the Middle Ages.* Princeton, New Jersey: Princeton University Press, 1956.

5 | The Search for New Meaning
An Early Christian Mosaic and a Basilica

The earliest Christians, the immediate followers of Jesus in Jerusalem, worshipped daily in the synagogue and performed that most Christian rite, the consuming of bread and wine, in private homes (Acts 2:46). Paul himself "preached Christ in the synagogue" (Acts 9:20, also 14:1, 17:1, 18:4, 26). We do not know exactly when structures were first built expressly for Christian worship, for none of the earliest churches has come down to us. Many of them were undoubtedly destroyed during the sporadic waves of persecution that began with Nero in 64 A.D. and flared up under Trajan, Marcus Aurelius, Valerian, and Diocletian. Many others were undoubtedly razed by the Christians themselves after 313, when the Emperor Constantine pronounced the Edict of Milan which made Christianity legal and encouraged the construction of new and larger buildings. And when, a few years later, Constantine himself was converted to the new faith, he personally saw to it that many magnificent basilicas were built in some of the holiest spots in Christendom, Rome, Constantinople, Jerusalem, and Bethlehem. In Rome he founded the basilicas of St. John Lateran and St. Paul's Outside the Walls which are still standing today, and St. Peter's which was demolished in the late fifteenth century to make room for the present church of St. Peter's. Many more basilicas were built in Rome during the following centuries. A number of them are still standing today and continue in use as churches. Old St. Peter's, which was built, like St. Paul's, over the grave of the saint for which it is named, was a gigantic structure 368 feet long. The width of its central space, excluding the four aisles, was 190 feet, and it could hold a congregation of five thousand worshippers!

The usual form of early Christian churches was based on a type of building which the Romans had developed much earlier, the basilica, although it differed in some of its features to fit the demands of Christian ritual of that time. Basically it was a rectangular hall, nearly twice as long as it was wide, with the front doors at one end and the altar, set on a

65

platform and in a semicircular space called an apse at the other. The interior space was divided into a large central area called the nave (because it seemed to resemble a ship, *navis*) and two or more aisles. The nave was covered with a gabled or A-shaped roof whose shingles were supported on a framework of timber called a truss. The aisles were covered by lean-tos, also of timber construction, at a level below the nave roof so that clearstory windows could be set into the wall between them (see figs. 25 and 26) to light the center of the church which would otherwise have been quite dark. This nave wall was invariably decorated with paintings or mosaics and rested on columns, so the worshipper could move between the nave and the aisles. The space between the bottom of the clearstories and the top of the colonnade is called the triforium. There were no seats or pews in these churches, and scholars believe that, in the early years anyway, the nave was reserved for the catechumens who had not yet been baptized, the left aisles for women and the right aisles for men. The altar, whose origin is the table at the Last Supper, was still shaped like a table with four legs. Behind it, on a bench which followed the curved wall of the semicircular apse, sat the clergy, and if the church was the seat of a bishop (a cathedral), the bishop's throne (cathedra) stood in the center immediately behind the altar. In a sense, then, the bishop represented Christ in the congregation, and the clergy on one side of the altar and the lay congregation on the other represented the communicants at the Holy Table.

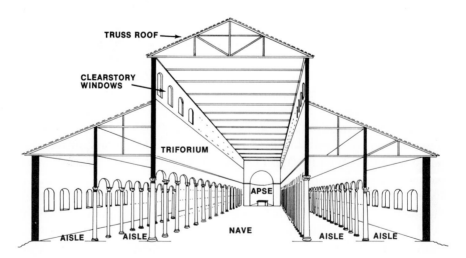

Figure 25 | Section through the nave and aisles of a truss-roofed basilica (after Old St. Peter's Rome. c. 333 A.D.)

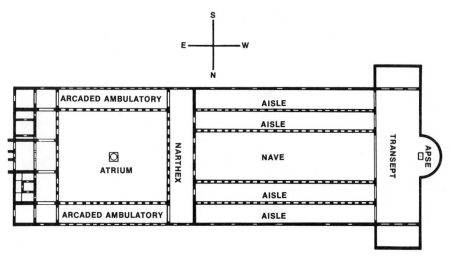

Figure 26 | Plan of Old St. Peters, Rome. Begun c. 333 A.D.

When in some of the larger churches the number of priests outgrew the space of the apse, the altar was sometimes moved forward and a space was extended to the left and to the right to form the beginning of what later became the transept, a kind of secondary nave set at right angles to the nave proper. This gave to the church building the suggestion of a cross shape which became a general characteristic of most Christian churches ever after. Old St. Peter's had transepts (fig. 26) as does St. Paul's Outside the Walls today, but the basilicas in Ravenna do not. The large churches in Rome were fronted by a courtyard called an atrium where new converts might gather until they were ready to attend services inside. On three sides of this atrium ran an arcaded, covered ambulatory. On the fourth side, a porch called the narthex led to the front doors of the church proper.

If the groined-vaulted basilica was a masterpiece of architectural invention, the truss-roofed basilica, though less spectacular, was an ingenious means of spanning a vast space with incomparably less trouble and cost. It was also a small triumph of engineering design. A stone beam, as we have noted, is limited in the space it can span because of the stone's tendency to crack in the middle. A wooden beam, though able to span a greater width, has its limits because of wood's tendency to bend. Now in a triangular arrangement of a beam and slanting rafters (as was used in the Parthenon), if all the corners are securely fastened, two forces are at work: the slanting rafters tend to press together at the top and to pull apart at the bottom, but they are held together by the connecting beam (fig. 27a). Since the triangle is the only geometric figure whose shape cannot be altered without changing the length of one of its sides, this structural system is extremely efficient, combining perfect stability with great economy.

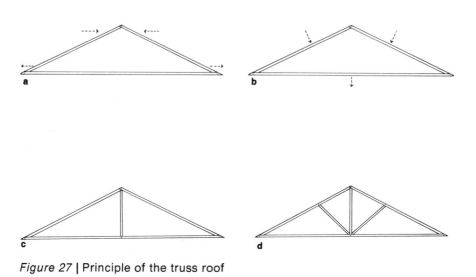

Figure 27 | Principle of the truss roof

If extended over too great a space, however, this construction develops certain weaknesses due to the sagging tendency mentioned above, in both the beam and in the diagonal rafters which must support heavy roof tiles (fig. 27b). But if a wooden strut is attached between the apex of the triangle and the center of the beam, the sagging beam may be pulled up. The resulting structure now consists of two triangles (fig 27c). If two or more struts are inserted between the center of the beam and the centers of each of the rafters, the latter may be made straight again. The resulting structure consists of four triangles (fig. 27d), all of whose parts neutralize the others' thrusts and thus produce an inert framework which functions like one single lintel. It will be seen that this construction can be made larger by merely adding more struts where needed and thereby multiplying the number of triangles. There is no reason why the horizontal beam need be one single piece of wood; it could be two (see fig. 27c and d) without weakening the construction, and in larger buildings even more. This structure is called a truss and a roof supported by it a trussed roof, the advantages of which were its economy and facility of construction. Comparatively light in weight, the truss roof could be supported by thin walls of brick or stone, and by the colonnades below it. Moreover, clearstory windows of adequate size could be set into this wall without imperiling the stability of the structure. Since the truss exerted no thrust but only downward weight, there was no need for heavy buttressing. The only real disadvantage of this roofing system was its vulnerability to fire, a constant threat in the congested, ramshackle cities of the time.

Like most Roman buildings, the early Christian basilicas were quite plain on their outsides. The tendency to embellish surfaces and achieve esthetic effects with color, texture, and visual rhythms was concentrated entirely on the interiors. The Constantinian churches were oriented with their fronts toward the east and their altars toward the west. This may be because Constantine, who was not converted until he was in his thirties, continued to regard the sun with that reverence which marked so many of the mystery religions of late Roman times and wanted the altar and the glittering, mosaic-covered apse to be illuminated by the rising sun. It is quite likely, too, that Constantine established the birthday of Christ on December 25, for on this date, when the sun began to rise earlier, was the pagan festival of the Invincible Sun. At any rate, the officiating priest, who stood behind the altar, could face his congregation and look toward the east at the same time. In the sixth century this orientation was reversed, but the priest continued to face east and therefore had to turn his back on the congregation during much of the service. The Vatican Council of 1964 directed priests to return to the early Christian practice, and it will be interesting to see whether this change will affect the architecture of future churches.

A new era began for Christianity when in 330 A.D., Constantine made it the official religion of the greatest empire in the world. A small, disorganized, and persecuted religion which had appealed chiefly to outcasts, foreigners, and slaves, Christianity now became a state religion and all the other sects became targets for disapproval and eventual persecution. This is why in many of the early Christian churches in Rome today we may see columns which do not match. They were taken from pagan temples which stood empty. Imperial favor meant new converts and a pressing need for large churches. The Roman temples were inadequate, because they were designed for small groups of individuals to burn incense at the statue of a god. The Christian church, however, required space for the communal worship of large congregations. And so early Christian architects based their church design on what, until the advent of the vaulted basilica, had been the largest enclosed space ever devised by man, the Roman civil basilica. These buildings, were like enclosed forums and served in a similar way for the negotiation of business, politics, and judicial functions. None of these vast structures has survived intact in our time, but we may see their foundations on the ground in the forums of Julius Caesar and Trajan in Rome, in the excavations at Pompeii, and elsewhere in the Roman world.

The Barbarians

In 476 A.D., a Germanic tribal leader named Odoacer forced Romulus Augustulus, Emperor of the Roman Empire in the West, to yield his throne to him, and, by pledging his allegiance to the Emperor of Byzantium, ended nearly a thousand years of Roman rule in Western Europe. But Rome had begun to fall long before that, partly because of internal troubles and partly because of the influx of the barbarians from across the Rhine. It is wrong, however, to think of these barbarians as fierce savages willfully overrunning the civilized Roman world. It was more a migration than an invasion, caused by the rise of an even fiercer people in the East, the Mongolian Huns, who suddenly swept out of the steppes of Asia and headed for Europe, after unsuccessfully attacking the Chinese Empire. Actually, the Germans admired the Romans, and many of their kings imitated Roman customs, adopted Roman laws, and tried to live like Roman rulers.

According to Tacitus, who wrote his *Germania* in 98 A.D., the Germans were tall, heavyset, and warlike. Their complexion was ruddy, their eyes clear blue, and their hair blond or reddish. Intensely individualistic, they were incapable of large political organization but lived in tribes. Women, children, and old people tilled the fields and did domestic work while the men reserved themselves for hunting, drinking, and warfare. As early as the fourth century the Visigoths, or West Goths, were converted to Christianity—the Arian variety which did not accept the doctrine of the Trinity. One of their bishops, Ulfilas, translated the Bible into Gothic and represented his diocese at the Council of Nicaea in 325 when the Nicene Creed was formulated and Arian Christianity was branded a heresy.

In 489 the Ostrogoths, or East Goths, invaded Italy and, under the leadership of Theodoric, set up a kingdom that eventually stretched from the Danube down to Sicily and from southwest France to what is today Yugoslavia. Theodoric visited Rome and so admired its architecture that he issued an edict for its preservation. He built many buildings in Verona and Pavia, but it is only in Ravenna that any of his architecture survives. For 33 years, between 493 and 526, Ravenna was the capital of Theodoric's kingdom, which came to an end when Justinian, the Byzantine Emperor in Constantinople, reconquered northwest Africa from the Vandals and most of Italy from the Ostrogoths. Justinian continued the buildings which Theodoric had begun in Ravenna, expunging the figures of the Arian Theodoric and his courtiers from the mosaics on the walls of one of these buildings, the church of Sant' Apollinare Nuovo.

The Church of Sant' Apollinare Nuovo

Unlike its Roman predecessor, the Christian basilica had its front door at one of the short ends, a feature which gave the building a more unified impact. The many horizontal lines in Sant' Apollinare (along the walls, along the ceiling, and, when the building had its patterned marble pavement, along the floor) all converge on a single point, the most important area in the entire building, the altar. Repetitive details like the capitals and the arches above the columns and the heavy bases below them, the clearstory windows, and the windows in the outer wall all seem to march down from the front door to the altar, as do the two processions of saints in the triforium mosaics. The sequence of semicircles here is particularly interesting. There are small dark ones between the columns and small light ones in the windows, all of which lead to the apse, a larger, darker space which is semicircular both in elevation and in plan.

Figure 28 | The south wall of Sant' Apollinare Nuovo, Ravenna, Italy. c. 500 A.D. Brick, marble, wood, and mosaic. 114' long, 41' wide, 48' high

The apse is pierced by three more semicircles, symbolic of God as the Three in One. Inside the apse and embraced by the curving wall—which contrasts so dramatically with the flat surfaces of the walls, floor, and ceiling—stands the altar where, according to the Church, bread and wine are miraculously transformed during every sacred service into the body and blood of Christ.

While there are still many early Christian basilicas in Rome, most of them have been renovated and redecorated, their venerable mosaics often replaced by Renaissance and Baroque decoration. Fortunately for the history of art, Ravenna did not prosper during those periods and, although her churches suffered some neglect, they were not drastically redone. Sant' Apollinare Nuovo has lost the mosaics in its apse, but its nave walls still glitter as they did fourteen centuries ago. Above and on the left side (where women were once segregated during services) twenty-two female saints, all virgins and all martyrs, led by three Magi in fanciful "oriental" costumes, march in solemn dignity from the town of Classe, the suburban seaport of Ravenna, to offer their crowns of martyrdom to the Mother and Child. Opposite them, twenty-six male saints, led by St. Martin of Tours to whom the church was once dedicated, proceed from Theodoric's palace in Ravenna and approach the enthroned Jesus who is flanked by four angels, obviously in Heaven. Between the clearstories stand thirty-two figures of prophets, apostles, and evangelists, and above them, extremely hard to see from the floor, are twenty-six scenes from the life of Jesus alternating with repeated scenes of two doves, symmetrically arranged on each side of a scallop shell, a motif that goes back to pre-Christian Persia. The church was not as empty looking in the sixth century as it is today, for there were ornate pulpits and other church furniture, numerous curtains of bright colors and patterns, and candles and oil lamps suspended from the ceiling that made the mosaics on the walls glitter with many colors.

Whenever they could afford it, the early Christians preferred a mosaic to a wall painting, because it sparkled when light struck it and the mosaic's colors were richer and more permanent than those of a painted surface. There was another important difference between the two media. In a painting a transition from light to dark could be gradual. In a mosaic, however, made as it is of thousands of cubes of colored glass, such transitions had to be achieved by short jumps. In a certain area, say Jesus' face (see colorplate 1), glass cubes of different shades of pink, rose, peach, salmon, orange, beige, tan, brown, white, and sometimes even green or blue, were placed next to one another. Each of these set its neighbor off and gave the area of color an unusual vitality, just as in a piece of gray cloth some threads of brown and blue running through it immediately enliven and enrich the gray by the contrast.

Moreover, the colors of each object in the mosaic are brighter than they would be in nature. The water in colorplate 1, for example, is green blue with splotches of various blues and streaks of white. The other large color area is the gold of the sky. Gold also pervades the rest of the picture, appearing on the borders of Christ's purple robe, on the boat, on the oar, and in the border around the picture. All through the Middle Ages, gold was equated with light, and light with the Kingdom of God.

Jesus Calling Peter and Andrew   Colorplate 1

The general composition of this mosaic is comparatively simple: two large vertical forms at the right are balanced by two smaller diagonal forms and a curved form at the left. Spatially the picture is flat with little distinction between foreground and background. Nor are the figures three-dimensional; the wrinkles of clothing do not follow around the bodies but stop when they get to the edges of the figures. The sharpness of these edges, moreover, makes the figures look more like cardboard cutouts than like real people. This sense of unreality is heightened by the fact that there seems to be no skeleton in the body of Jesus. There appears to be no skull behind Christ's face, and the shoulders do not press against the drapery as they would in a real person; his right arm curves as if it were made of putty instead of flesh and blood, and the position of his left arm is not clear. There is no expression on any of the faces, and, instead of looking at the men he is talking to, Christ's eyes stare into space. Finally, the colors are too bright and unmodulated to be real. In these and many other respects this picture departs from natural appearances.

One more thing that removes this picture from the realm of believability is the relationship of light and shadow. From earliest infancy we comprehend the form and shapes of objects by the way light strikes them. In the statue of Zeus the sculptor modeled his material so that light and dark combine to give us the illusion of muscles and the bone structure in a human body. In this respect the figures in the mosaic are more like the Dogon statue. The light and dark folds of Christ's robe do not articulate the body under it by defining the form of the shoulders, the hips, or the knees. Instead, these folds are merely stripes of light and dark color, some of them vertical, some of them diagonal, some of them arranged in a zig-zag sequence. They are visual rhythms which, like those on the Sudanese statue, generate energy, tensions, and oppositions. They dramatize rather than describe the figure of Jesus. Light and dark, then, in the Ravenna mosaic achieve a pattern which, like everything else in the picture, is symbolic rather than realistic in effect.

Our first reaction to this picture is: "It looks like something a ten-year-old child might have done." The boat is much too small to hold the two men in it. The men are much too big to be out in the water away from the shore. The figure of Jesus is badly drawn, inaccurate and clumsy as far as human anatomy goes. One reason that it looks like a child's drawing is that children's minds do not work like adults'. They ignore certain aspects of realism that make things "true" for us, such as the relationship of a distant boat to the nearby land. Children ignore such factual truths in their eagerness to convey certain ideas: Jesus is important, and so he should be big. The fishermen are next most important, and so they are the next in size. The boat is necessary to the story but otherwise is not important, and so it is too small to be true for an adult but it is perfectly true for the child. This, of course, is exactly the point: the early Christian artist who did this was not interested in showing how Jesus looked about five hundred years before, on the day he first met Peter and Andrew. Medieval man was not concerned with historical or scientific facts. For him the test of truth lay not in verifiable facts or else he could not have believed in the unicorns, mermaids, and all the scaly, winged monsters that he depicted in his manuscripts and churches. Things were true if they served a purpose in what was the most important thing in his life, not science or history or logic, or even the problem of feeding and clothing himself and his family, but the salvation of his soul and its resurrection in the hereafter. And so the episode of Christ calling Peter and Andrew was not a historical event for him but, like everything else in his life—like the mermaids and the dragons that filled his world—it was a symbol. This is why Christ does not look at his future disciples as he calls them. As a matter of fact, he is not even looking at us. (An artist can make a painted face look in one direction by relating the pupil of the eye to the rest of the eye in a certain way. Thus a person painted to look at us will look directly at us even if we move to the left or to the right of the painting.) In this mosaic, Christ's eyes look beyond us. They are focussed on space, on the world at large. In other words, he is not calling Peter and Andrew to leave their way of life and go with him. He is not even calling us, the spectators. He is calling all of mankind to arise and follow him.

In order to function as a symbol the boat does not have to look big enough to hold two adults. The relationship of water to land does not have to be believable; distant figures do not have to be smaller than close ones; figures do not even have to look as if they had skeletons inside them, or elbows and knees. Such things belong to our world, not to the world of spiritual truth, divinely ordained and revealed. And so, gravity does not make the water lie down as it does in our world. Skies are a miraculous and precious gold color, not ordinary everyday blue. If Jesus' feet were firmly planted on the ground, he would be just like the ordinary men we see around us every day. In the world of eternal truth we cannot expect things to look as they do in the finite and fallible world we live in.

Some may argue that the picture looks as though a child had done it, because, after the disintegration of the Roman world, the artist had lost the knowledge of how to represent the human body and nature. In a way this is true, but he lost his skills of representing appearances precisely because he no longer cared how things look. The physical realism of Greco-Roman art no longer satisfied him as a vehicle to convey his new *Weltanschauung;* a materialistic art was inadequate to express a spiritual message. What the early Christian artist did was to go back to preclassic art, the art of ancient Egypt, Mesopotamia, and Persia whose religions, incidentally, were also strongly mystical, ritualistic, and concerned with a life hereafter. As far as artistic skill goes, there is little, if any, loss of manual dexterity or technical sophistication between the art of classical Greece and Rome and that of these mosaics. The grandeur and richness of these mosaics, their beauty of color and pattern, attest to the artist's imaginative and technical gifts.

The Concept of Design

The chief qualities that distinguish the arts of painting, sculpture, and architecture from the performing and literary arts are in the language by which they communicate to us, a language that is primarily visual. Unfortunately there is no Webster's Dictionary in which we can look up the vocabulary of this language. Men in every era have tried to formulate such a dictionary and to lay down rules of a visual grammar, so to speak, but the next generation has always disagreed with their formulations and has gone ahead to do all the things their predecessors had declared artistically invalid. Yet if the principles of the visual arts are impossible to codify, it does not mean that they do not exist. They are simply very elusive and variable, but we can see them and point them out.

The word "design" is sometimes used to designate merely the arrangement of shapes, like the design of a poster, but there is a larger, more comprehensive meaning of the word. In designing a house, for example, an architect does not merely put together some nice looking stones and shingles and add some attractive windows and doors. His design depends on how he wants the house to work: where to put the front door in relation to the living room, the coat closet, and the back door; where to locate the bathrooms and the kitchen to cut down plumbing costs; how to place the windows so that ventilation is adequate and the glare of the sun is avoided.

Design in a painting does not involve such practical considerations but stems from another kind of logic which we might call pictorial logic. A certain straight line, for example, might lead our eye straight out of a painting unless the painter halted this movement with some curves or a perpendicular accent. One color might clash with its neighbors and perhaps destroy the particular mood of the picture. On the other hand, the discordant color may enhance the design if it was the painter's object to strike a jarring note. It will be seen, then, that design includes more than composition which refers merely to the arrangement of forms and patterns in space. In its fullest sense, design involves all of the components in a painting: line, pattern, color, light, perspective, texture, and so on, in short, all the pictorial means by which the artist has achieved his effect. It would include other elements, of course, in the arts of sculpture and architecture.

In the Ravenna mosaic, the composition is comparatively simple because there are only a few clean-cut shapes and they are related in a clear and simple way: principally two verticals at the right and two or three diagonally arranged shapes at the left. The two at the right are both the darkest and the lightest shapes in the picture. Not only that, but they are next to each other. This juxtaposition of the lightest and darkest tones heightens their importance. They are the focal area of the picture in size, direction, and tone, as well as in religious significance. We feel an axis running through each of these figures (their bodies are quite rigid and their heads do not bend), an axis which is parallel to two sides of the picture and, of course, perpendicular to the others. We feel the resulting immobility of these figures. They are firmly anchored to the frame of the picture, so to speak, while the men in the boat are adrift both visually and in terms of the narrative. In this way, therefore, the composition plays a dynamic role in the design of this mosaic.

The background has a logic of its own. The sky might easily have been one solid tone, because gold cubes in mosaics are not a natural color like the rest of the cubes. An actual fragment of gold leaf was put over one face of each cube and then a thin coat of glass was put over that to make it glisten like the rest. It would have been no trouble, therefore, to make the sky all the same tone of gold. The artist (or team of artists under a master artist's direction) must have intended the various cubes to be different shades of gold. Why? We do not know what was in the artist's mind, of course, but since contrasts of light and dark tones and bright and dull colors give the illusion of receding and projecting in space, the result is that the sky is not a flat, impenetrable curtain of gold, but something more like a golden mist. The broad expanse of water, on the other hand, has much more variety of effect: flat and placid at the right, broken up into waves of line and color at the left, and intersected by the diagonal oar and what is visually the most turbulent area in the picture—the net full of fish.

We have spoken about the stability of vertical shapes and the movement implied by diagonals. Outline, too, can suggest motion. The undulating line of the Zeus statue endows the figure with a sense of movement similar to that of a real human being. Compared to that graceful, smoothly curving line, the outlines in the Ravenna mosaic are hard, heavy, and clumsy. If one's eye begins to follow a line, one runs immediately into a dead stop or across an opposing line. The resulting effect is a lack of movement. Moreover, the lines are like wires which are rigid and stiff. This rigidity is not inappropriate to the solemn and highly symbolic mood of the mosaic. An elegant, graceful, or more human Jesus in this picture would have produced an effect which is quite different and quite unsuited to the spirit of the early Middle Ages. The suggestion of change, of movement through change, would contradict the solemn, unchanging, and eternal implication of this picture. There is, however, another kind of movement inherent in this mosaic which does agree with its mood and meaning. Since each cube of glass is set individually into the cement, each of them slants at a slightly different angle. Moreover, the cubes are not flat and rectangular but random shaped, just as the glass cracked. The result is that light reflects from their surfaces as from the facets of a diamond. The mosaic may lack movement in the character of its lines, but as we move through the church, light moves in various ways across that flickering surface, whose forms suddenly acquire a movement and a mysterious life of their own.

These are only a few of the elements of this mosaic's design. Now the question naturally arises: is the design of a picture connected with or independent of the content (the subject and meaning) of the picture? Design may be relatively independent of subject matter, but generally it agrees with it and augments the impact of that content. The fact that Jesus is the largest and most stable form in the picture, and the only spot of purple in the mosaic, cannot help but enhance the picture's meaning to the worshipper for whom it was intended. If verticals generally suggest stability, diagonals frequently convey a sense of movement. Not being parallel or perpendicular to the frame, the diagonals of the two men in the boat, and the boat itself, epitomize instability. The two fishermen incline diagonally toward the solid verticality of Jesus as if pulled toward him by some mysterious magnetic force. Even the boat seems to be lifted out of the water to follow the Fisher of Men. In contrast to them the man at the right has already found his stability in Christ in a visual as well as a narrative sense. Moreover, the repetition in each group, their exact parallelism, adds power to the idea, as the repetition of a word does in a poem.

The gold of the upper background removes this scene from the everyday world, for except in a very unusual sunset, such a sky is not a familiar sight to us. In contrast to this golden mist of heaven, the earth and water are turbulent and troubled. Again, we may question whether the artist who designed this mosaic (a team of mosaicists actually performed the manual work) did all of these things on purpose. Of course, there were no books on the rules of art, or art schools where such principles might be taught. The medieval artist was trained as an apprentice in a workshop. Design was based on tradition. This mosaic may have been based on others elsewhere, perhaps in Constantinople or in Rome, or on some manuscript illumination or ivory carving, all of them lost to us. It can be argued, however, that a creative artist uses his means creatively, just as a natural-born storyteller knows all the tricks with which to dramatize his narrative, devices which he may have picked up from other storytellers and recognized intuitively as effective elements of his art. The rules which govern composition, perspective, anatomy, balance, movement, color relationships, etc., may be and are taught in art schools today. But the effective use of these elements of art is something completely personal with each artist, however ignorant he may be of formal theory and esthetics.

Projects

1. Investigate the general form, structural principle, and decoration of the church of San Vitale in Ravenna. How does its axial arrangement make its impact upon the beholder different from that of Sant' Apollinare Nuovo?
2. Analyze the design of the apse mosaic in the church of San Vitale in Ravenna which depicts the Emperor Justinian and his followers, paying particular attention to the placement of the heads, hands, and feet. Does the flow of the composition follow the implied movement of the figures?
3. Select one page from each of the following medieval manuscripts: *The Book of Kells,* the *Beatus Apocalypse* in Gerona, the *Utrecht Psalter,* and the *Gospels of Otto III.* In each case describe how the artist has arranged the lines, patterns, colors, repetitions, and contrasts to achieve his effect. How much of this effect is appropriate to the subject of the picture and how much is independent of it?
4. Look at four color reproductions of Roman mosaics. How does the artist produce the effects of three-dimensional form, the recession of things in space, and the semblance of light and shadow?

Suggested Reading

Beckwith, John. *Early Medieval Art.**New York: Frederick A. Praeger, Inc., 1964.

Grabar, André. *Byzantine Painting.* New York: Skira, Inc., Publishers, 1953.

Grabar, André, and Carl Nordenfalk. *Early Medieval Painting.* New York: Skira, Inc., Publishers, 1964.

Lassus, Jean. *The Early Christian and Byzantine World.* New York: McGraw-Hill Book Co., Inc., 1967.

Lowrie, Walter, *Art of the Early Church.**New York: Harper and Row, Publishers, 1958.

Maiuri, Amadeo. *Roman Painting.* New York: Skira, Inc., Publishers, 1953.

Volbach, W. F. *Early Christian Art.* New York: Harry N. Abrams, Inc., 1962.

*Available in a paperback edition.

6 | Art for Meditation
A Romanesque Relief, a Statue from India, and a Chinese Landscape

Life in the medieval village was lived pretty much from day to day without much thought for the past or the future. There were other communities, however, where the past and the future were more in mind than the present. These were the monasteries where monks spent their lives in prayer, meditation, and work. The abbey church was the focus of the community, not only the largest building in it but the tallest as well, often built on a rise so that its towers could be seen from miles away. Around this church, which was a basilica in form though usually covered by a stone vault rather than a truss roof, were the monks' dormitory, chapter house for meetings, refectory for eating, kitchen, storerooms, bathroom and other washing facilities, and a cloister (an enclosed garden, arcaded and shady, where the monks could walk or sit as they read their devotional books, or could pray and meditate in relative seclusion). Around this nucleus there were buildings for a variety of functions: schools, chapels, infirmary, workshops, stables, and service buildings. There were gardens for food, sheds for livestock, a cemetery, quarters for novices who were not yet monks, and a hostelry for travelers, for in those unsettled days monasteries became places to spend the night without fear of being robbed or even murdered. Monks not only copied and illuminated (decorated) manuscripts, but engaged in architectural projects, sculpture, and other arts, and crafts such as goldsmithing, enameling, silk and carpet weaving, glassmaking and ceramics, as well as trades such as bookbinding and bell casting. In the monastery of St. Riquier in northeastern France there were rows of streets lined with shops of armorers, saddlemakers, cobblers, and other tradesmen. There are still monasteries today that are famous for some specialty such as making cheeses or liqueurs.

Life in a Monastery

The daily life of the monk was (and is, in monasteries still today) an existence that seems unbelievably severe to the average man in the twentieth century. Each day began with a period of prayer at Matins before the sun rose, and continued with others at Prime just after sunrise, Tierce two hours later, and six more prayer sessions before the sun rose again. Solemn High Mass, the service that included the Eucharist or Communion sacrament, was celebrated several times in between. In other words, the basilica was in use almost constantly both day and night, even though pilgrims and other visitors might be worshipping in various other parts of the building. For the most part these prayers and services were sung to melodies which we call Gregorian chants, because they were first written down at the order of Pope Gregory the Great about 600. Still used in the Catholic church today, these Gregorian chants are sung in unison by male voices only. They are chanted unaccompanied by any instrument, and have no meter, that is, no regular rhythm. Moreover, they conform to a modal system of music of which only the major and the minor modes survive today (except in authentic folk music or imitations of it). This practice of frequent singing must undoubtedly have had a part in forming church architecture, particularly in the height of the barrel or groined vaults from which the sound could reverberate, rising and falling in meterless purity, endlessly repetitive, and seemingly without beginning or end, impelling the singer and anyone who heard it to shut out the external world and look inward in near hypnotic contemplation.

As in many monastic institutions then and now, the rule of silence was rigidly maintained except for two half-hour periods when conversation was allowed. Even meals were taken in silence except for the lector who read aloud from the lives of the saints and the writings of the church fathers. Each monk lived in a cell which was lit by a small window at one end. There was no heat anywhere in the monastery except in the kitchen. This was why the monks wore woolen robes with long sleeves that could serve as hand muffs and a hood that could keep the head warm in the cold stone rooms. Such hardship might seem unnecessarily severe to us except that it is basic to the whole concept of freeing the soul from the body through renunciation. A monk, according to the Rule of St. Benedict, should own absolutely nothing, "neither a book, nor tablets, nor pen— nothing at all. For indeed it is not allowed to the monks to own even their bodies or their own wills." This is, after all, only a literal interpretation of Christ's own words according to St. Luke: "Whoever will lose his life for my sake, the same shall save it."

The Pilgrimage Roads

The period from about 1000 to 1150, the era we call Romanesque, saw a great surge of artistic activity during which countless new churches were built and old ones either replaced or enlarged. The fronts of churches, their interiors, and the capitals of the columns in their cloisters were richly ornamented with sculpture. Much metalwork was produced then —sculptured bronze doors, baptismal fonts, and candlesticks—as well as a wealth of gold, enameled, and jewel-encrusted chalices and other ecclesiastical objects, but most of these have disappeared because of their valuable materials. The interiors of churches were covered with vast wall paintings most of which, alas, have been covered over or destroyed later by people who thought them ugly. So many new churches were built during this era and so sturdy was their construction that still today almost every town and village in Europe has one or more churches that are either entirely in the Romanesque style or that have Romanesque portions still discernible.

One factor that helped disseminate art styles, symbolism, and iconography (the conventions of symbolism at a given time or in a certain locale) was the practice of making pilgrimages. Every devout Christian wanted, at some time during his life, to visit certain places that were held in particular veneration. After Rome and the Holy Land, the most noted of these shrines was the town of Compostela in the remote northwestern tip of Spain where Santiago, or St. James, one of Christ's twelve disciples, was believed to be buried. There were four main roads across France and over the Pyrenees to Santiago de Compostela, and along each road, as hundreds of pilgrims from all over Europe stopped at the abbeys and towns, churches were enlarged or rebuilt; for this was the age of relics, and every church had a number of treasured items—garments or other belongings of a saint, his body, or a portion thereof—before which the pilgrim could offer up prayers. Such relics were kept in reliquaries that were frequently made of gold and decorated with enamel and jewels, often in the shape of little houses, or sometimes in a shape that conformed to the relic inside it—a head, for example, for a portion of the saint's head, or a hand for a finger bone.

Returning Crusaders brought back many of these relics from the Holy Land, so that every church accumulated a number of them. Many churches boasted pieces of the true cross, thorns from the crown which Jesus wore, and other objects of veneration. A vial of Christ's blood was exhibited in Bruges in the twelfth century, and the coat he wore was claimed to be in the possession of two separate churches, one in Trier and one in Argenteuil. The remains of Mary Magdalen are still claimed by at least two churches in France today. Churchmen themselves sometimes questioned the authenticity of these relics, but popular imagination thrived on them and countless miracles were attributed to their powers. Some churches displayed racks full of crutches left by cripples who had been cured there, and one church dedicated to Saint Leonard, the patron saint of prisoners, was festooned inside and out with the chains of those whom he had delivered from prison.

On the road the pilgrim could be identified by his garb which included a walking staff and a scrip—a small pouch in which he carried his valuables. On his hat he wore an emblem to identify the shrine he had seen: a shell if he had visited Compostela; a human head if he had been to Amiens (because the severed head of John the Baptist had been taken there in 1206). During his journey, he came under the special protection of the Church, and the lands and goods he left behind were held in keeping for him. When he at last returned to his village, he became a celebrity and was regarded by his colleagues with awe.

Emile Mâle, who wrote so eloquently about the art of the Middle Ages, describes what a pilgrim might have encountered, according to the twelfth-century *Guide for the Pilgrim of Santiago*, along the road that led through western France:

> Beyond Bordeaux, the pilgrims entered the great desert of the Landes, a wild country, where the traveler who strayed an instant from the path sank in the sand up to his knees. At Belin, one of the halting-places, a great tomb contained the bodies of the holy martyrs Olivier, Gondebaud, Ogier the Dane, Arastain of Brittany, Garin of Lorraine, and many other companions of Charlemagne, killed in Spain for the Christian faith. The pilgrim then passed through Labouheyre, Dax, Sorde, and reached the Pyrenees at Ostabat, not far from the Port de Cize. There the three great roads to Compostela joined. On the mountain stood a huge cross, raised up, it was said, by Charlemagne. The Emperor had prayed there, his face turned toward Santiago, and the pilgrims followed his example, each one planting in the earth, near the stone cross, a little wooden cross. From Cize the way led to Roncevaux, near which passed all pilgrims who did not pass the Pyrenees at Somport. In the church at Roncevaux they stood entranced before the stone that Roland had cleaved through with his sword. Crossing the famous battlefield, they came down toward Navarre and the most dangerous part of their journey. Here they met mountain people with bare legs, short, fringed coats, and sandals of hairy leather; each man carried two javelins, and a horn suspended from his waist. Some-

times they would howl like wolves or hoot like owls, and comrades would surge up beside them. They were Basques, a most inhospitable and dangerous race. . . .

The two mountain routes, the one coming by way of Somport and the other by Port de Cize, merged at Puenta la Reina. From that point on, a single road led through Estella, Burgois, Frómista, Carrión, Sahagún, León, Astorga to Santiago. From Monte San Marcos the pilgrims could see for the first time the towers of the Basilica of Santiago. The first to catch sight of the church was proclaimed "king of the pilgrims," and the title passed from father to son, like a noble rank. Finally, after months of difficult and dangerous traveling, the pilgrims could kneel down at the apostle's tomb.[1]

The Abbey of Moissac

Located near Toulouse on one of the pilgrimage roads that led across south central France and joined the two eastern roads near Roncevaux, the Benedictine abbey at Moissac was founded before 650. The basic shape and the lower portions of the church as we see it today date from 1063, but since the church was rebuilt in the fifteenth century, the vaults are late Gothic. In the thirteenth century the sculptured porch was moved from the west end to the south transept portal. On the left wall of this porch are depicted several scenes from the New Testament story of the rich man, Dives, who would give the beggar Lazarus nothing but the crumbs from his table. In one scene, Lazarus expires and angels take his soul (depicted as a little baby coming out of Lazarus' mouth) up to Paradise, where Abraham clasps it to his bosom. Below this, on the ground level, terrifying demons personify Luxury and Greed, while other monsters torment the miserly Dives. On the right-hand wall are depicted scenes from the life of Jesus, including the Annunciation, the Adoration of the Magi, and the Flight into Egypt.

In the semicircle above the door, a large and crowded relief represents the Second Coming of Christ as described in the New Testament book of Revelation. Jesus is shown flanked by the winged figures which, in the Middle Ages, were taken as the symbols of the Four Evangelists (the lion for St. Mark, the ox for St. Luke, the eagle for St. John, and the winged man for St. Matthew). Below these sit the twenty-four elders described in

---

1. From *Religious Art from the Twelfth to the Eighteenth Century,* by Emile Mâle. Copyright 1948 by Pantheon Books, Inc. Reprinted by permission of Pantheon Books, A Division of Random House, Inc.

Revelation, who wear crowns and hold goblets and musical instruments in their hands. Below this scene, on the *trumeau,* the vertical pillar which divides the door into halves and supports the lintel above the door, three pairs of lions are represented standing one atop the other. Elsewhere in the porch the faces of monsters and demons make grimaces, rats and birds of prey scurry along moldings, and in one capital a grotesque old man pursues a fish-tailed mermaid.

The cloister at Moissac, one of the most famous in France, contains more than fifty capitals with figures on them as well as about thirty with flowered and foliate patterns, animal heads, mythical beasts, and other grotesque subjects. If the presence of so many hideous details seems to us inappropriate for church decoration, we must remember two things: ferocious animals were part of the barbarian tradition which was one of the sources of Romanesque art, and the religion of this period was governed by fear and the belief that Hell's emissaries lay everywhere in wait for the careless Christian. Even the images of Christ and the saints were not kindly, but stern and fearful.

Part of the impact which the relief in figure 29 makes on the beholder is due to its location on the side of the *trumeau,* the stone shaft that divides the door in two. From outside the church, we see only the six lions on the front surface of the *trumeau.* It is not until we cross the threshold that we see the elongated figure of the Apostle, whose head towers high above ours and whose eyes are not focussed on us but stare into the dark interior of the church. Besides contributing to its impact on the beholder, the position of the relief has one other significant result. The source of illumination is fixed, since the daylight comes always from the right, and the interior of the church is dimly lighted. The effect of this oblique light upon the carved surface is like that of a theatrical spotlight, and the carving has been done in such a way as to make the most of this circumstance. Instead of the gentle flow of one volume into another such as we saw in the Zeus, we have in the Moissac sculpture a surface broken up into separate units, more in the manner of the Sudanese carving. Yet this fragmentation of the surface is not here so much in terms of volumes as it is in the African statue. The Moissac relief is conceived as an arrangement of well-defined planes. Strictly speaking, the word plane refers to a flat, two-dimensional area, either actual, as in the arts of sculpture and architecture, or apparent, as in a painting. The word is also used, however, to denote surfaces which are only relatively flat, so that we can speak of the planes of the figure from Mali as angular and highly contrasted, and those of the Zeus statue as more numerous and less sharply defined. Neither of these two statues is conceived primarily in terms of planes, however, as is the Romanesque relief.

This reliance on planes is not due merely to the fact that the St. Paul is a relief. The drapery folds on figures in Greek and Roman reliefs are rounded volumes that fall across the body like real cloth. St. Paul's robe, on the contrary, is arranged in flat pleats that seem to overlap each other like the segments of a lobster's shell, even over the shoulder and on the elbow, where full folds of drapery might be expected. The hand that holds the book, moreover, is drastically reduced to two major planes which are separated by the knuckles of the fingers.

Everywhere one looks in this relief, one encounters similar sharp divisions between lighted planes and planes in shadow. The rhythm which this pattern of light and dark makes suggests neither the thundering drumbeats nor the mellow sound of a stringed instrument that we mentioned in connection with the African and Greek statues. Instead, it might be compared to the sound of a trumpet, sharp and brittle, by turns abrupt and sustained. The artist has taken the human figure and has neither dehumanized it completely nor reproduced it as humans look. He has done somewhat as the Ravenna mosaicist did: he has distorted the details of the human body sufficiently to remove it from our everyday experience, and he has transformed these details into a rhythmic design, a design which is not of lines and color (although the relief was probably painted originally), but which depends largely upon the arrangement of shallow planes.

Our pleasure in looking at this relief is derived not so much from our recognizing a hand with a book in it, a robe with a jeweled border, or a face with a long, flowing beard. We are moved more by the interrelationship of the planes. Observe St. Paul's other hand, for example. It seems to have been broken off at the wrist, and its fingers appear to have no bones inside them. But by twisting it into an unnatural position, the sculptor has emphasized the pattern of light and shadow made by the four parallel fingers. The three tendons in the wrist, which might seem like incongruously realistic details in this otherwise stylized relief, are made to echo the three troughs of shadow that separate the fingers. On the arm to the left of these fingers, over the abdomen, across the chest, everywhere in the relief, one can see repetitions with slight variations of this light-dark motif, sometimes in a sequence of three, sometimes of four, sometimes of more numerous accents. The most remarkable transformation of this elaboration occurs in the hair and beard, where the separate strands are treated in parallel grooves, very unlike real hair, but wonderfully suitable to the total design of the relief.

Figure 29 | *St. Paul,* a stone relief from Moissac, France. c. 1125. Stone, 6′ high

Compared to the irregular geometry of this descriptive detail, the jeweled border around the neck and over the left wrist seems unusually precise and regular. With great deliberateness, the sculptor has carved the pattern of raised dots on the edges of the border. Yet in their roles as repetitive accents, they harmonize with the rest of the carving. So do the diamond-shaped jewels on the border, which, though startling in their contrast with the stripes and grooves that dominate the relief, nevertheless relate to one very important detail in the figure, the large, staring eyes. These eyes, below the arched brows and furrowed forehead, seem to be focussed on something far away, as if they were meditating on the apocalyptic scene of Christ's Second Coming which is depicted above the door.

Aside from its strange elongation, one of the most notable qualities of this carving is the movement of its main volumes and the tension which seems to exist between its various parts. The head is turned one way, the shoulders another; the hips are not directly below the head but project on one side; and the legs seem to be in motion. The tendency to geometrize, to make natural forms flatter, simpler, and more harmonious to one another, is also characteristic of Byzantine art—the mosaics, manuscripts, and ivory carvings made in Constantinople or under the influence of the Eastern Christian or Orthodox Church. But Byzantine art is static. Movement is frozen and figures seem to be eternally fixed in the flat space they occupy. What has here given so much energy and dynamism to the figure of St. Paul?

We need only look at his face for our answer. This is not a Latin physiognomy, not the Mediterranean type with thick, curly hair, certainly not the smooth-shaven Roman. This hair is long and gently wavy, and its texture is thin and light; it is fine blond hair rather than coarse brown or black. Clearly, the face of St. Paul and those of all the statues on this sculptured porch are of twelfth-century monks in the abbey at Moissac, the descendants of the Visigoths who once ruled this region. And just as the Church Universal had absorbed many diverse peoples, so also had it assimilated the art styles of many cultures. The graceful curling acanthus leaves above St. Paul are derived from classical Greco-Roman art; the rhythmic grace of the figure, from Byzantium; the vigor and intensity of the forms, from the barbarians; and the paired lions on the front of the *trumeau,* from the art of Mesopotamia and Persia that had flourished long before either Greek or Roman civilization existed. Even the art of the Moslem Moors in Spain seems to have left its mark in the strange scalloped edges of the door jambs.

One might wonder why there should be elements of ancient Mesopotamian, Persian, and even Egyptian art forms in the Christian art of the

Middle Ages. After rejecting the art of one pagan culture, that of the Greco-Roman world, why should the medieval Christians have sought inspiration in the art of other pagan peoples? The answer lies in the fact that the religion of the Greeks and Romans was worldly and centered on man, whereas the religions of the Near East, including Christianity, were strongly supernatural and antirational. The values inherent in the art of the latter were therefore closer to medieval Christianity than were those of Greco-Roman art.

Sculpture in India

The otherworldliness implicit in the Ravenna mosaic and in the St. Paul relief is rare in the history of Western art but dominates art in the Far East. The Hindu faith, which has pervaded India's thought and way of life for an incredible thirty-four centuries, is centered around one basic tenet, that Brahman is the supreme spirit, the generating force of everything in the universe. Brahman is ultimate reality. All else is illusion. The material world and all physical desires are vain, temporal, and ephemeral.

The goal of the Hindu's life is enlightenment—the realization of ultimate reality, the understanding of absolute truth, and therefore complete identification with Brahman. This union of man with God may be achieved through self-discipline by means of spiritual exercises, meditation, and the cultivation of virtues such as charity, nonviolence, and compassion for all living things. Yoga, or the yoking of the soul to God, comprises more than the physical exercises about which we hear so much. It involves mental and spiritual exercises as well. The achievement of enlightenment takes many many lifetimes, countless cycles of births, deaths, and reincarnations. Time for the Hindu does not move in a straight line as it does for us, from past to present to future, but in ever repeating cycles.

Centuries have added to these basic precepts a complex accretion of practices and beliefs. Unlike Judaism, Christianity, and the Moslem faith, Hinduism is not an exclusive religion but tolerates and tends to absorb the ideas of other religions. Even Buddhism, which originated in India as an outgrowth of Hinduism, was so reassimilated that it has virtually disappeared in India, whereas it continues as a major religion elsewhere in the Far East. Through the centuries, moreover, countless regional and tribal gods were incorporated into Hinduism on the theory that all gods, since they are part of Brahman, are worthy of reverence.

Since Brahman is not a person but a life force, it is not representable in an image; but its various manifestations are, and so the walls and roofs of

Hindu temples often swarm with sculptured figures of gods and goddesses, semidivine spirits, and animal forms. Each one of these divinities, moreover, may be represented in a variety of guises and reincarnations. Shiva, for example, the God of Destruction, is sometimes shown wearing a necklace of skulls and performing his dance of cosmic destruction. But since rebirth inevitably follows destruction, Shiva also incorporates Brahman as the creator, and so he is often shown embracing his wife as a symbol of fertility and procreation. Or he may be depicted with three faces, one representing the male force in nature, one the female, and one the union of these polarities. Quite frequently he has four arms, each of them representing a different aspect of his power.

Although Hinduism stresses self-denial, it considers the sensual aspects of life, though they belong to the physical world of illusion, as part of the divine plan. Instead of dehumanizing and dematerializing his sacred images, as did the Christian artists in Moissac and Ravenna, the Hindu artist emphasizes the physical characteristics of his figures, celebrating their sensual, often erotic, voluptuousness. Sculptured reliefs teem with curvaceous bodies amid a profusion of fruits and flowers, which, in their uniformity of treatment, imply at once the fertility of nature and the pervasiveness of the divine spirit in all things.

A Stone Relief from India

Part of a larger temple decoration, the pink sandstone relief of Shiva illustrated in figure 30 is conceived in rounded volumes rather than in flat planes. A horizontal slice through any part of it would reveal a circular section, whereas a similar slice through the Moissac relief would yield only slight curves that approach straight lines. In its rounded forms, moreover, the figure of Shiva also differs from the African and Greek statues in its interplay of large, plain, curved surfaces and smaller, narrow, and highly decorated ridges of stone, both of which elements are set against deep voids filled with shadow. As a composition, the relief moves in a fluid, swelling rhythm which is dominated by undulating, serpentine curves.

Shiva's pose suggests both rest and motion, and forms a sinuous S-shaped curve suggesting, but not actually depicting, a dance. In the Zeus we are shown an instant in a sequence of time in which the god throws his thunderbolt; we can imagine what his pose was before that

Figure 30 | *Shiva,* a sculptural relief from India. Eighth century. Pink sandstone, 37″ high, 10″ deep. Virginia Museum of Fine Arts, Richmond. Virginia

instant and what it will be afterwards. Moreover, the Greek god is subject
to the force of gravity; his feet are planted firmly on the ground and his
body reveals the pressure of the skeleton against the flesh and of the
muscles against each other. Shiva, on the other hand, exists in a timeless
and weightless world. His swelling limbs are not subject to an external,
physical force, but respond to an energy which seems to press outward
from within the stone.

Iconographically, Shiva is here represented with four arms, one of
which is unfortunately broken off. One arm is encircled by a snake. The
other two are entwined with a garland. He has a third eye arranged
vertically into his forehead, through which he can look into eternity.
Flanked by small figures of lesser spirits, he stands before his worshippers, his eyes half closed in meditation, his radiant face and smiling
mouth revealing the bliss of inner peace and contentment that comes with
enlightenment.

Painting in China

The art of painting has been called the preeminent art of the Chinese
culture, particularly landscape painting, which allowed the artist to
combine his introspective impulses with the representation of natural
forms. The very word for painting in Chinese is formed by two syllables,
one meaning water and the other, land. One quality which is a constant in
Chinese art, and the quality which perhaps distinguishes it most sharply
from art in the West, is its self-sufficiency. The painting of a landscape on
a scroll, for example, was not principally something to decorate the wall
of someone's house, or to tell a story, or even to reproduce the appearance
of some particular place or a specific variety of tree or plant. It was
instead a cherished possession that was kept rolled up in a tubular
container and taken out and unrolled only on certain occasions when
those who looked at it wished to meditate on its meaning, as we might
open a book of poetry and read, perhaps for the hundredth time, a poem
that has particular significance for us.

This significance lay not only in the objects depicted but also in the
qualities of the painting itself, in the vitality of its lines, the gradation of
its tones, and the subtlety and power of the artist's touch. Still, the
Chinese artist did not regard himself as a craftsman, but as a philosopher
and poet, almost a seer or prophet. Before touching his brush to paper, he
prepared himself spiritually for the act of painting by emptying himself of
all disquietude and concentrating on certain ideas. His hand, whose
dexterity had been prepared by years of rigorous exercise and discipline,
set down a visible account of these thoughts which can be understood

through the eyes but not expressed in words. Every touch of his brush, therefore, was charged with meaning, and nothing he did was superfluous. The picture he painted is more than what he saw. It is a visual transcription of an emotional and intellectual experience which he felt.

This is not to say that the subject matter depicted in the painting was not significant in the experience of the picture. A complex set of symbols was elaborated over the centuries. Clouds, mist, and haze are in Buddhism as well as in Taoism the very image of universal impermanence and insubstantiality. Mountains rise into the sky as if aspiring to perfection, trees bend to the adverse forces of the wind, rocks are worn away by the patient trickle of a stream of water which also serves to fertilize and purify. The comparative smallness of man in many Chinese landscapes is a self-explanatory symbol. Western art as a whole has been dominated by Greco-Roman thought, in which man was the central subject and nature usually of secondary importance. In some periods, indeed, a painting was not considered art at all unless the image of man was preeminent in it and highly idealized. In Chinese landscape painting, human figures are generally shown as mere specks of light and shadow no more remarkable than the root of an old tree, an inert stone, or a clump of grass.

The mystic and meditative tendency was especially strong among the painters of the Sung dynasty, from 960 to 1276. The twelfth and fourteenth centuries particularly saw the rise of the Ch'an sect of Buddhism, which we know by its Japanese name, Zen, both words derived from the Sanskrit word for meditation. Rejecting the role of ritual and scriptures in the search for spiritual enlightenment, Ch'an relied instead on inner discipline, intuition born of meditation, and the direct personal confrontation of ultimate reality, often brought about through the surprising statement of a paradox or even a physical blow.

As to technique, Chinese painting is closely related to writing. The brush is the same as that used in writing, and is held in the same way—straight up and down, more in the fist than by the fingers alone. And in both writing and painting the hand is held without resting the arm on the paper or cloth surface. As in writing, too, instead of paint of various colors, black ink is used, what we call India ink and what the French more correctly refer to as *encre de Chine.* The ink, diluted with water to produce various shades of gray, is applied to either silk or paper.

Chinese Landscape

Without a doubt the most striking quality of this picture is the remarkable illusion of atmosphere. Not only are portions of forms hidden by a veil of mist that makes the distant mountains appear to float in space,

but the forms which one sees completely are modulated and often slightly blurred by the atmosphere. The clump of shrubbery at the lower center of the picture is an extreme example of this blurring. The tall trees, on the other hand, are more sharply outlined. And some forms, like the towering cliffs on the right, move gradually from a sharply outlined area to a more blurred one. Then there are other volumes in which crisp, sharp lines separate one part from another, for example the edge of the headland also at the lower center of the picture.

There seem actually to be three devices that separate one form from another—sharp edges, blurred contours, and crisp lines—but these are used in many different combinations, so that the total effect of the picture is of an infinite variety of transitions. The mass of land on the lower left, for example, changes gradually from light to dark. Its upper contour is separated from the water beyond it by sharp lines. Its lower boundary, on the other hand, involves a simple dark edge against the lighter water.

Our eye moves across the bridge in a series of jogs because the wooden planks of the bridge are represented by crisp, strongly isolated strokes of the brush. Below the bridge, a number of isolated volumes, many of them surrounded by strong outlines, set up another kind of rhythmic movement across the water. Once over the bridge, we encounter a wealth of new effects. The bush with the blurred edges is stippled with light dots on the dark foliage. Below the bush, some dark dots on the ground echo the stippled effect, but this time dark on light. As we move on to the right hand corner of the picture we encounter the points of the rocks indicated by sharp lines, a whole series of jagged peaks of various sizes, each one overlapping its neighbor and separated from its neighbor by intermittent pockets of shadow. Here, too, there is white stippling on dark areas and dark spots on light areas. But each time these elements are repeated they appear in new combinations and produce new effects, as if the artist were trying to impress the viewer with the boundless variety and inexhaustible configurations of which nature is capable. Yet he does this while imposing severe restrictions on his means of expression.

The severest of these restrictions is in the area of color. Yen Tzu-Yu has ignored the gamut of hues which nature generally displays. He has purged this panorama of all the hues which this scene must certainly have had: the blue of sky and water, the green of the vegetation, the many-shaded browns of earth and rocks. Instead, he has rendered this picture entirely in various shades of gray brown. (Today the picture is embellished with

Figure 31 | YEN TZU-YU. *A Hostelry in the Mountains.* Sung dynasty, late twelfth century. Chinese ink on silk, 10″ high, 10½″ wide. Freer Gallery of Art, Washington, D. C.

nine stamped monograms in different shades of red, the marks of various collectors who once owned the painting.) Yet the picture is not monochrome in the strict sense of that word. There is a greenish tint in the gray-brown trees. There are warm grays and cool grays, areas in which brown pervades the gray to a greater or a lesser degree. Why the Chinese landscape painter ignored colors we do not know. What is obvious, however, is that he has chosen the pattern of things as his primary means of describing natural objects and their relationship to each other. Perhaps this preference of pattern over color allowed him better to comply with the first of the six canons of painting laid down in the fifth century by Hsieh Ho, namely, that a painting must express the life spirit or the rhythm which all life possesses.

Yet if the painting seeks to express the rhythm of nature, it does so without certain qualities which a photograph of this scene would reveal. The perspective effect, particularly, is different. In a photograph the objects in the foreground would not only be larger than similar objects farther away, but they would be clearer in detail and stronger in the contrast of light and dark. Conversely, objects in the distance would be smaller and more blurred. Here, however, the people on the bridge are no larger than those up on the hill under the tall trees, the rocks in the foreground are no sharper in detail than those in the distance, and the contrasts of light and dark seem deliberately to have been reversed: some of the sharpest and most dramatic juxtapositions of light and dark areas are in the lower center of the picture, where the foot of the headland and the three rocks are set starkly against the light water.

This vehement contrast of light and dark, which causes our eye to return again and again to the center of the picture, also makes this area come out toward us more strongly than the foreground. And the rocks at the bottom of the picture, being blurred and uncontrasted, seem to recede in space. If the painter has here violated the normal behavior of optical phenomena, he has, nevertheless, achieved a remarkable esthetic effect. The foreground has been pushed back and the middle ground has been pulled forward to contrive a strange compression of space (a compression which is borne out by the way the rocks are piled up in front of each other without really receding into the distance). There results an effect like that of tightening a spring, a densely packed mass of latent energy which is in tension but at rest. As a counterpoint to this compressed mass of volumes there is the large expanse of empty space, more than half of the picture's surface, a vast void which seems, strangely enough, to be capable of holding in equilibrium these active and passive energies. And so the painting as a whole consists roughly of two triangles which, like positive and negative electric charges, hold each other in suspension.

Projects

1. Compare the relief of St. Paul with either a painting, a mosaic, or an ivory carving from Byzantine art. In what ways does the Romanesque relief resemble it in style and spirit?
2. Find some photographs of the reliefs on the Ara Pacis, the Altar of Peace, which was erected in Rome by the Emperor Augustus. What accounts for the illusion of space in these reliefs? Characterize the difference of mood generated by the Roman and the Romanesque works. Explain how this difference lies in the way the artist has handled his material.
3. Select an example of stone sculpture from India, preferably from the tenth, eleventh, or twelfth centuries. Describe how the artist has treated the anatomy of the figure, its costume, and other descriptive and decorative detail. Does this treatment serve to accentuate the spiritual or the physical aspects of the work, or both?
4. Look for a color reproduction of a Chinese landscape of the Sung period. Contrast it with color reproductions of a Roman landscape mural from Pompeii and a seventeenth-century Dutch landscape. Point out differences in the use of light and space and in the artists' attitudes toward nature.

Suggested Reading

Cahill, James. *The Art of Southern Sung China.* Connecticut: Asia House Gallery, 1962.

Dupont, Jacques, and François Mathey. *The Seventeenth Century.* New York: Skira, Inc., Publishers, 1951.

Frédéric, Louis. *The Art of India.* New York: Harry N. Abrams, Inc., 1960.

Goetz, Hermann. *India.* New York: McGraw-Hill Book Co., Inc., 1959.

Kidson, Peter. *The Medieval World.* New York: McGraw-Hill Book Co., Inc., 1967.

Kramrisch, Stella. *The Art of India.* London: Phaidon Press, Ltd., 1965.

Lee, Sherman. *Chinese Landscape Painting.* New York: Prentice-Hall, Inc. and Harry N. Abrams, Inc., 1962.

Lee, Sherman. *A History of Far Eastern Art.* New York: Prentice-Hall, Inc. and Harry N. Abrams, Inc., 1964.

Mâle, Emile. *Religious Art from the Twelfth to the Eighteenth Century.** New York: Pantheon Books, 1948.

Rowland, Benjamin. *The Art and Architecture of India.* Baltimore: Penguin Books, Inc., 1953.

*Available in a paperback edition.

7 | Structure and Decoration
Amiens Cathedral and the Alhambra Palace

The art term *Gothic* has nothing to do with the Germanic barbarians who overran Europe in the early Middle Ages. It originated with Renaissance writers who considered the art of the late twelfth and thirteenth centuries crude, irregular, and deficient in that grace and serenity which they admired in the art of antiquity.

The cathedral of the city of Amiens in France is like the Parthenon in that it marks the culmination of the best ideas of its predecessors; it was begun after the principles of Gothic construction had been thoroughly mastered, and most of it was finished before the taste for overembellishment and pointless elaboration of forms had set in. It is unlike the Parthenon, however, in that it is not governed by a single, preconceived, unifying style but grew like a living plant, in whatever way the winds of architectural style and the rainfall of building funds happened to come. Different parts of the cathedral are different in design and detail. The most striking example of this lack of uniformity is the dissimilarity of the two towers of the façade, one of which is thirteen feet taller than the other and different in its decoration (see fig. 37).

Amiens Cathedral: Its Plan

If we compare the plan of Amiens Cathedral (fig. 32) with that of Old St. Peter's (fig. 26), we will be struck particularly by one remarkable difference between them. Instead of forming a sharp rectangle with transept and apse breaking its rectilinear character, Amiens is a more unified, comprehensive, and one might say, organic whole. The various spaces do not exist as separate, sharply demarcated compartments, but seem to flow into one another and around the slender vertical supports (the small, cross-shaped black dots in the diagram).

The large areas of black on the left in figure 32 indicate the very thick walls which are needed to support the two heavy towers on the front of the church. But before we enter there, we must ascend two flights of steps, an act which gives us time to experience the effect of the richly sculptured façade as a whole and from different eye levels. Next we enter one of the three sheltered porches to examine a smaller part of the façade at close range. Inside the tower area a shallow narthex, very dark because the heavy supporting walls under the towers will not tolerate large windows, leads us to the nave or to one of the aisles, depending on which door we have chosen to enter. Here tall piers divide the nave and aisles into bays which are covered not by a truss roof, but by groined vaults; hence the X-shaped lines in each bay in figure 32.

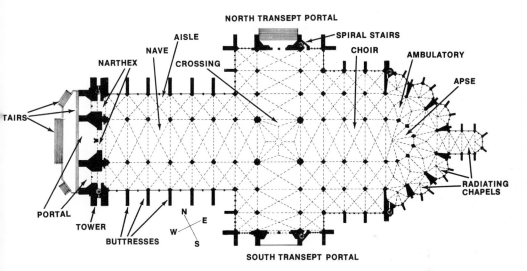

Figure 32 | Plan of Amiens Cathedral, before addition of chapels to nave

One of the most radical changes in the plans of earlier and later churches is the position of the transept, which in most Romanesque and Gothic churches has moved westward nearly to the midsection of the building. This transept, like the nave that leads us to it, consists of a central space with two side aisles. At the extremities of the transept are doors which lead to the outside and which, like the front portals, are ornamented with sculptured porches. The square formed by the intersection of nave and transept, an area called the crossing, is covered with a dome-shaped vault of remarkably complicated construction. The piers that bound the crossing are larger than any of the rest in order to support the thin spire which rises above the crossing to a height of 370 feet. The large space between the transept and the aisle, which is missing in the Early Christian basilica, is called the choir. At Amiens the choir is flanked by two sets of aisles, the inner of which is a continuation of the aisles in the front of the church. But it is in the section east of the choir, the section which the French call the *chevet* because it resembles the curved form of a cradle, that the builders of Amiens created a masterpiece of planning and construction. The apse, first of all, is not covered by a half dome as in the Early Christian basilica, but by a vault made of seven wedge-shaped sections. Behind this apse runs a circular corridor, or ambulatory, whose seven bays grow naturally out of the apse arcade, although it is separated from the apse by a decorated screen. Each of the ambulatory bays, in turn, opens on one of the seven radiating chapels which contain the altars and often the relics of particular saints. An invention of the Romanesque era, the ambulatory allowed pilgrims or other visitors to visit and pray at these altars without disturbing the service that may have been in progress at the main altar. Since the bays of the ambulatory are trapezoidal rather than square, they were difficult to cover with groined vaults, as were the radiating chapels, which are heptagonal in general form.

The Ribbed Vault

We saw in connection with Roman architecture that the groined vault permitted the thrust of the vaults to be concentrated at the four corners of each bay instead of along the entire length of a wall. This principle lies at the very basis of the Gothic style, but we must go back to the Romanesque era to understand its new aspects. Between the years 1000 and 1150 architects in the Lombardy region of northern Italy and in Normandy in northern France began using groined vaults over the naves as well as over the aisles of their churches, thus adding one further elaboration to the Roman system. These vaults were like the Roman groined vaults discussed in Chapter 4 with one new feature: they were built over a framework of arches which were allowed to project like moldings on the undersides of the vaults. These ribs divided the vault into four sections, each of which could be constructed separately and consequently, with a minimum of scaffolding and centering (see fig. 33).

Besides providing an actual skeleton upon which the vaults might be built, these ribs served an esthetic purpose as well in providing a framework along which our eyes may follow the structural lines of the vault. Transverse ribs run across the nave, marking the limits of each bay on the east and west. Longitudinal ribs run from the front to the rear of the church, framing the clearstory windows. Diagonal ribs follow the groins, accenting these intersections and forming X-shaped patterns overhead.

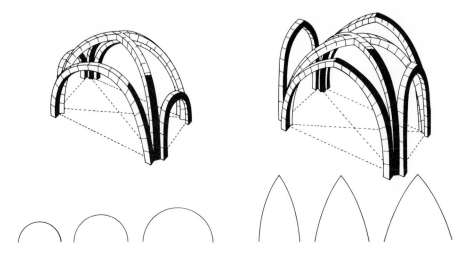

Figure 33 I Groined vault ribbing, Romanesque and Gothic

Each of these ribs comes down on an engaged column called a shaft, and several of the shafts cluster around each of the piers in the nave to form what we call a compound pier. At Amiens each nave pier, except the four in the crossing, consists of a large cylinder surrounded by four smaller cylinders.

The Pointed Arch

Just as each of the intersecting vaults in the Roman groined vault had to be the same height in order to meet evenly and form a ceiling of a uniform height, so it was with the Romanesque vault. Both transverse and longitudinal ribs, therefore, had to be of equal diameter, a simple task as long as the bay was square. But since the nave of a church was wider than the aisle, a square in the nave would form a rectangle in the aisle, and vice versa (see fig. 32). The arches constructed over the short sides of the rectangle would obviously not reach as high as those built over the long sides, unless the former were raised on stilts or the latter depressed. Neither of these solutions was very satisfactory from a visual standpoint. And diagonal ribs, having a larger diameter than the transverse or the longitudinal ribs, rose higher than the others and gave each bay a slightly domed character (see fig. 33). It was the architects of the Gothic period who first realized that the pointed arch, having no fixed diameter, could span any given width and still be raised to any required height. It could be used to cover any space—square, rectangular, triangular, pentagonal, or even trapezoidal—and the crown of each arch could be made to rise to the same height (see fig. 33). Moreover, the pointed arch and vault system, being more vertical in shape, exerts less sideward thrust and therefore needs less buttressing.

Gothic Buttressing

The groined vaults of the basilica in the Baths of Caracalla were buttressed by three barrel vaults on each side, a system which made each of the barrel-vaulted areas a separate spatial unit. Such a system worked well for a building with no strong axial orientation and no principal focus. A number of spaces could be used for various purposes in the Roman basilica. In a Christian church, one single event, the service, was paramount, and one special space, the altar-enclosing apse, was focal. The rest of the interior space had to lead to this focus. The aisles, like the nave, had to participate in this spatial flow, besides fulfilling the practical function of letting people move from the front doors to the altar. Architects during the Romanesque period had solved this problem by opening up the space between the bays of the aisles and moving the buttresses out to the exterior of the church. The thrust of the nave vaults was thus conducted to the aisle vaults, and then on to the buttresses which reinforced the exterior wall at the juncture of each bay. Architects eventually realized that the heavier they made these buttresses, the thinner they could make the actual walls of the church and the larger they could make the windows. Finally, in a High Gothic church like Amiens ("High Gothic" refers to the climax of the Gothic style, not to the physical height of the building), it seems almost as though the walls had been broken into short sections and turned around at right angles to the church's axis (see fig. 32).

Up to the aisle roof these external buttresses are solid walls of masonry, but above this point there is no necessity for making them solid walls. It suffices to have only thin, bridge-shaped arches that "fly" through the air from the exterior buttresses outside the aisle walls to the piers that hold up the nave vault (see fig. 34), somewhat like the diaphragm walls in the Roman vaulted basilica (see fig. 22). In the nave at Amiens these flying buttresses are on two levels, one reaching up to the springing of the vault—the point where it begins to curve— and the other to its crown. Far from looking like unsightly crutches, these flying buttresses were made into graceful elements of the total design. They were decorated with carved pinnacles (very sharply pointed pyramidal spires), colonnettes, and sometimes delicate arcades, carved foliage, and gargoyles—rainspouts with monsters' heads that threw rainwater away from the building's foundation.

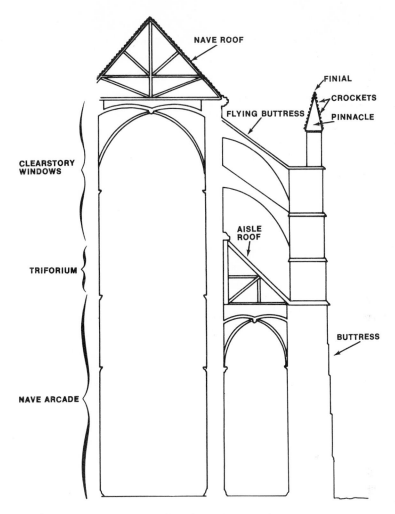

NAVE ROOF

FINIAL

CROCKETS

FLYING BUTTRESS

PINNACLE

CLEARSTORY
WINDOWS

AISLE
ROOF

TRIFORIUM

BUTTRESS

NAVE ARCADE

Figure 34 | Section of the nave of Amiens Cathedral

Once the relationship between the thrust of the vaults and the counter-thrust of the flying buttresses was understood, Gothic architects began to raise their vaults higher and higher off the ground. In Sens Cathedral, which was begun in 1140, the ratio between the width of the nave and its height was 1 to 1.4. At Noyon it was 1 to 2; at Chartres, 1 to 2.6; at Notre Dame in Paris, 1 to 2.75; at Amiens, 1 to 3; at Beauvais, 1 to 3.4; and at Cologne the nave is nearly four times as high as it is wide (1 to 3.8). This development is all the more remarkable when we consider the fact that it was achieved intuitively rather than through scientific calculation, simply by means of trial and error. A dramatic example of such an error occurred at Beauvais Cathedral, which was begun just five years after Amiens with vaults just a few feet higher. The choir vaults were finished and stayed up until 1284, when they collapsed. Reconstruction proved to be so costly and slow that it was decided not to build a nave at all, but to erect a high tower over the crossing. Again the architects tried to outdo every other church in Christendom and raised a tower more than 500 feet into the air. In 1573 it too toppled and the church remains to this day an unfinished but still impressive piece of architecture.

Amiens Cathedral was begun in 1220 on the ruins of a Romanesque structure which had been struck by lightning four years before and had been badly damaged by fire. The construction of churches usually commenced at the altar end and progressed westward, but since the choir of the old cathedral was still intact, the builders at Amiens began with the façade and worked eastward, eventually replacing the Romanesque choir with Gothic construction. It took them sixteen years to finish the façade up to the top of the rose window and to raise the nave and aisles complete with their vaults. The ambulatory and the radiating chapels were completed by 1247 and the light, airy apse by 1269. The choir was rebuilt by 1270, and between 1292 and 1375 the spaces between the buttresses on the nave were enclosed to form side chapels (which are not shown on the plan in fig. 32). The two towers were finished in the fourteenth and fifteenth centuries, but the daring spire over the crossing was not added until 1529. As in all European churches that have been in continuous use through the centuries, much alteration and redecoration were done in Renaissance, Baroque, Rococo, and even modern styles.

Amiens Cathedral: Interior

The nave vaults at Amiens rise to 140 feet above the floor. As one enters the nave, one is quite overwhelmed not only by its sheer size, but also by the upward pull of its design (see fig. 35). Everywhere one looks, vertical elements dominate horizontal ones. The horizontal divisions between the nave arcade, triforium, and clearstory are still clearly marked, but in every case their horizontal movement is interrupted by the vertical shafts which rise from floor to ceiling. Like the Roman half-columns, these shafts have little structural function. The church could easily stand if they were chiseled away. But from an esthetic standpoint they function as supports, tying in with the ribs of the vault and forming a stone framework upon which the vaults and the walls seem to hang like membranes stretched

Figure 35 | Amiens Cathedral, interior, looking east. 1220–1288. Stone. Nave, including choir, 140' high, 370' long, 49' wide

over a skeleton. But they serve another end as well. Without them, each pier would be a single, cylindrical support—one vertical accent—like the columns in the Early Christian basilica. The four shafts that cluster around each pier multiply its vertical lines, giving our eyes that much more upward impetus.

Each of the four shafts, moreover, has its separate destiny: those on the east and west join the arches of the nave arcade; the one on the aisle side ties in with the ribs of the aisle vaults; and the shafts on the nave rise, as has been mentioned, to join the main vault's ribs. Moreover, the shafts serve to divide the wall into precisely measurable units whose repetitive cadence is one of the outstanding characteristics of this interior. The precision of this rhythmic articulation is further elaborated. Above the capitals of the nave arcade, two more shafts join the main shaft, and above the triforium, two more, so that the shafts seem to grow, like the limbs of a tree, until five shafts arrive at the springing of the vault. There each shaft begins to move in a different direction as branches do, one across the nave in the form of the transverse rib, two diagonally across the nave, and two along the nave wall above the clearstory windows.

Between this framework made of piers, shafts, and ribs, space opens up to varying depths. Deepest and darkest are the openings of the nave arcades that lead to the aisles. Next deepest and not quite as dark is the space of the triforium, which is screened off from the main space by a line of columns and pierced tracery. Shallowest and lightest of all is the clearstory wall whose glass windows are physically flat but which allow light to penetrate from one space to another. This vertical graduation of depth and light is paralleled numerically as well (see figs. 35 and 36). The single arch of the nave arcade becomes two arches in the triforium, each of which in turn is subdivided into three. The bays of the clearstory have something in common with each of the levels below them. They form single units like the arch of the nave arcade; but are subdivided into two like the triforium bay, and again into four openings.

The neat distinctness of elements, of shafts, capitals, architrave, frieze, and cornice, which we noted in Greek and Roman buildings, is here obliterated; it is not eliminated completely but transformed so that the various elements merge and mesh. Some of the shafts rise higher than others. Capitals are set at different levels. Arches enclose other arches of varying sizes and heights. We do not feel an irrevocable relationship among units. The arrangement is not static but kinetic. Various elements could be made smaller or larger, moved upward or lowered without greatly changing the character of the wall. The arrangement of parts, in other words, is more fluid than in the Parthenon, more intuitively arrived at than rationally conceived.

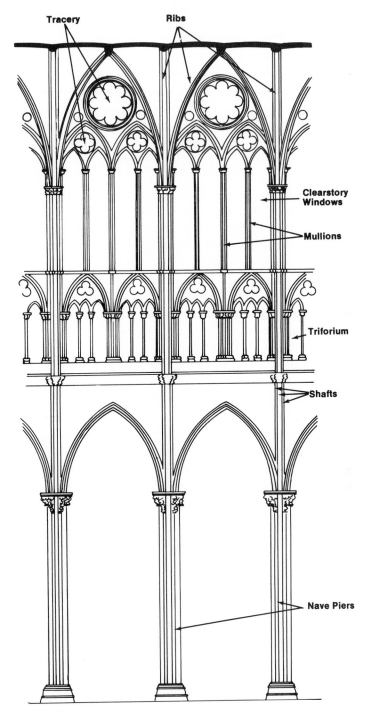

Figure 36 | Elevation of two bays in the nave of Amiens Cathedral

As our eye moves from the front door toward the altar, we are struck by the insistent, repetitive rhythm of these elements—a rhythm whose monotony is very much like the repetition of certain portions of the liturgy and church music of the thirteenth century. And just as this music now involved many voice parts and a complicated pattern of melodies and rhythms, so also was the architectural rhythm strongly varied within each unit, varied in spatial depth, in degree of illumination, and in the number and heaviness of its subdivisions. The illumination, which is rich in color, comes down into the church from above. It is of equal intensity for each bay until we reach the crossing, where it suddenly becomes dim. Beyond the crossing, however, its intensity increases again, first in the choir and then in the apse, where it pours down in a torrent of multicolored light, the apse having more stained glass and less stone support than any other part of the church.

Amiens Cathedral: West Façade

Despite the profusion of carved ornament, the façade (fig. 37) clearly reveals the internal arrangement of the church. The large central portal heralds the broad nave, as the smaller doors do the aisles. The decorated bands above the portals echo the interior triforium, and the round rose window marks the front end of the groined vaults. The same clarity of thought and frankness of expression which led the architects of Amiens to reveal the internal structure in the external design is also present in an ingenious integration of decorative detail and structural members. At the outer corners of the towers (which were meant eventually to be carried up to pointed spires) four huge buttresses divide the façade into three vertical sections. They also form a prominent surface for some of the sculpture on the ground level, where they function as dividing walls between the portals.

Yet despite the happy wedding of decorative and structural elements, the sheer profusion of ornament on the façade defies logic and reason. Pinnacles rise everywhere, often in front of other forms, particularly the horizontal moldings. A variety of arches and columns break up the flat surfaces, catching the light and casting shadows. Not only the west end but every side of the exterior is ornamented with carving. Finials (small flower-shaped ornaments) crown the tops of pinnacles. Small rooflike canopies overhang statues, niches and arched openings, and larger triangular gables cover the porches; the sharpness of their contours is broken by protruding crockets, those short curved projections that seem to blossom out of the stone. Some of this carving denies the very character of its material, stone, and looks more like wrought iron or the work of goldsmiths than carved stone. This is particularly true of the round rose window whose tracery reminds one of lace or a filigree spun of gold or silver thread.

The profusion of this carving produces a glittering effect when light strikes it, an effect which denies the materiality of the wall, as if it were not stone at all but a shimmering screen of gossamer floating weightlessly in the sunlight. And when the rays of the setting sun struck this palpitating surface of saints and heavenly beings, it must have seemed to the thirteenth-century inhabitants of Amiens that this was indeed the Heavenly Jerusalem described in the twenty-first chapter of Revelation, a passage which, incidentally, was read at the dedication of cathedrals:

> And I John saw the holy city, new Jerusalem, coming down from God out of heaven, prepared as a bride adorned for her husband.

> And I heard a great voice out of heaven saying, "Behold, the tabernacle of God is with men, and he will dwell with them, and they shall be his people, and God himself shall be with them, and be their God.

> And God shall wipe away all tears from their eyes; and there shall be no more death, neither sorrow, nor crying, neither shall there be any more pain: for the former things are passed away."

If Romanesque art was monastic in origin, the Gothic cathedral was a product of an urban society. The rapid growth of commerce and manufacturing in the eleventh and twelfth centuries increased the wealth of certain cities, and although the Crusades failed to recapture the Holy Land from the Moslems, they introduced new ideas from the Near East, fostered the prosperity of the merchant classes, and increased the power of the French monarchy. A special consequence of the latter was the growing importance of Paris and the area around that city known as the Ile-de-France. It was here that the architecture we call Gothic was born.

Economic prosperity brought with it an intellectual ferment, the growth of universities, and the creative thought of the scholastic philosophers such as Albertus Magnus, Duns Scotus, and Thomas Aquinas. Arabic translations of Greek manuscripts which had come into Europe in the twelfth century brought classical philosophy to bear on Christian theology and impelled churchmen to synthesize the ideas of the past in a logical, orderly cosmology. The sculptured cathedrals of the Ile-de-France—at Chartres, Paris, Amiens, Reims, and Bourges—are direct reflections of this tendency to sum up all knowledge, sacred and secular, that had been revealed to man by God through the ages.

And so, as the worshipper ascended the steps of Amiens Cathedral, he could see in detail what had from a distance been a shimmering screen of lights and darks. Over the south portal he could see scenes from the life of Mary, the Queen of Heaven, to whom the church was dedicated. What seems to us like an incongruous inclusion of Adam and Eve near the Annunciation and the Nativity, was understood by him as a reminder that it was original sin which made necessary Christ's coming. Over the door of the central portal he saw Christ enthroned at the Last Judgment. Above him, on the underside of the porch, one hundred and fifty figures represented the celestial hierarchy. At Christ's left hand, he saw the damned led off by bestial demons to the gaping jaws of Hell, while on the other side, the blessed received new garments and crowns before entering the Paradise. Such choices of subjects in art, their manner of representation, and their arrangement is called iconography. Medieval iconography was not original with the artist, of course, but was dictated to him by churchmen who included in it the latest thoughts of contemporary theologians.

Beneath the terrifying Last Judgment, on the *trumeau* of the central door, stands a ten-foot statue of Jesus, whose gentle countenance and graceful pose have earned him the popular name of *le Beau Dieu.* This is not the stern image of Christ so often depicted on the fronts of Romanesque churches and in Byzantine apse mosaics, or even on the awesome Last Judgment above. This is a new image of Christ as the loving Savior and Teacher whose left hand holds the Gospels and whose right hand is raised in the sign of benediction.

Beside Christ on the oblique walls of the central porch, stand the twelve Apostles, each of them recognizable by some identifying symbol. Saint James, for example, wears the scallop shell which is the emblem worn by pilgrims to his tomb in Compostela. In each of these figures, as in the central statue of Christ, the artist has made an effort to humanize the holy personages. Unlike the Romanesque St. Paul at Moissac, these figures have normal proportions. Details of clothing have been studied and imitated. Even distinctions in the textures of various kinds of cloth have been rendered in stone. When these statues still had their colors they must have seemed startlingly real to the citizens of Amiens.

This frieze of large standing statues is continued across the walls of the other portals, thus giving a visual unity to the lower level of the façade. But there is another kind of unity in subject matter which pervades all of the portals. On the fronts of the four huge buttresses are represented the

Figure 37 I Amiens Cathedral, façade. 1220–1288

twelve minor prophets. In the Portal of the Virgin stand the twelve major prophets. The north portal includes the statues of St. Firmin, the first bishop of Amiens, and other saints who figure in the Christianization of Amiens. This frieze of large, almost freestanding statues therefore stresses the continuity of Christianity from ancient to modern times. And below these statues, in a double row of small reliefs, are depicted scenes from the Bible and from the lives of the saints; the signs of the zodiac and the various occupations appropriate to the months of the year; personifications of the virtues and the vices; and even scenes from Aesop's fables. The façades of the Gothic cathedrals have been called Bibles in stone, but they are more like encyclopedias from which the medieval worshipper could glean, as much as he was able, the most profound thoughts of the church scholars. What he could not understand on a rational level must still have overwhelmed him on a sensuous level. When he finally left the bright colored portals, he entered first the cool darkness of the narthex of the church and then the seemingly limitless interior whose vaulted spaces glowed with the vibrant, multicolored light of the great stained glass windows.

The Gothic Window

As the ingenious network of ribs, piers, and buttresses came to bear more and more of the building's weight and thrust, the wall between the buttresses lost its load-bearing function and became merely a screen that separated the space within from that without, a screen that might just as well be made of glass as of stone. Windows, therefore, became larger, and the great age of stained glassmaking began. Like the sculpture on the outside, the windows were also intended to instruct the worshipper. The designs were made of numerous pieces of glass, each piece having a specific color and attached to its neighbor with grooved bands of lead. For the sake of stability, large windows were subdivided into smaller units by stone columns called mullions, which rose and supported a network of arches and multilobed openings called tracery (see the clearstory windows in figs. 35 and 36).

It will be remembered that the basilica had originally been chosen as a model for the Christian church partly because its clearstory windows served to illuminate the nave, which would otherwise have been quite gloomy. Moreover, light had a symbolic significance, as we saw in connection with the glittering mosaics of the Early Christian basilica. That this light shone downward from above must also have had significance for the medieval worshipper. It was a challenge to the ingenuity of the Romanesque architect to devise means of putting windows into the nave wall of the stone-vaulted church by means of groined vaulting and external buttresses. It seems like a paradox, then, that when the architects of the Gothic period discovered how to erect vast expanses of glass by means of their buttressing system, they colored the glass so that the light inside the church was still dim. Obviously, the light that was wanted was not daylight, but a mysterious, vibrating, many-colored light unlike the light on earth.

Equally paradoxical is the compulsion to make the vaults of each new church higher than its predecessor, even though a high church like Amiens held no more people than one of the large truss-roofed basilicas in Rome. It was evidently spiritual impulse rather than practical consideration that produced the soaring height of these churches, an impulse that overrode even the fear of collapsing masonry and the labor of devising ever more complex systems of buttressing.

The combined effect of the architecture, the sculpture, and the stained glass windows has often been praised as a perfect expression of a triumphant Christianity and regarded as the antithesis of the classical spirit in architecture. The rectangle formed by the Greek post and lintel is a static unit. It rests and remains immobile. It implies no movement, either to the right or to the left. The round arch of the Romans carries our eye from side to side in an arc. Our eye rises toward the center and falls again thereafter, but this rising and falling and this movement from side to side are controlled and confined; we never move further than the radius of that semicircle permits us. Thus both the Parthenon and the Colosseum are static in their design. Their façades are at rest, producing a repeated rhythm of forms in equilibrium. The one follows the module of the rectangle as a unit; the other uses a semicircle as a module or unit of measurement.

The Gothic cathedral has no such module. Its arches conform to no common radius, the various parts of the building do not follow a related system of proportions, and the combination of curves and rectilinear forms is determined not by an all-governing system but by the particular circumstances in each case. Compared to the Greek or Roman temple, the Gothic church seems to have been improvised, and in a sense it was. This is not to say that it was not planned. Robert de Luzarches, the first designer of Amiens, and each of his successors, worked out their plans before construction began, but each time construction was halted and resumed the current builder discovered new ways of proceeding, ways in which he could more fully express his feeling for God.

The effect of Amiens, as one enters the building, is correspondingly unclassical. The multiplicity of the forms and their movement and countermovement, the sweep of curves, perpetually interrupted by and intersecting one another in unexpected and highly complicated ways—all this serves to excite and elate rather than relax the senses. The lines of the architecture seem to pull the worshipper into their vertical exultation.

As the German art historian Wilhelm Worringer wrote in 1912:

> To enter the Pantheon is to feel freed from individual isolation: voiceless, solemn music of space leads to a beneficent, liberating, sensuous composure: one is swayed by the unspeakably blissful rhythm of spatial life: one feels a clarification of the senses. And what more did Classical man require in all his art than this lofty bliss of ideal, sensuous clarification? On the other hand, anyone entering a Gothic cathedral encounters something far removed from sensuous *clarification.* He encounters an *intoxication* of the senses . . . a mystical intoxication of the senses which is not of this world.[1]

The Architecture of Islam

Before the architects of the twelfth and thirteenth centuries realized the possibilities of the pointed arch, it had been used in Persia, in Egypt, and in other parts of the Moslem world for centuries, but only for decorative purposes, for its grace and elegance. One of the best preserved examples of Moslem architecture is the Alhambra Palace in Granada in southern Spain, which was built in the mid-fourteenth century.

Mohammed died in 632, and in the next twelve years the Arabs, heretofore a collection of scattered and quarreling tribes, united in a crusade that eventually swept over Egypt, Syria, Iraq, and Persia to the borders of India in the east and across Spain in the west. After conquering Spain from the Visigoths, the Arabs traversed the Pyrenees and marched across France until they were stopped outside Poitiers by Charles Martel in 732, just a hundred years after the death of the Prophet. Although they made raids into France and Italy for centuries thereafter, their rule in Europe was confined to Spain, where they were called Moors, and to southern Italy, where they were known as Saracens. It was not until 1492 that Ferdinand and Isabella drove the last Arab rulers out of Spain, although large numbers of Arabs continued to live there and to leave their imprint on the character of Spanish art and music.

Although the Koran, the holy book of Islam, does not specifically prohibit the representation of man or animals in religious art, Moslem artists and craftsmen avoided it and developed in its stead a remarkable

---

1. | Wilhelm Worringer, *Form in Gothic,* trans. Herbert Read (New York, 1964), p. 159.

vocabulary of ornament based partly on geometric patterns, partly on vegetable forms, and partly on Arabic calligraphy or handwriting. In architecture the Arab genius lay not in devising structural systems but rather in inventing decorative forms and contriving wonderfully picturesque effects: rich surface ornamentation, subtle color combinations, dramatic contrasts of sun-drenched spaces with shaded arcades, sparkling fountains, and pools of water. Roofs were generally wooden and shingled with tiles. Arches were used merely as decorative openings, and were made interesting through the variety of their forms, which might be horseshoe shaped, multilobed, polygonal, or, as has been said, pointed. Vaults were occasionally used; and domes, often faced with colored tiles or encrusted with stucco ornament, were popular.

Stucco allowed artists to fashion with ease and great speed the flowing, curvilinear forms which mark Islamic ornament, and to shape the projections and depressions which, when light strikes them, make surfaces glitter with highlights and shadows. Most characteristic of these decorative systems is the arabesque, a delicate pattern made of flowing, interlacing, ribbonlike lines which frequently turn into branches or leaves and which are sometimes interspersed with stars, octagons, triangles, and fruit or flower shapes.

The Alhambra Palace

Perched on a promontory outside Granada in southern Spain, high above the city and cooled by the breeze that comes down from the snowcapped Sierra Nevada mountains, stands the Alhambra, the palace of the sultans who ruled this portion of Andalusia. It consists of an asymmetrical, rather rambling arrangement of halls, rooms, and corridors, grouped around two large and several smaller open courts, sometimes on one level and sometimes on two. The palace consists of three parts: first a public section where affairs of administration and justice were conducted, next the official residence of the sultan, and last his private residence and the harem, or apartments of his wives and concubines. As one walks through the palace, now almost empty of furniture and, of course, lacking the richness of carved woodwork, damask curtains, Persian carpets, glittering glass and metal utensils and vessels, one is still astounded at the richness of surface and subtlety of color harmonies. Brightly lit courtyards contrast abruptly with the dark, cool rooms into which light is sometimes filtered through grilled windows. Almost everywhere one looks one can see through a window or balcony a cool garden patio where the splashing of a fountain adds to the magic of the architecture.

Figure 38 | The Alhambra Palace, Granada, Spain. One of two porticoes in the Court of the Lions. 1354–1391. Brick, stucco, stone, and wood. Courtyard: 115´ long, and 66´ wide

The Court of the Lions

The heart of the harem, or private apartments of the sultan, was the large court whose central fountain, supported on the backs of twelve lions, gives the court its name. It is rectangular, measures 115 by 66 feet, and is surrounded on the sides by an arcade whose arches rest alternately on single and double columns (see fig. 38). The great number of these columns (eighteen in each portico alone) and their thinness remind one of a line of young saplings whose sunlit trunks stand out against the cool shade of the forest beyond them. The spreading of the arches above them and the vegetal forms of the decoration heighten this impression.

Visitors to this court marvel at the lightness and the delicacy of its architecture. Part of the lightness is due to the thinness of the columns and the surface elaboration on the walls which suggests lace or metalwork rather than stone. Actually, the construction is light to begin with. The core of the wall is brick and the decoration is done in stucco, not stone. Moreover, this is post and lintel construction with the real support provided by the wooden beams rather than the purely decorative arches.

The color of the stucco and the stone varies from a creamy pink to a golden tan, with occasional accents of dark in the stucco work, or blue on the underside of the star-studded domes that cover the centers of the two porticos. Most of the color is given to the surface by the play of light, not only direct sunlight and shadow but also the reflected light thrown by one surface upon another. In some places the stucco wall is pierced so that it is really a screen rather than a wall, a screen that lets in air while keeping out the hot light. Occasionally, therefore, one may see blue sky through such a wall or, more remarkable still, seemingly unexplained splotches of light in otherwise shady areas as sunlight streams through the perforations. (See fig. 38 under the arches at the upper left.)

But it is the ornamentation which most strikes the visitor to the Court of the Lions. The capitals of the columns are decorated with vegetal patterns. Above them rise two tall stilts which add to the feeling of lightness and delicacy; these are decorated with panels of interlaced ribbon design flanked by small engaged columns. Filling the rectangle above the three arches is a repetitive pattern of trilobes which project and cast shadows on the flatter surface of stylized palm leaves and pine cones, a surface which is further enriched by the dark patterns of perforated areas.

Surrounding this rectangular area is a band of Arabic script, an inscription of poetry. Such inscriptions are quite common in Islamic art and sometimes pass unnoticed because Arab calligraphy blends so well with the lacework patterns. The undersides of the arches are interesting because each of the trilobes on its outer and inner edges lets one of its sides hang downward like an icicle on a roof or a stalactite in a cave. This stalactite motif occurs elsewhere in the palace.

On the floor under the portico are fountains whose circular basins are connected by channels cut into the pavement, so that one basin leads to another and to the large fountain with the twelve stone lions at the center of the court.

The Alhambra, exquisite as it is, is the final flowering of a gradually degenerating culture. The power of the Moors had begun to wane long before the Christians drove them southward. And when, in 1492, the armies of Ferdinand and Isabella stormed the walls of the Alhambra, the last Moorish ruler was expelled from European soil.

Projects

1. Salisbury Cathedral in England was begun in the same year as Amiens Cathedral—1220. Find photographs, plans, sections, and elevations of Salisbury, and compare its various characteristics with those of Amiens.
2. Find an example of either Persian or Turkish metalwork, pottery, or rug weaving. How do the patterns in this object compare with those in figure 38, with certain portions of stone carving of the Romanesque era, and with the ornament on the temples of Central America such as those in Mitla and Chichén Itzá in Mexico?
3. Examine the photographs of several Moslem tombs in India such as the Tomb of Humayun in Delhi, Akbar's Tomb in Sikandra, and the famous Taj Mahal in Agra. Can you relate them to what you have learned about the architecture of ancient Rome, medieval Europe, and Islam? Point out some similarities and differences.
4. Investigate the character of castle architecture in Romanesque and Gothic Europe. What is the relationship between the functional requirements and the general plan of the castle, its various parts, and the characteristics of each part?

Suggested Reading

Busch, Harald, and Bernd Lohse, eds. *Gothic Europe,* trans. Peter Gorge. New York: The Macmillian Co., 1959.
Branner, Robert. *Gothic Architecture.** New York: George Braziller, Inc., 1961.
Frankl, Paul. *Gothic Architecture.* Baltimore: Penguin Books, Inc., 1963.
Hoag, John D. *Western Islamic Architecture.** New York: George Braziller, Inc., 1963.
Sordo, Enrique. *Moorish Spain.* New York: Crown Publishers, 1963.
Worringer, Wilhelm. *Form in Gothic.** New York: Schocken Books, Inc. 1964.

*Available in a paperback edition.

8 | The Rediscovery of the Earth
Giotto and Memling

During the twelfth and thirteenth centuries certain cities in central and northern Italy became centers of manufacturing, commerce, and banking. Venice, Genoa, and Pisa grew rich through their monopoly of outfitting and transporting the European armies during the Crusades. Situated on trade routes between the countries north of the Alps and the Near East, these cities, as well as Milan and Florence, grew in wealth, population, and power.

The city of Florence specialized in the production of silk, wool, and leather goods. By the end of the thirteenth century she had grown from six to over seventy thousand inhabitants, and the agents of her banking houses resided in Paris, London, Bruges in Flanders, and Constantinople. This material prosperity brought with it an intellectual and artistic ferment that was to make Florence the cradle of the Renaissance.

Giotto di Bondone   c. 1266–1337

Although art was still predominantly religious in subject matter and destination, it was frequently commissioned and paid for by private individuals. The artist was the master of a *bottega* or studio full of assistants and apprentices. He considered himself a craftsman and worked according to a contract which set forth in specifics the subject matter of the art object, the materials to be used, the dimensions of the work, and so on. Such a master was Giotto di Bondone (c. 1266-1337) who was a mosaicist, painter, sculptor, and architect. Like all the artists of his time, Giotto was trained in the Italo-Byzantine manner which was prevalent in Italy at that time. Somewhat like the mosaic of *Jesus Calling Peter and Andrew,* this art was spatially flat, decorative, simplifies, and resplendent with gold. Above all, it was decidedly austere and dehuman- ized. Those who practiced this manner did not look at and then paint what they saw around them, but they copied the works of their predecessors and followed approved rules of style and iconography.

During Giotto's lifetime this Byzantinism began to lose some of its severity and to acquire some of the humanism which St. Francis of Assisi had injected into Christianity a half century previously. Some of Giotto's predecessors had carved reliefs which were strongly inspired by Greco-Roman sculpture. Giotto was undoubtedly interested in this "modern art," and he may also have traveled during his journeyman years to the Île-de-France region and seen *le Beau Dieu* or any of the other relatively realistic sculpture on the fronts of French Gothic churches. During his long life Giotto succeeded in synthesizing the realistic trends of his time with its spiritual impulses. Thus he not only ended an artistic tradition but also heralded a new era in western art which lasted for the next six centuries.

Giotto: *The Lamentation*   Colorplate 2

Although this painting by Giotto and the mosaic from Ravenna both decorated the walls of churches, and although both depict episodes from the life of Jesus, they differ radically in style and spirit. Where the mosaic is flat, this picture suggests three-dimensional space, and where the former stresses the symbolism of the story, the emphasis here is dramatic. Compared to the mosaic, whose artist tried to communicate its meaning largely through the abstract form of the work, Giotto's painting speaks to us more through its concrete images and illustrative details. In other words, Giotto has tried to create the illusion of actually being present at the time Christ's body is taken down from the cross.

Spatially, Giotto has created a painted world that we can enter, to a limited degree at least. We read space into the picture, because some of the figures are standing in front of others and because the pattern of lights and darks has been contrived so that the figures appear to be three-dimensional. Yet we know that objects in nature get smaller as they recede from our eyes. In Giotto's picture, however, all the figures are about the same size, and the rocky ledge behind them does not seem to lie back far enough.

The illusion of space is therefore ambiguous. The seeming roundness of the figures conflicts with the shallowness of the space they inhabit. In this respect the painting is reminiscent of a sculptured relief such as the St. Paul at Moissac, but in other respects it is closer to natural appearances than the Romanesque relief.

What gives the painting its greatest aspect of realism is Giotto's psychological insight into the people he has painted here. He has conceived this scene as if it were a dramatic performance, and he may well have been inspired by one of those church-sponsored passion plays or mystery dramas which were current in the late Middle Ages. Notice, for example, the facial contortions of the weeping women, their squinting eyes and parted lips. Not only by their faces, but in the rendering of gesture and the posture of the entire body Giotto has endeavored to make us feel the grief of each person. Unlike Early Christian and Byzantine artists who repeated a traditional repertoire of poses, Giotto has deliberately varied the movements of his figures in the interest of greater realism. Mary embraces the dead Christ's head; Mary Magdalen weeps at his feet. One woman, in the center of the picture, holds up Christ's limp arms. Above her, John, the Beloved Disciple, flings his arms out at his sides in a desperate grief that befits his youth and his temperament as suggested by the Scriptures. The two older men at the right, more controlled in their sorrow, stand mute and downcast, in direct contrast to the two distraught women at the far left.

In each of these characters, Giotto has created a separate individual, specific in age and distinct in personality. To each he has assigned a part to play in his drama, and he has made the scene additionally believable by a most remarkable and hitherto unheard-of device. He has painted two mourners seated with their backs to us, practically blocking our view, so that we, too, become spectators at this solemn scene and feel almost impelled to crane our necks to see more of the tragic event.

For further evidence of Giotto's ability to use the human body to communicate emotion, we should consider those two seated figures. Without showing their faces to us, without revealing their bodies very plainly, Giotto makes us feel the intensity of their grief through the huddled, keening poses of their shrouded forms whose very simplicity and clumsiness make them additionally eloquent. All through the picture, as a matter of fact, there is this sort of simplicity, and a remarkable absence of illustrative detail. It was customary for painters of Giotto's time to burden their pictures with details of costume, for example, jewelry, buckles, belts, sandal straps, and elaborate patterns on cloaks and tunics. In the *Lamentation* Giotto rejected such decoration as distracting from the dramatic unity of the scene. Instead, he relied on the rocky ledge, the tree, and the angels to decorate his picture. Decoration, therefore, is not extrinsic in Giotto's picture, something added onto the painting; it is an integral element, inseparable from the descriptive and dramatic aspects of the painting. Take the figure of the woman on the left who wrings her hands in grief. The folds of her purple robe form vertical patterns of light and dark stripes which simultaneously ornament that portion of the picture, describe the material of the robe, and augment the visual excitement which encompasses the tragic aspects of the heads of Jesus and Mary.

The colors of this painting are relatively high-keyed. That is, much white has been added to all the hues. There are actually few abrupt contrasts of color, no very dark areas next to very light areas. Blue is the dominating color, at least insofar as it covers more space than any other single color. In addition to the sky, two other areas are painted blue: Mary's robe at the left and the undergarment of the man at the far right. Three red accents—St. John's robe, the cloth Mary Magdalen has draped over her lap, and the tunic of the man with the white shawl at the right—serve to pull our eyes to the right and thereby reduce the asymmetry of the composition whose main subject, Christ's head, is set dramatically off-center. Fainter colors, grayish purples and pale lavenders, appear in the rest of the figures except for the seated woman at the left who is dressed in a yellow that approaches white, and the seated woman at the center whose robe is olive green. The colors of the angels' robes are almost unidentifiable because of their pallor, for Giotto obviously did not want them to distract us from the principal episode below. The rocky ledge with its leafless tree is a neutral tan color. As in many frescoes of the time, the haloes are sculptured in the plaster so that they project slightly from the wall, and they are covered with gold leaf. Gold has also been applied to the borders of nearly all of the robes.

Each of the colors in the painting occupies a given area, a compartment surrounded by a line. Every volume, as a matter of fact, is bounded by a line, but unlike the lines in the sixth-century mosaic, these are less rigid and wirelike. Giotto's lines move not only in a flat plane like the line in an arabesque, but also in and out of space—around the apparent bulk of each figure. Our eyes, therefore, move over each compartment of color until they encounter a boundary line which they must leap to go on to the next volume. The resulting rhythm is one of gentle stops and starts. We travel from one figure to another, perhaps along the ellipse formed by the two standing figures on each side and the three seated women in the foreground. We may enter the space of the ellipse to examine the figures at the center. Or we may follow the diagonal ledge of rock toward the right until, with the form of the solitary tree, we travel across the sky (with the flying angels as stepping stones) and back down to the women at the left.

Within each figure the various volumes—arms, shoulders, heads—are defined by a combination of line and modeling. The expressiveness of Giotto's drawing and modeling would indicate that Giotto, unlike the mosaicist in Ravenna, was very conscious of the bodies under the robes. But that he had investigated anatomy to the point of having dissected the human body is unlikely. The Church, interpreting literally the resurrection of the body, forbade the mutilation of the dead, and even Leonardo da Vinci two hundred years later found it difficult to study the construction of the human skeleton and musculature. The result in the *Lamentation* is some awkward anatomy, for example the wide-flung arms of John, whose right hand seems to be growing out of his neck. In the angels who wheel and dive through the air overhead, Giotto's reach exceeded his grasp. But when we consider the repetitive and stiffly arranged angels in earlier Italian paintings, we can see very clearly what Giotto was trying to do. He was attempting to make these heavenly beings as believable as the human ones. Today, we who are conditioned by photography may consider them naive and charming, but to Giotto's contemporaries, who had never before confronted a three-dimensional representation on a two-dimensional surface (mirrors were rare then and far from the excellence of ours), this whole scene must have appeared startlingly real.

The question naturally arises: with so many imperfections, why is this painting considered to be great art? An even more pertinent and bothersome question is: supposing we did not know that Giotto was a daring innovator and that he came closer to the natural appearance of things than anyone since ancient times, would his picture still move us and speak to us? Or conversely, hundreds of other painters since Giotto's time have painted facial expressions more convincingly and have arranged their painted figures more cleverly. Why then is the *Lamentation* called a great work of art and dozens of more realistic pictures by later artists considered inferior to it? The answer is the same as the answer we must give with regard to any other great artist: everything Giotto touched he managed to infuse with a power that moves us as it has moved thousands of others before us. Compare the major works of Giotto with those of his contemporaries, or with those of his immediate followers, and the power of Giotto to tell a story vividly, to endow his scene with monumentality and his personages with dignity, and his ability to combine spirituality with physical conviction are not matched by any of them.

What it is that generates this power is a complicated matter, one that has concerned art critics and philosophers for centuries. It is partly technique, but not entirely so, or else the best technician would be the greatest artist. It is partly ideas, though an idea unsupported by pictorial means does not constitute great visual art. There is no certain answer to this problem but only a constant search for and discovery of the sources of this power which each age must seek and discover for itself. Each of us must take part in this search and discovery, for each of us is a judge of the art of the past and the art of our time, and each of us adds his vote to the cumulative verdict of our age. If, one day, the power of Giotto's *Lamentation* is no longer felt by the people who confront it, then that work will have ceased to be art even though it may have been praised for centuries. The storerooms of museums throughout the world are filled with works that were once considered to be great art and are without significance to us today. Conversely, there were times in the past when certain artists—El Greco and Rembrandt, for example, and even Giotto—were considered inferior, although today we rank them among the greatest artists who ever lived. This means that people in one century discovered and felt their power while the people in another era did not. The paintings themselves have changed very little through the ages, but people's way of seeing and reacting to ideas (both pictorial and intellectual ideas) do change. The paintings of Giotto may not say the same thing to us that they did to the artist's contemporaries, but they do still speak to us, we still feel their power, and the values they express are still meaningful to us. This is why they are considered to be great works of art today, despite Giotto's ignorance of human anatomy and other technical devices.

Wherever the power of a painting may be said to originate, certainly some of its roots are in the picture's design. We have already mentioned the feeling of space in the *Lamentation* that allows our eye to move from volume to volume and to feel a limited degree of depth. We have mentioned the variety of the poses in the figures, as well as the repetitions which add a rhythmic element to the picture. We must also point to a device which Giotto has employed and which affects both the dramatic impact and the formal design of his painting—the use of the human eye. The eyes have always been the focal points of the human face. In our daily lives we look at a person's eyes when we speak to him, and we are bothered if someone avoids looking back into ours. Moreover, when we look at a person's eyes and find him looking at something else, we immediately and instinctively glance in the direction of his gaze. The story about the practical joker who stands on a busy street and looks intently upwards until he is joined by one, then several, and finally a crowd of passersby, each trying to see what his neighbor is looking at, is perfectly true, and may be demonstrated any time one cares to try it.

Giotto realized that when we see a painted figure looking in a given direction, we, too, follow his gaze. In the *Lamentation* Giotto has used this device for several purposes. He understood first of all that the human eye, along with the mouth, is the principal mirror of the emotions, and that the compressed eyes which he gives his sorrowing figures could do much to heighten our emotional response to the drama of this scene. Secondly, Giotto knew that he could emphasize the focal part of his painting—Christ's head—by having the majority of the painted personages look at it. So sure was he of his ability to do this that he moved this important detail daringly to the left of the picture's central axis, thereby giving to his composition an element of surprise, as well as contributing to the informality and naturalism of the scene. Moreover, Giotto has used the painted eyes to steer us along a strictly controlled and strongly unifying path through the composition. Again and again, as we let our eyes wander through the scene, we are directed by the glances of the various faces, either back to the head of Christ, or to another part of the composition where, eventually, we encounter another glance that leads us back to the principal subject and dramatic focus of the painting—the grief-stricken Mary and the dead Jesus.

Fresco and Tempera Painting

The churches of Giotto's day were embellished with two kinds of pictures, wall paintings and paintings on wooden panels, usually altar-pieces, which were set on altars or attached to walls. Such panel paintings were done in tempera, a medium which usually consisted of pigments mixed with water and egg yolk, a combination which produced a brightly colored surface of great durability and permanence. Besides the paint, much gold leaf was applied to such paintings, on haloes, on details of clothing, on backgrounds, and on the elaborately carved frames and Gothic arches which often surround these panels.

Wall paintings were generally done in the fresco technique which was inherited from the ancient Romans. In such paintings colored pigment was mixed with water and applied to a wall while the plaster was still wet, so that the paint could soak into the plaster and become an inseparable part of the wall itself. The great number of frescoes that have come down to us in relatively good condition from Roman times as well as from the Middle Ages and the Renaissance attests to the permanence of this medium.

In order to execute a fresco properly, however, the painter must work fast and be quite sure of what he is doing. All later corrections and alterations made after the plaster is dry must be done in tempera and are therefore subject to peeling and flaking. The painter must work the wall in sections, plastering only as far as he knows he can go before the surface dries, or else he must chip away the dried plaster that he has not painted on before he can go on. In many fresco paintings we can see the boundaries that separate one section from another, usually along the edge of a human figure or some other detail where the boundary would be as imperceptible as possible.

One more obstacle lay in the path of the fresco painter of Giotto's day. He could use only those pigments which made stable chemical combinations with the lime in the plaster, a condition which made it impossible for him to use blue, for example. Blue backgrounds, therefore, and Mary's robe, which is traditionally blue, had to be painted on in tempera, and since such blue areas are impermanent, they have had to be repainted through the centuries. Hence the splotched character of the blues in Giotto's frescoes.

Painting in Flanders

While the mercantile cities of Italy rose to prominence in the Mediterranean world during the later Middle Ages, certain cities in Flanders (today the southwestern portion of Belgium) also became centers of manufacturing and banking. Textile mills in towns like Ypres and Ghent took raw wool from England and transformed it into quality cloth which was then exported either via the North Sea or overland to various parts of the Continent, including Italy. By the fifteenth century, Bruges had become the financial clearinghouse for all of northern Europe. Prosperity produced a flowering of art and architecture, not to mention literature and music. Many of the Gothic churches, city halls, guild halls, and private homes built at this time are still standing, and the painting of the fifteenth-century Flemings constitutes a sort of proto-Renaissance in the arts.

Between 1400 and 1450 what we call the Renaissance had begun in Florence and had spread to other parts of the Italian peninsula. Contemporary architects in Flanders, however, were just reaching their peak in the Gothic style, and Flemish painters like Jan van Eyck and Roger van der Weyden were finding much of their inspiration in Gothic sculpture. Such sculpture, it will be remembered in connection with Amiens Cathedral, showed a keen study of natural appearances, and this, coupled with a heritage of manuscript illumination that stressed minute detail and a great richness of color, produced a style of panel painting in Flanders completely different from that of either Italian Gothic painters like Giotto or Italian Renaissance artists of the fifteenth century like Filippo Lippi. One of the causes of this great difference is the development in Flanders of oil paint.

Oil Painting in Flanders

Tempera paint, as has been said, was bright and high-keyed, but rather opaque, so that only the top layer of paint was discernible to the eye. Pigments ground into oil, however, may be made opaque if used thick, or transparent if diluted with additional linseed oil and/or turpentine. The general technique of oil painting as practiced by the fifteenth-century

Flemings was to execute a picture, complete with details and masses of light and shadow, but in a grayish brown monochrome, then to lay in bright colors, and finally to cover this underpainting with transparent coats of color called glazes until the desired color effects were achieved. The special quality of such a painting is that the light rays which strike the surface penetrate through several layers of paint before they are reflected and return to our eye. Instead of giving back merely the simple surface color, as does a tempera painting, a picture built up in oil glazes achieves a subtly modulated effect, richer and more resonant (also much darker), because it combines within itself the hues of many strata of paint. According to how the artist uses his glazes, colors can be made to glow almost as if lit up from within; and a wide variety of textures can be simulated by the way the glazes are applied.

As a descendant of Greco-Roman classicism, Giotto sought realism in the structure of his figures, in the measured arrangement of objects in space, and in the psychological interpretation of his figures in terms of human relationships. Flemish artists, remote from the classical world, made their painted scenes real in other ways, relying first of all upon a profusion and an exactitude of recognizable detail, and secondly on a variety and a convincing rendering of the textures of things. Thus they depicted costumes to the very stitches that hold them together, and hands are painted complete with fingernails and wrinkles over the knuckles. They delighted in reproducing the material character of objects: the polished or rough grain of wood, the silky or wooly feel of cloth, the cold glitter of metal, the softness of flesh, the sheen of hair, and the transparency or translucency of glass.

Hans Memling   c. 1430–1494

Although he lacked the vigor of his predecessor Jan van Eyck and the passion of Roger van der Weyden, Hans Memling painted gentle and lyrical pictures of considerable charm. Born in Germany, actually, about 1430, he learned his craft in Flanders and worked for Roger van der Weyden before settling in Bruges, where he lived until his death in 1494.

Hans Memling: *Madonna and Child with Angels*   Colorplate 3

Two things above everything else in this painting distinguish it from frescoes like Giotto's *Lamentation:* its amazingly rich colors and the startling clarity with which the details are painted. The glowing, jewel-like colors are due to the way artists in fifteenth-century Flanders used their newly discovered medium of oil paint. Transparent glazes of paint were laid down over bright colors, so that the latter would shine through with an almost phosphorescent effect. Not only luminosity but a great variety of textural effects could be achieved in this way, a feature which the Flemish painters used to full advantage. In this painting the textures of various kinds of cloth, wood, and stone offer a real feast to the eye. Notice, for example, the contrast between the polished stone columns and the rougher limestone of the archway and between the metallic embroidery of the angel's robe and the softer nap of the oriental rug at Mary's feet. Such textural contrasts make this picture appeal to our tactile imagination, that faculty which allows us to enjoy the feel of materials simply by looking at them. Neither a black and white reproduction or a color slide can, of course, convey these textural distinctions; to appreciate them we must be able to see the actual paint surface of the picture.

We also enjoy in this picture its many minutely observed and carefully painted details, many of which function on two levels, the actual and the symbolic. To the fifteenth-century Fleming an apple in a painting with the Christ Child immediately recalled the original sin in the Garden of Eden, the reason for Christ's coming into the world to save mankind. But for most modern viewers, such symbols are meaningless. Even if we go to the trouble of looking them up in books, we are not conditioned like medieval man to feel these symbols emotionally. We are more likely to enjoy them on another level of meaning; we delight in seeing the angel playing with the Infant Jesus who reaches out for the apple with childish delight. For Memling's contemporaries, however, every object in this picture probably had a double significance (modern scholars have not rediscovered all these meanings), but to us the ornately carved Gothic arch and the sunlit landscape offer pleasures of another sort.

One of these pleasures is spatial. We perceive the floor slanting back, the angels standing at different distances from us, the arch and the dais behind Mary forming a brief barrier, and the windows at her sides catapulting us through a landscape that reaches into infinity. The chief means by which this spatial effect is achieved is called perspective: linear perspective in the way the floor tiles converge like railroad tracks as they recede, and in the way objects get smaller as they are further removed from our eye; and aerial perspective in the way colors become paler, more grayish, and details less sharp as they recede into the distance.

Another way of suggesting the three-dimensionality of an object is to distribute the light and dark colors on it so as to imitate natural light and shadow. Since the light in this painting seems to come from a single source, the upper left, the right-hand side of all of the objects is veiled in shadow—very slightly because the light is gentle—and the harp actually casts a faint shadow on the angel's chest. This gentleness of light is in keeping with the gentleness of the painting as a whole: the graceful poses of the angels, the dreamy languor of the Virgin, even the carefully groomed, fairytale landscape in the distance. Indeed, we feel this is a fairytale world and not the real world we live in. One reason we get this feeling is that the artist's approach to perspective and lighting effects is intuitive rather than scientific. The floor slants upward, as it should, but too much. The angel at our right is obviously closer to us than the angel at the left, yet they are both the same size. And if Mary stood up, her head would almost touch the top of the arch. The spatial contrasts between the objects in the foreground and those in the distant landscape are so abrupt that the two windows look almost like two pictures hanging on the walls of the Gothic chapel. The figures are nicely modeled in light and dark, but nevertheless they seem unsubstantial and doll-like. They seem to have no skulls behind their faces, no bones inside their hands, or real bodies under their lovely clothing. The artist has looked at the world around him and painted what he saw, but he does not seem to have observed things analytically or to have found out why things look as they do. In his unscientific attitude toward visual phenomena, Memling belongs to the Middle Ages, to the late Gothic era rather than to the Renaissance.

Projects

1. Examine a narrative painting by Giotto's contemporary, Duccio, or by Giotto's follower, Simone Martini, with regard to the dramatic unity and the impact of the picture.
2. Find a color reproduction of a painting by Jan van Eyck or Roger van der Weyden. What are the factors that contribute to the picture's realism? Name some factors which you think detract from its realism.
3. Draw a rectangle and imagine that it is the ground upon which the people in Giotto's Lamentation are situated. Indicate by means of circles or ovals where each of the figures is located, beginning with the seated woman in the center and working back. Draw a similar diagram for Memling's Madonna, this time including the rug and the arch.
4. Piero della Francesca was an almost exact contemporary of Hans Memling. Examine a color reproduction of one of Piero's wall paintings. How does its style of execution compare with Giotto's? In what ways is it similar in style to Memling's picture; in what ways is it different?

Suggested Reading

Battisti, Eugenio. Giotto, trans. James Emmons. New York: Skira, Inc., 1960.
Clark, Kenneth. Piero della Francesca. New York: Phaidon Art Books, Inc., 1951.
Dumont, Georges-Henri. Memling.* New York: Barnes and Noble, Inc., 1966.
Dupont, Jacques, and Cesare Gnudi. Gothic Painting, trans. Stuart Gilbert. New York: Skira, Inc., Publishers, 1954.

Eimerl, Sarel. *The World of Giotto.* New York: Time-Life Books, 1968.

Giotto. *Frescoes.* New York: Oxford University Press, 1950.

Lassaigne, Jacques, and Giulio Argan. *The Fifteenth Century,* trans. Stuart Gilbert. New York: Skira, Inc., Publishers, 1955.

Semenzato, Camillo. *Giotto.* *New York: Barnes & Noble, Inc., 1964.

Vasari, Giorgio. *Lives of the Artists,* *ed. Betty Burroughs. New York: Simon & Schuster, Inc., 1959.

*Available in a paperback edition

9 | The Artist as a Scientist
Filippo Lippi and Albrecht Dürer

Whereas medieval man saw the world around him in symbolic terms and life on earth as preparation for a life hereafter, man in fifteenth-century Italy began more and more to explain the world around him in terms of rational causes and effects, to feel that the goal of existence was the enjoyment of life on earth, and to use his energies to make himself master of his environment. As life became more secular and wealth and power more desirable, art was more and more often commissioned by private individuals, even art destined for the adornment of a church. Portraiture, though not unknown in the Middle Ages, became more general and art as a whole more the exact reproduction of what the eye perceived. Since such an art required careful observation of the structure and appearance of natural forms, art and science became closely linked. Not only Leonardo da Vinci but many other artists were both artists and scientists, devoting as much energy to the study of human and animal anatomy, botany, geology, optics, and other physical sciences as to the problem of transcribing this three-dimensional world onto a two-dimensional surface.

Combined with this tendency toward realism was the fifteenth-century Italians' admiration for the art of antiquity, mostly Roman copies of Greek statues. With this rediscovery of antique art there was a corresponding revival and imitation of the classical poets and philosophers, especially of Plato, who had not been known during most of the Middle Ages. As a matter of fact, Renaissance man saw his era as a continuation of classical civilization, whose progress had been interrupted by ten centuries of ignorance and barbarism—the "middle ages" between the antique and the modern eras. The word "humanism," which originally referred to the study of Greek and Roman writers, has come to denote an emphasis on the individual, the centrality of man in the universe, and the importance of human values—all of which were cardinal in the Greco-Roman world and have become fundamental to Western thought from Renaissance times to ours.

The wealth and the privileges of leisure enjoyed by the newly risen upper middle class townsman produced in him a desire to build stately town houses, to decorate and furnish them in the latest style, inspired, of course, by classical art, and to commission works of art for his church, partly for the good of his soul and partly, to be sure, for his social status. As a consequence of this patronage, the artist became less of a manual laborer, less a member of the proletariat, and more a respected master. Some of these master artists established privileged positions at a ducal court and became personal friends of the sovereign and his circle of intellectuals. Some of them amassed wealth and property of their own and, like Leonardo, Raphael, and Michelangelo in the High Renaissance, were treated as social equals by princes and churchmen, even by the Pope himself. It was inevitable that such conditions should effect a change in the artist's opinion of himself and his work. After all, he could do something quite remarkable: by means of his learning and science he could turn a flat surface into something so realistic that one could hardly tell painted objects from actual ones. We who are used to photography miss this aspect of Renaissance art, of which artists at the time were very proud. In the Renaissance it was regarded as an achievement quite as remarkable and as much beyond the understanding of the layman as, say, the ability to send a satellite around the moon is in our day.

We saw how late Gothic artists like Memling in 1480 tried to develop linear perspective in their pictures by observation and guesswork. In Florence at the same time the search for a scientific explanation of physical phenomena impelled artists to find a mathematical basis for linear perspective. According to the principles of geometric perspective, all lines parallel to each other come to one point in infinity. Most Renaissance painting before the early 1500's used this one-point perspective. That is, the spectator is so placed in front of the painted scene that the major lines of the buildings and streets come together at one point and that is within the boundaries of the painting, generally at its very center. Such an arrangement was employed in interiors as well, for example in Leonardo's *Last Supper,* where the lines of the ceiling, the walls, and the table meet at one point just above Christ's head, or in Raphael's *School of Athens,* where the lines of the architecture converge on the central figures of Plato and Aristotle. The centrality of this arrangement resulted in a symmetry and a simplicity of relationships which enhanced the serenity, the clarity, and the monumentality of the painting. It meant, moreover, that the spectator knew exactly where he stood, how far he was away from each object depicted in the painting, and how far each of those objects was from the others. Such a picture represented an ordered world, a universe that was clearly measured and comprehensible. The artist had discovered, explored, and, so to speak, conquered the world around him in a pictorial way just as the scientists, geographers, and mariners of his time were doing in a literal sense.

Like their ancient counterparts, Renaissance artists made the image of man primary in their art and sought those proportions of the human body which were most pleasing and ideal. As for the posture of the human figure in their painting and sculpture, they imitated that graceful interaction of motion and rest which classical statues often exhibited, that S-shaped disposition of the body which the Italians called *contrapposto*. Their favorite compositional arrangement for a picture or a sculptured group was the isosceles triangle or pyramid, one of the most stable of all geometric figures both visually and actually. Such a triangle encloses within itself a highly concentrated yet varied field whose center is focal and axial and whose sides diminish in height as they approach the lateral corners. This centrality and unity of focus, combined with just enough repetition and variety, seemed particularly appealing to the Renaissance artist who, like his classical Greek and Roman counterpart, generally conceived a work of art as a totality rather than piecemeal. A Gothic church, as we have seen, was begun with one idea in mind and continued through different stages in a diversity of styles until the church as a whole became a free-flowing, constantly evolving organism. A Renaissance building, however, followed a preconceived plan, each part of which was worked out with regard to its relationship to every other part. Similarly, medieval mosaics, wall paintings, and manuscript illuminations often appear to be random and seemingly spontaneous in their composition, intuitive rather than preconsidered in their arrangement. When symmetry was employed, as in the countless altarpieces of the Madonna with saints and angels, the arrangement was strictly bilateral with an equal number of figures on each side of the central axis (except for the Christ Child, who was always located on our right of center). Renaissance artists tried to achieve symmetry and balance within the framework of a natural and believable arrangement. Objects on either side of an axis were not identical, but differed in shape, size, or position. The resultant effect is one that Phidias would have admired: movement within a fixed order, variety within unity, stylization without a loss of naturalness.

Filippo Lippi 1406–1469

Foremost among those who added this element of naturalness and believability to art, especially to art with sacred subject matter, was Fra Filippo Lippi. Orphaned at an early age, Lippi was placed, when only eight years old, in a monastery of the Carmelite Order; here his artistic

talent was recognized, and he was trained as a painter. In 1434 he did
some work for Cosimo de' Medici, grandfather of Lorenzo the Magnificent. At the age of fifty Lippi fell in love with a young novice in the
convent where he was painting and succeeded in persuading her to run
off with him, along with her sister and three of her girl friends. Through
Cosimo de' Medici's influence he got the Pope to release both himself and
his sweetheart from their monastic vows and to solemnize their marriage.
Lippi was working on a fresco in the cathedral at Spoleto when he died in
1469, and that city petitioned Florence to let it keep the painter's remains,
arguing that Florence already had so many famous artists' tombs. Florence
granted this request. Lorenzo de' Medici had a monument erected over the
painter's tomb and had his chief poet, Poliziano, compose couplets in
Latin to honor the artist.

Filippo Lippi was not a great innovator. He left to others the task of
scientific research and problems of perspective. He was satisfied to use
what others had discovered and to make the holy personages in his
pictures look believable: his Madonnas are like the Florentine girls he so
admired; his saints look like the people he saw every day; and his angels
resemble the street urchins he encountered. In a long, dramatic poem
called "Fra Lippo Lippi" (Lippo is short for Filippo), Robert Browning has
Lippi's conservative superiors find fault with his paintings as follows:

> Your business is not to catch men with show,
> With homage to the perishable clay,
> But lift them over it, ignore it all,
> Make them forget there's such a thing as flesh,
> Your business is to paint the souls of men— . . .
> Give us no more of body than shows soul!
> Here's Giotto, with his Saint a-praising God
> That sets you praising—why not stop with him?
> Why put all thoughts of praise out of our head
> With wonder at lines, colours, and what not?
> Paint the soul, never mind the legs and arms!

Lippi, on the other hand, claims that he can paint the soul by painting
people as they really appear to our eye. He wants to represent:

> The beauty and the wonder and the power,
> The shapes of things, their colours, lights, and shades,
> Changes, surprises—and God made it all!

Lippi does not want to "stop with Giotto." He sees no conflict between
the physical and the spiritual in his work. Why can't a painter do both, he

asks—first make the body look lifelike "And then add soul and heighten them threefold!"

Filippo Lippi: *Madonna and Child*   Colorplate 4

Compared to Memling's Madonna, Lippi's Mary is much more sharply drawn, more sculptural, and more filled with psychological life. That is, her eyes look directly into ours and her face reveals an awareness of our presence. Incomparably simpler than Memling's picture, devoid of all but the most essential details, this painting is also radically different in its color, being done in tempera instead of oil. The quality of the color is flat: we see the topmost layer of paint and that is all. There is therefore little difference, for example, between the cloth of the Christ Child's robe and the texture of his skin. Only in the stroking—a stippled effect in several places and different types of brushstrokes elsewhere—was Lippi able to give a little textural variety to the work.

The figures are sharply outlined in their external contours and also in their interior detail—fingers, drapery folds, facial features. The painting resembles a tinted drawing, for line is everywhere more important than color. One reason for this is that Florentine artists, more than artists elsewhere in Italy, were fascinated by antique sculpture (which was linear and colorless), and Lippi's Madonna and Child do in a way resemble stone statues more than living humans. Their affinity to sculpture is heightened by the presence behind them of a scallop shell niche, a favorite setting for sculpture in ancient Rome. This niche is rendered in linear perspective (for example, the molding that seems to go into space behind Mary's shoulders) and in light and shadow (notice how the shadows in the upper corners of the picture make the recessed moldings look three-dimensional). This is the second great interest of the Renaissance artist: besides his inspiration from ancient sculpture, there is his passion for investigating the world he lived in and formulating methods of rendering the visible world in his art. To make his painted people more like living humans, he studied the human skeleton and musculature, the mechanical way parts of the body move. Filippo Lippi was not as scientifically inclined as many Renaissance artists, but the contorted pose of the Christ Child shows him trying to solve rather complicated problems in anatomy and foreshortening (the method of representing something as if seen from above or pointing toward the spectator).

Filippo Lippi's passion, according to his biographers, was to make saints and other holy people as real as the people he saw around him. It is said that he used his own wife as a model for Mary and his son for Jesus and angels. Certainly the Madonna in this picture, who glances at us so casually, must have looked like a young Florentine woman to Lippi's contemporaries. The most usual way of depicting Mary and the Christ Child before the fifteenth century was as a queen on a throne with a baby who looked more like a diminutive adult, his right hand raised in the traditional sign of benediction. Even Memling's Madonna still has many of these medieval characteristics. Lippi's Jesus, however, squirms impatiently at his Mother's side, playing with her fingers and, like most human babies when they are supposed to be at their best, ignores us completely. Only their haloes, not solid gold disks as in Italian medieval paintings, but diaphanous, almost imperceptible ellipses, suggest that this is more than an ordinary mother and her baby.

Next to the triangle (and its three-dimensional extension, the pyramid) the most restful of all shapes is the semicircle, whose unchanging radius suggests constancy and restraint. The very compositional arrangement that Lippi chose for his Madonna, a pyramid set into a semicircle (which is semicircular in both elevation and plan) is calculated to communicate the sense of serenity and quiet monumentality which was part of the Renaissance ideal.

Yet the liveliness of this painting is not due merely to the lifelike postures and expressions of the Mother and Child. It is also due to the design of the picture, especially to the rhythmic interplay of its curves. The dominant semicircle of the niche above Mary's head and its projection into space behind her shoulders find a diminutive echo in the edges of the fifteen grooves inside the top of the niche. The roundness of these curves is recalled by other parts of the design: the neckline of Mary's robe, the edge of her face, the convolutions of her hairdo, and many other details of both figures. As a counterpoint to these larger curves, there are many repetitions of smaller elements. The parallel folds of Mary's robe as they are gathered by her high-waisted belt recall the grooves inside the niche, while various parts of the veil around her head and shoulders repeat this multiplicity in a more random way, as do the wrinkles on the heavy cloak on the left and the jumble of fingers just beside them. Finally, by setting the free-flowing curves of the figures against the rigid, geometric framework, the artist has polarized the identity of each: the cold, hard, inanimate character of the architecture and the supple, graceful, and human aspect of the figures.

Albrecht Dürer   1471–1528

The Renaissance was slow in crossing the Alps. When Albrecht Dürer was born in Nuremberg, artists in Germany were still treated like mere craftsmen. Trained as a goldsmith in his father's workshop, Dürer distressed his father when, at the age of fifteen, he chose art as a career and apprenticed himself to an engraver who, besides painting altarpieces and doing other odd jobs, made woodcuts for printed books.

After serving his apprenticeship, he traveled for four years, working for and learning from various masters in different parts of Germany. In 1494 he visited Italy, where he studied the various developments in art and made sketches of works that he admired. On his second visit to Italy in 1505, he was almost tempted to stay, partly because of the honors accorded him in Venice and partly because of the respect artists received there. But he returned to Nuremberg where he lived for the rest of his life except for shorter sojourns to the Netherlands and elsewhere.

In Nuremberg he frequented a circle of humanists and scholars, and drew upon himself some measure of the respect which his counterparts in Italy received. Besides filling an enormous number of commissions, he devoted himself to intellectual and scientific pursuits, studying natural phenomena, plants and animals, the principles of perspective, fore-shortening, and other technical matters. He wrote books on geometry, military fortifications, and human proportions and set down his ideas on the theory and practice of the arts. In the 1520's he became an ardent admirer of Martin Luther, who wrote an epitaph for him when Dürer died in 1528.

The Art of Printmaking

The word "print" has come to have several very distinct meanings which have only one thing in common: the mechanical process of being stamped or reproduced in numerous identical copies. When someone says that he has a print of Leonardo's *Mona Lisa* or Giotto's *Lamentation*, we understand it to be a reproduction which, though it may have cost as much as ten or twenty dollars, is not an original work of art and has no real artistic value. The kind of prints that artists make—woodcuts, engravings, etchings, or lithographs, for example—are works of art made by treating a block of wood, a metal plate, or some other material in such a way that it may be inked and printed.

In the case of a woodcut print, the surface of a flat block of wood is carved so that when ink is applied to it the portions of the surface that were not cut away will be stained with the ink; when the block is pressed against a piece of paper, this inked design will be transferred to the paper, reversed, of course, like a mirror image. The majority of prints are done in black ink on white paper, but, of course, colored ink or colored paper may be used. If the artist wishes to make a print which involves more than one color, he generally makes a separate woodblock for each color, and prints one block over the other on the same piece of paper.

In past centuries, the chief reason for making prints was the practical one of having many copies of a work rather than just one. The Chinese, the first people to discover how to make paper, were making woodblock prints many centuries before the Europeans. It was not until the invention of the printing press that printmaking became a major art form in the West, and then again because an artist needed to cut only one block instead of laboriously painting a picture in each copy of a book.

In our day of easy duplication methods, prints are bought by collectors for another reason. Each of the graphic media has its particular characteristics, just as the fresco, tempera, and oil media of painting have theirs.

One of the charms of a woodcut print is the particular quality of the lines and shapes which result from the cutting—the actual path of the knife or gouge through the fibers of the wood. The resistance of the wood, the effect of the grain on the cutting edge—all this endows the woodcut with its particular character which is different, for example, from a linoleum cut in which there is no grain and the surface yields slightly under the pressure of the knife; it differs as well from the etching where the acid makes the grooves instead of a cutting edge.

Compared to painting, however, a woodcut or an etching might seem to be limited in its expressive possibilities. Yet it is these very limitations that appeal to the print collector. The printmaker is like a basketball player, for example, who can catch the ball but not run with it, throw the ball but not kick it. The limitations are the essence of the game. So it is with the print.

Albrecht Dürer: *The Angel with the Key*

The variety of line possible in a woodcut is decidedly limited. Lines can be thick or thin, relatively straight or undulating, continuing some length or short and interrupted. They may also be separated by areas of white paper or they can be set close to each other, thus achieving various tones of gray. Considering the limitations of the medium, therefore, Dürer has achieved a remarkable amount of variety in the great diversity of his linear effects in the woodcut reproduced in figure 39.

The lines on the robe of the angel, for example, describe the character of the cloth, suggest the angel's movement, model the volume of his body, and pull him forward toward us by contrasting the rounded mass of his body with the flatter and less modeled area immediately behind him. In the hair of his head and in the feathers of his wings, the lines have the character that best describes those surfaces. Sometimes these lines function simply as outlines and sometimes they suggest shadow as well. If we let our eyes move from the lines on the angel to the lines of the distant city, we receive the sensation of moving through space: the lines become thinner as they approach the distant mountains. This, of course, is the aerial perspective that we discussed in relation to Memling's painting, but Dürer has here achieved the effect with lines alone. And in their variety and complexity, the lines also endow this woodcut print with a richness of patterned effects. The birds in the sky and the branches of the tree, the forest on the distant hills and the stones of the city walls, the parallel strokes of the ground and the streaks and spikes of the nearby vegetation, all these serve to excite the eye as purely visual rhythms.

Dürer's lines, therefore, perform a variety of functions. They describe objects, they imply movement, they model volumes, they suggest effects of light and shadow, they depict textures, they intimate various degrees of distance, and they proffer a richness of pattern which is one of the picture's major charms. If we allow our eyes to range over the print, we will savor this aspect of the picture on a purely sensuous level. In some places Dürer's line sweeps along in graceful curves, often in parallel groupings with other curves. Sometimes it curls and twists in sinuous contortions. Elsewhere it starts, stops, changes direction, and collides with other groups of lines with a restless, nervous energy.

Dürer's *Apocalypse* is interesting because it is the earliest book we know which was designed and published by an artist exclusively as his own undertaking. There are fourteen prints in the book, of which the best known is *The Four Horsemen of the Apocalypse* (Hunger, Pestilence, War, and Death riding over a multitude that includes rich and poor, kings and clergymen). The word "apocalypse" refers to any prophetic, highly symbolic, and supernatural vision. Specifically, it refers to the visions of St. John as described in the book of Revelation in the New Testament. Besides seeing God and other holy personages, St. John saw monsters and symbolic objects like candlesticks and stars. The last print in Dürer's book refers to three passages in the book of Revelation:

> And I saw an angel come down from heaven, having the key of the bottomless pit and a great chain in his hand.
>
> And he laid hold on the dragon, that old serpent, which is the Devil, and Satan, and bound him a thousand years.
>
> And cast him into the bottomless pit, and shut him up, and set a seal upon him, that he should deceive the nations no more, till the thousand years should be fulfilled: and after that he must be loosed a little season. . . .

And there came unto me one of the seven angels which had the seven vials full of the seven last plagues, and talked with me, saying, Come hither, I will shew thee the bride, the Lamb's wife.

And he carried me away in the spirit to a great and high mountain, and shewed me that great city, the holy Jerusalem, descending out of heaven from God,

Having the glory of God: and her light was like unto a stone most precious, even like a jasper stone, clear as crystal;

And had a wall great and high, and had twelve gates, and at the gates twelve angels, and names written thereon, which are the names of the twelve tribes of the children of Israel: . . .

And I John saw these things, and heard them. And when I had heard and seen, I fell down to worship before the feet of the angel which shewed me these things.

(Rev. 20:1–3; 21:9–12; 22:8)

Dürer's devil is a disgusting beast but hardly impressive enough to be Satan himself. Nor does the angel have to struggle with him. All seem to be following a preordained plan, obeying God's will. The entrance to the pit is just a hole in the ground that is evidently closed by the round object which looks like a manhole cover except that it has a lock mechanism on it to which the angel has the key.

The hill on which St. John stands is hardly a "great and high mountain," but a promontory across the river from the walled town which, moreover, is not a Near Eastern city but a medieval German city like Nuremberg, where Dürer lived. It seems as if Durer, having depicted dreadful scenes of horror and catastrophe in some of the other prints, were trying to end the sequence on a note of serenity and comforting security. Moreover, the simplicity of the design here appeals more to the modern viewer than the cluttered abundance of details and episodes which appears on some of the *Apocalypse* prints. But even in this, the gentlest of the prints, there is a restless energy which we do not find in the works of Giotto or Filippo Lippi. It is useless, of course, to compare the contrasts of color and modeling in these pictures, because the print is done in black and white only. We must compare what they all have in common, their line. Compared with the simplicity of line in the pictures by Giotto and Lippi, there is a nervous restlessness in Durer's lines. Only a

Figure 39 | ALBRECHT DÜRER. *The Angel with the Key to the Bottomless Pit.* c. 1496. Woodcut print from the Apocalypse series. 16″ high, 11″ wide. National Gallery of Art, Washington, D.C.

few of the lines are straight—those of the architecture mostly. Only a few of them are simple—the folds of drapery and a few blades of grass. The majority of lines are dynamic. They wiggle and curl like snakes, bend and stretch like wires under tension, or cut into each other, overlap, and interweave. Everywhere our eye looks, it is confronted with linear conflicts and complications. The simple form of the tree at the top center of the page is squirming like a tortured snake. Everything in the picture, even the inert stones and blades of grass, seems to be moving or throbbing with potential movement. This linear energy invades even the clothing on the angel in the foreground. The wrinkles on his right arm resemble crumpled paper which has been thrown into a fire. And the angel's face is as alive with squirming linear forms as his hair. Instead of calm, gently undulating lines forming graceful patterns and round, convex forms, we have just the opposite. Notice how many sharp, thorny, aggressive forms there are, not only in the devil's horns and spines, but also in the angel's wings and clothing, in the vegetation on the left, and in the distant city.

In short, we have here a picture which is far removed from the classical ideals of serenity and restraint. This is partly due to the absence of the classical tradition in northern Europe, including the absence of Roman statuary and architectural decoration, and partly due to the barbarian heritage in northern art, the energy of geometrized animal and abstract forms.

Projects

1. Find a color reproduction of a painting by either Masaccio, Fra Angelico, Mantegna, Botticelli, or Perugino. Point out specific details that bespeak the artist's interest in (1) perspective, (2) human anatomy, and (3) classical art.
2. Look through the drawings of Leonardo da Vinci's notebooks. Describe in some detail the wide range of his interests as evidenced in these drawings.
3. Point out some medieval and some Renaissance characteristics in a painting by either Hieronymus Bosch or Matthias Grünewald. How can you account for these characteristics of style?
4. Describe how line and color function in a painting, preferably a portrait, by Hans Holbein, the Younger. In what ways are they like the line and color of other painters we have discussed? In what ways are they different?

Suggested Reading

Bosch, Jerome. *The Complete Paintings of Bosch,* ed. Michael Levey. New York: World Publishing Co., 1967.

Bosman, Anthony. *Bosch,* trans. Albert J. Fransella. New York: Barnes & Noble, Inc., 1963.

Bussagli, Mario. *Bosch,* trans. Claire Pace. New York: Grosset & Dunlap, Inc., 1967.

Chastel, André. *The Age of Humanism.* Landmarks of Art Series. New York: McGraw-Hill Book Co., Inc., 1963.

Clark, Kenneth. *Leonardo da Vinci.** Baltimore: Penguin Books, Inc., 1967.

Dürer, Albrecht. *Dürer: Complete Engravings, Etchings, and Woodcuts,* ed. Karl-Adolf Knappe. New York: Harry N. Abrams, Inc., 1965.

Holbein, Hans. *Holbein,** ed. Karl T. Parker. New York: Phaidon Art Books, 1967.

Leonardo da Vinci. *The Drawings of Leonardo da Vinci,** ed. Arthur E. Popham. New York: Harcourt, Brace & World, Inc., 1963.

Leonardo da Vinci. *The Genius of Leonardo da Vinci,* ed. André Chastel. New York: Orion Press, Inc., 1961.

Pevsner, Nikolaus, and Michael Meier. *Grünewald.* New York: Harry N. Abrams, Inc., 1958.

Russell, Francis. *The World of Dürer.* New York: Time-Life Books, 1968.

Steck, Max. *Dürer and His World,* trans. J. Maxwell Brownjohn. New York: The Viking Press, Inc., 1964.

Venturi, Lionello. *The Renaissance.* Italian Painting, vol. 2. New York: Skira, Inc., Publishers, 1950.

White, John. *The Birth and Rebirth of Pictorial Space.* Boston, Massachusetts: Boston Book and Art Shop, 1967.

*Available in a paperback edition.

10 | An Age of Transition
The Farnese Palace, Titian, and El Greco

It was customary for prominent families in the Renaissance to own one or more town houses such as the Farnese Palace (fig. 40) which was begun in 1515 for a cardinal who was a member of the Farnese family. In 1534, when the cardinal was elected to the papacy as Pope Paul III, Antonio da San Gallo was asked to enlarge it. Upon San Gallo's death in 1546 Michelangelo added the third floor and changed certain other parts.

In general form, the Farnese Palace is typical of palaces in central Italy: a large three-story block of rooms arranged around an open central courtyard (see fig. 41). In this respect it is related to the ancient Greek and Roman houses which were arranged around a central garden or a room that was open to the sky, an idea which spread throughout Mediterranean lands and to the New World; we see examples of this architectural style in Latin America and the United States in California, New Orleans, and other areas where Spaniards or Frenchmen settled. In warm, mild climates this arrangement was ideal, for every room had at least one window on the street and a door on the *loggia* or gallery that opened onto the court. Lighting and ventilation were thus provided and one side was always shaded no matter where the sun was. By proper adjustment of the shutters at different times of the day, cool air could be let in from the shady side and the hot sun shut out, an important factor in days before air conditioning.

The Farnese Palace: Exterior

The outside façade of the Farnese Palace (185 feet long and 96½ feet high) is marked by its symmetry on all three levels. A large central door, high enough for a man on horseback to pass through, stresses the very center of the façade on the ground floor. Six windows are arranged on each side of this door, all of them identical and rectangular in shape to contrast with the semicircular arch that forms the doorway. Although these windows were later altered and enlarged, they are not too different from San Gallo's original ones. This ground floor was occupied by servants, stables, and offices. The second story was inhabited by members of the Farnese family.

The center of the second floor is also pronounced, being marked by a window whose opening is as large as the rest but whose outlines distinguish it from the others in that it has two extra columns and lacks a pediment. This window is actually a door that opens on a balcony and thus accentuates even more the centrality of the façade, as does the sculptured coat of arms of the Farnese family which replaces the pediment. The remaining twelve windows on the second floor have alternately triangular and curved pediments, a feature found occasionally in Roman Imperial architecture. All of these windows rest, visually that is, on a molding which connects them and which is suggestive of a balustrade on each of the three levels.

The windows of the third floor (as well as the central window of the second) were designed by Michelangelo after San Gallo's death. All thirteen are alike, with triangular pediments and columns that rest, most unstably from a visual point of view, on S-shaped scrolls or consoles, a favorite motif of Michelangelo's. What distinguishes these windows most radically from the lower ones is that their tops are round and rise unexpectedly into the space where the entablature should be. Crowning the façade is a huge cornice which extends five feet over the sides of the building and casts a deep shadow, thus stressing the finality of the façade.

Shadow is important in the effect of the façade as a whole, for the very three-dimensional windows make an abrupt contrast to the otherwise smooth wall which is made of yellow brown brick. The only exceptions to this are the projecting stones around the entrance and at the corners which are of travertine plundered from the Colosseum. These quoins project slightly less on the second than on the ground floor, and less on the third floor than on the second. This rustication (the use of relatively rough, projecting stone in a wall) is repeated in the area around the front door and thus gives additional unity to the façade.

In the clarity of its design, in the logic of its repeated and contrasting parts, and in the harmony and predictability of its proportions, the façade of the Farnese Palace is very classical in spirit. The effect upon the spectator is that of magnificence tempered by restraint, of unity without monotony, of opulence and splendor without ostentation or extravagance. It is undoubtedly for these reasons that architects of the nineteenth century—that period of stylistic copying and paraphrase—used variations of the Farnese Palace as a model for men's clubs and banks throughout the Western world. The most famous of these is the Reform Club in London by Sir Charles Barry, who also designed the Houses of Parliament in the Gothic style.

Figure 41 | ANTONIO DA SAN GALLO THE YOUNGER
and MICHELANGELO. The Courtyard
of the Farnese Palace. Limestone,
96½′ high, 81′ wide, 81′ deep

Figure 40 | ANTONIO DA SAN GALLO THE YOUNGER
and MICHELANGELO. The Farnese Palace,
Rome. 1534-1548.
Brick, limestone trim,
96½′ high, 185′ wide

The Farnese Palace: The Courtyard

One enters the palace through a barrel-vaulted passageway which is flanked by narrower passages intended for pedestrians. The central passageway is high enough to admit a man on horseback. From the dark of the passageway one emerges into the groin-vaulted ambulatory that surrounds the courtyard where, of course, one sees daylight again. Here one may enter the courtyard, walk around it in the shaded ambulatory, or mount to the second floor by means of the stairway at the left. The courtyard façade is, strangely enough, more elaborately decorated than the exterior façade. For one thing, besides the three entablatures that crown each story, engaged columns divide these horizontal spaces into rectangular areas, thereby establishing an even clearer system of proportions. Each compartment, then, stresses its ratio of height to width and becomes part of a rectilinear framework which, visually at least, forms a supporting skeleton for each wall. The half columns of the ground floor are engaged to piers. That is, they do not form supports for the arches but rise between the arches and tie together the horizontals of the ground and entablature. This, of course, is the system used in the Colosseum.

The second floor was once open to the court, but the arches of the *loggia* were filled in and the windows built by Michelangelo when he added the third floor. These windows all have triangular pediments. Those on the third floor have round ones. As in the Colosseum, the orders used are Doric, Ionic, and Corinthian, with friezes decorated accordingly. Needless to say, all the details are strongly Roman.

In several details, however, Michelangelo's refusal to merely copy becomes apparent. The pilasters on the third floor, for example, are multiplied so that each one projects in several layers, and the heavy pediments, which one would expect to be supported by half-columns or pilasters, sit on those very unsubstantial looking consoles.

Like the front façade, the courtyard of the Farnese Palace is highly symmetrical. A strong horizontal pull is introduced by the vaulted entrance tunnel and completed by the elaborate entrance to the garden which once lay behind the palace. A secondary axis moves at right angles from one side entrance to the other. The pavement pattern of the square court reaffirms these axes and suggests still more axial directions in the form of diagonal lines that lead to the four corners of the courtyard.

A glance at the floor plan of the Farnese Palace reveals the three-part barrel-vaulted entrance (a), the groin-vaulted ambulatory around the courtyard (b), the courtyard itself (c), and the stairway (d) that leads to the second floor. The plan shows also that despite the symmetry of its façade and court, the interior disposition is not strictly symmetrical. In the

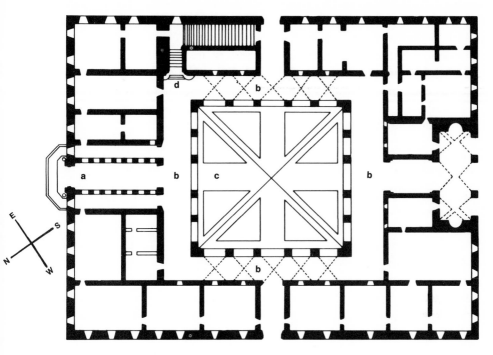

Figure 42 | Plan of the ground floor of the Farnese Palace

interest of conserving space, the stairway at the left is not duplicated at the right. Even in the front of the building the rooms do not fulfill the idea of symmetry which is suggested by the exterior. One has the distinct feeling, therefore, that the utilitarian requirements of the building as a place for living were forced into a preconceived scheme which fulfilled certain esthetic ideals of the time, especially the desire to impress the passerby with an imposing façade.

Titian   1488/90–1576

The painter we call Titian was born Tiziano Vecellio in the Alpine region of Italy. He was trained in Venice and lived there all of his life except when special commissions called him to Rome or elsewhere. On the whole, his art is strongly materialistic and sensuous. Many of his pictures have mythological subjects and stress their voluptuous aspects. Even his religious paintings are dramatic in human rather than spiritual terms, and are quite worldly, relying for their effect on the lush rendering of materials and textures. These qualities made him a popular portrait painter. His many portraits for the Farnese family made him a favorite of Pope Paul III.

He received many commissions from the Emperor Charles V, who honored him with knighthood, and from his son, Philip II of Spain.

Titian's skill brought him wealth and fame. He lived in a princely *palazzo* in Venice and ran a studio with numerous assistants to help him fill his many orders. It used to be said that Titian lived to be ninety-nine, but modern scholars believe he was about eighty-eight when he died during an epidemic of the plague in 1576.

Titian: *Venus with a Mirror*   Colorplate 5

As a city built on islands off the Adriatic coast of Italy, Venice lagged behind such centers of the Renaissance as Florence and Rome. When in the late fifteenth century the Renaissance did come to Venice, the research in anatomy, perspective, and light, which culminated in the art and writings of Leonardo da Vinci, had already been achieved. Venetian painting, therefore, rarely has that diagrammatic look that so much Florentine art has, in which muscles are itemized one by one and surfaces are modeled as if the artist were trying to prove his mastery of the latest scientific disciplines. In Titian's *Venus* some of the outlines are blurred or even disappear completely, and parts of the figure merge with the background. As a matter of fact, the goddess seems more real to us because she has been painted more the way a female figure in real life would appear to our eyes. Of the three paintings—Memling's, Lippi's, and Titian's—the latter is most like a photograph in which lights and shadows appear wherever they happen to be when the shutter clicks. Note how the shadow of Venus falls across the arm and face of the cupid who reaches up to put the floral crown on her head.

Where in Lippi's painting every fold of drapery is carefully drawn and separately modeled in light and dark, Titian suggests wrinkles with just a few, seemingly random, strokes of the brush. In Lippi's picture Mary's dress, her cloak, her veil, her hand—every object in the picture—has its own color and is sharply separated from its neighbor by a distinct line which our eye must hurdle as it jumps in a staccato rhythm from one compartment of color to the next. In Titian's painting the color of one area flows into the next, and most of the contours are blurred, so that our eye moves smoothly around the picture in a graceful rhythm.

The grace and elegance which this picture projects, and which Venetian painting as a whole exemplifies, is due only partly to Venus' graceful pose and gesture. It is in larger measure due to the richness of texture which Titian achieves with his paint—the soft, warm flesh, the silken blond hair with its adornment of shiny pearls, the glowing crimson velvet cloth with its sparkling embroidered border and its fur trim. The Venetian painters adopted the use of oil based pigments from Flanders, but they painted on canvas instead of wooden panels and went far beyond the Flemings in exploring the possibilities of this medium. Titian often laid down a flat coat of red before he sketched his picture on the canvas. The colors and glazes which he put over this red ground produced a golden glow which was particularly effective in his representation of flesh tones. But what distinguished Titian most radically from both Flemings and Florentines was that instead of drawing his forms and then coloring them in, he did both simultaneously. With a few touches of his brush he could suggest and hint at details without systematically drawing them out. A few strokes of the brush suffice for Venus' fingernails, the pearls in her hair, her bracelet, and the ring on her finger. The figures of the two cupids are even more sketchy in their execution, so different from the Christ Child of Lippi or the one by Memling.

The triangular composition, which Titian often used in his Madonnas, his portraits, and even in larger, mural-size canvases, is here less rigid than in Lippi's picture. The head of Venus, which marks the apex of the triangle, is to the left of center, and the base of the triangle is only vaguely accentuated by the striped bedclothes on the lower right and the red velvet at the left. We can almost discern an inverted triangle superimposed on the picture, a triangle whose lower point is Venus' hand and whose sides extend upward to the left and to the right. Or perhaps we can discern an oval movement rising through Venus' arm, through her head, the wreath, and down again through the body of the cupid at the right. Whichever disposition we prefer to see, the result is a much more fluid composition, still serene and monumental, but less rigid, less classical, more prophetic of art in the next century.

Part of our experience of things is tactile. As infants, we began to understand the world around us by touching objects which were up to then unfamiliar to us. As adults we no longer need to touch objects in order to experience them. We have learned to tell what is smooth to the touch, hard or soft to our pressure, light or heavy in weight, even cool to the touch like ice or polished marble, simply by looking at it. We can even imagine what an object would sound like if we were to tap it with our knuckles—a piece of wood, for instance, or a pane of glass, a tin can, or the tire of an automobile—simply by looking at it. This tactile imagination may be stimulated by an artist to a greater or lesser degree. In the Giotto fresco there is virtually no difference in texture between the faces and the clothing of the figures or the rocks behind them. Nor is there much textural variety in the Lippi Madonna, a tempera painting. The Flemings of the fifteenth century first exploited this textural appeal in painting, because, we are tempted to say, they used oil paint. The reverse is true, of course. They began using oil and perfected the glazing technique precisely because they were searching for ways to make their pictures more imitative of the world around them. The technique is a result, not a cause, of the way they looked at their universe.

The sixteenth-century Venetians were even more explicit in their simulation of natural textures. Theirs was a frankly materialistic impulse without that mysterious clarity that removes Flemish paintings from the realm of everyday nature. The Venetian love of textures was highly physical, sensuous, and hedonistic. One is ravished by the sheen on the red velvet cloth around Venus' hips and the contrast it makes with the metallic embroidery on its border. The warmth and suppleness of the flesh tones have a strongly sensuous appeal. The picture celebrates the physical beauty of existence, as Venice herself, the Queen of the Adriatic as she has been called, celebrated the joys which financial prosperity and the admiration of the whole world made hers.

The Style Called Mannerism

The Farnese Palace, we have seen, was begun by Antonio da San Gallo in the High Renaissance style, a style which, in the Imperial Roman manner, expresses grandeur and self-confidence. In the later additions and alterations to the palace, Michelangelo injected a new note by using the classical vocabulary in a very unclassical way—heavy pediments that rest on consoles instead of columns, windows that break into the space of the entablatures above them, and so on. A similar change in feeling may be seen in the paintings of Titian, whose life spanned nearly a century. In his early work we find the linear, sculptural sharpness of his Florentine predecessors. In the paintings of his middle years, brushstrokes became freer, colors richer, and textures more varied and lush. During the three decades before his death in 1576, restlessness and tension replaced the calm serenity of his former work; compositions became more agitated, the poses of his figures more strenuous, and the proportions of his painted people slightly abnormal. Heads, hands, and feet seem too small for the tall, bulky bodies; we can see this in the *Venus with a Mirror* which Titian painted about 1555, when he was in his late sixties. We have already noted the relative complexity of this picture's composition, especially its deviation from the stable, triangular disposition. We might also point out the ambiguous placement of the cupids in space. Where are they located in relation to Venus? There is no clear indication of what they are standing on. Nor are their proportions a clue as to their placement in space: the head of the distant cupid, being larger than his companion's, forces him forward toward us. Deep space, therefore, has been denied or, at least, made unimportant. The precision of spatial placement that marks earlier Renaissance painting is here repudiated (by an artist who once delighted in that precision himself) and is replaced with what seems like deliberate ambivalence. All these tendencies make up a style which has acquired the name of Mannerism because many of the artists and architects in the sixteenth century executed works in the *manner* of certain High Renaissance artists, particularly that of Michelangelo.

El Greco   1541–1614

Titian cannot rightly be called a Mannerist, although the work done in the last decades of his long life shows some Mannerist traits. Perhaps the best example of the Mannerist tendencies in painting was a man who was born Domenikos Theotokopoulos in 1541 on the Greek island of Crete, then governed by the Venetian Republic. As a colonial, the young Cretan went to Venice to study art—in Titian's studio according to tradition—and eventually settled in Toledo, Spain, where he was called El Greco, the Greek. What little we know about his private life comes from later chroniclers and from legal documents, mostly of law suits in which the painter was frequently embroiled. His personality seems to have been eccentric, combining religious mysticism with a love of physical pleasures that made him persist in living beyond his means. Most of his paintings are of religious subjects, although he was also in demand as a portrait painter. His art seemed strange to some of his contemporaries, and in succeeding centuries he was neglected as being ignorant of the rules of art. He was rediscovered in the twentieth century, although one still hears it said that the distortions in his pictures are due to astigmatic vision. Only a few years ago an ophthalmologist devised a pair of glasses through which the proportions of the figures in El Greco's paintings looked more normal.

Toledo in El Greco's day was the religious and spiritual capital of Spain in a century when that country rose to become the most powerful nation on earth. With the Low Countries, the Germanies, Austria, and most of South, Central, and North America under his rule, Charles V of Spain, Emperor of the Holy Roman Empire, invaded Italy, sacked and plundered Rome, and imprisoned Pope Clement VII. In a Europe split into Protestant and Catholic camps, Spain saw herself in the role of a crusader for the faith, fighting not only an external foe, but the enemy within. The ensuing investigations, persecutions, imprisonments, and public executions of nonconformists have made the Spanish Inquisition infamous in history, but they were little worse than the hangings and burnings perpetrated by the witch hunters in Protestant lands. Adding to the political and religious upheavals of the sixteenth century, the inflation caused by the influx of New World gold aggravated the general anxiety and frustration.

Now, a style of art must, as has been said, fulfill some need and express the major ideas and ideals of an era, or else it becomes replaced by another style. The spirit of the Renaissance, on the whole, was one of optimism and self-confidence. Man was discovered to be a being of limitless possibilities, and the world was an oyster to be opened by anyone with a sharp enough sword. Such a spirit can be related directly to the very elements of painting. Perspective, for example, is measured and measurable. Parallel lines converge on one point and almost every geometric object in a painting has an edge that is parallel to another so that objects have simple and uniform relationships, easily perceived, even felt, by the viewer. The vanishing point, moreover, usually falls within the bounds of a picture, often at its center, as in Leonardo's *Last Supper* and Raphael's *School of Athens,* to name only two. If not perpendicular to the picture plane, then objects are parallel to it, progressing in logical and easily grasped stages from nearby to far away.

Logical, too, is the distribution of light in Renaissance painting, which originates most often at a point outside of the picture and illuminates one side of all the painted objects more than another. A sense of unity is therefore effected by both a single source of light and a single perspective system, and the visual rhythm produced by these elements stresses regularity and a certain predictability that leaves the viewer satisfied and sure about what he sees. The more human aspects of a painting—the proportions and poses of the body, the expression of faces and the gestures of hands—are as simple, convincing, and unambiguous as possible. Long years of research into all these aspects of painting were spent by men like Uccello, Pollaiuolo, Signorelli, Piero della Francesca, and Leonardo da Vinci to achieve this clarity of effect and contentment of spirit in the arts of the Renaissance. In the painting of El Greco we see a total rejection of this Renaissance ideal and the substitution therefor of very different artistic ideals.

El Greco: *Madonna and Child with Saints*   Colorplate 6

Whereas the light in the two paintings by Lippi and Titian comes from a single and unifying source, the illumination in El Greco's picture seems to have no natural or logical origin. It seems rather to flicker over the forms as if produced by flashes of lightning or by a mysterious inner phosphorescence. Nor is space any more logical than illumination. Our first assumption as we look at the painting is that the two saints are closest to our eyes and that Mary and the two angels at her sides are further removed from us. If we let our eyes move from the two saints to the angels we get a sensation of moving back through space. But when we move to the figure of Mary, we are propelled forward again because of her large size, the strong colors of her robes, and the abrupt contrast between her lower silhouette and the adjoining light-colored clouds. All through the picture, as a matter of fact, space is as ambiguous and bewildering as the illumination.

The purpose of perspective in Renaissance painting was to clarify spatial relationships. Pictures were usually painted as if the spectator were viewing them from a normal position in front of the scene, not perched on a rooftop or standing in a hole. El Greco's picture, on the other hand, is painted as if our eyes were on about the level of the two saints' hands. Their heads appear to be above us, and Mary, the Christ Child, and the angels even higher. The fact that the two saints' hands are so much larger than their heads augments this illusion of foreshortening. Yet Mary is not painted as if seen from below. Nor is the angel at the right. As for the angel at our left, he is painted as if we were looking at him from above. Instead of a coherent and comprehensible spatial arrangement, we have here a fluid shifting of forms which we experience in different ways at different times as we confront the picture.

Adding to this fluidity of movement is the general composition, the basic arrangement of the picture. If the triangle with a solid base and sides that taper to a point above it is the most stable of geometric shapes, then El Greco here has chosen the least stable compositional form: the inverted triangle, or more precisely, a diamond-shape poised on one of its points. Notice how strongly that lower V-shape has been emphasized by the saints' hands, and the area between the two saints. The resultant effect is one of precarious balance, of supernatural buoyancy, of many separate hovering forms that suggest electrically charged particles suspended in a magnetic field.

The pull of this magnetic field is clearly upward, for not only is the picture vertical in its format but the people in it seem to have been stretched and elongated. Heads are tiny compared to the rest of the body; necks, arms, and hands are overly long; and torsos are large and bulky. And in keeping with the tensions produced by the light, space, and composition in the picture, El Greco has achieved a dynamic polarity of coloring. On the whole, this picture consists of neutral colors—mostly cool grays, blues, and browns—except for three zones of strong, vibrant color. Mary wears a cloak of deep, luminous blue, and a crimson robe which is visible on her upraised arm and on her left leg. The other accents of brilliant color are in the two saints, one of whom—St. Inés (or Agnes) who holds the lamb—wears a cloak of fiery red orange. St. Tecla, whose symbol is the lion and the palm frond, wears a cloak of deep lemon yellow over a sky blue robe.

A close examination of this picture will reveal a remarkable vigor in the application of paint. In many places brushstrokes are left plainly visible, so that we are not aware of the distinctive textures of cloth, clouds, or flesh as much as we are of the texture of the paint as paint. On the red cloak of St. Inés, the paint has been applied in a jagged pattern that does not describe the cloth. Instead, it enacts a rhythmic dance of its own. In some parts of the picture the marks of the brushes' bristles are clearly discernible. In some places the brush has been dragged across the surface and has pulled the color of one area into another. Many colors are sometimes juxtaposed in one area. The heads of the cherubs under Mary's feet, for example, show splotches of blue, tan, yellow, and what looks like some of the crimson of Mary's gown, as if the artist had painted them in the heat of inspired ecstasy.

Throughout the painting, in its light, space, composition, color, and brush stroke, there is a close connection between its emotional content and the painter's method, a fact which accounts for El Greco's popularity in the twentieth century, particularly among those who respond to the more abstract aspects of the art of painting.

Historically, Mannerism is interesting as an example of the artist's role as a reflector of his times. After more than a century of study and patient search by Renaissance artist-scientists for the most perfect human proportion, the Mannerists rejected their predecessors' findings and resorted to purely arbitrary, even abnormal, canons. It seems almost as if they were saying: "Visual reality is one thing, but we are interested in a reality beyond the physical world—a spiritual reality." Where Filippo Lippi, Leonardo, and others saw Mary as a human mother in a familiar and believable setting, El Greco conceives of her as a supernatural being, surrounded by other transcendental spirits and set in a world where light and space are totally unlike ours.

Projects

1. Pieter Bruegel, the Elder, was a sixteenth-century painter whose work falls into three general categories: landscapes, scenes of peasant life (including Flemish proverbs and folklore), and fantastic scenes of monsters and demons. Choose a picture from the first two categories. How does the design of the painting exemplify what you have learned about Mannerism?
2. Contrast the character of line in a painting by Sandro Botticelli and in one by Titian other than the *Venus with a Mirror*.
3. Describe and analyze the design in a painting by one of the following Mannerist painters: Tintoretto, Bronzino, Pontormo, or Parmigianino.

4. Study a color reproduction of a Titian portrait, preferably a half-length portrait. How strong is the impact of the sitter as a human being, as a piece of abstract design, as a stimulus to your tactile imagination?

Suggested Reading

Bousquet, Jacques. *Mannerism,* trans. Simon W. Taylor. New York: George Braziller, Inc., 1964.

Bronstein, Léo. *El Greco.* New York: Harry N. Abrams, Inc., 1950.

Bruegel, Pieter. *Bruegel,* ed. Emil R. Meijer. Greenwich, Conn.: Fawcett World Library, 1967.

Bruegel, Pieter. *The Paintings of Bruegel,* ed. Fritz Grossmann. New York: Phaidon Art Books, 1966.

Lowry, Bates. *Renaissance Architecture.* New York: George Braziller, Inc., 1962.

Martindale, Andrew. *Man and the Renaissance.* New York: McGraw-Hill Book Co., Inc., 1966.

Puppi, Lionello. *El Greco.* New York: Grosset & Dunlap, Inc., 1967.

Sutton, Denys. *Titian.* New York: Barnes & Noble, Inc., 1963.

Tietze, Hans. *Tiziano Vecellio.* New York: Phaidon Art Books, 1950.

Venturi, Lionello. *The Sixteenth Century: From Leonardo to El Greco,* trans. Stuart Gilbert. New York: Skira, Inc., Publishers, 1956.

Wentinck, Charles. *El Greco,* trans. Albert J. Fransella. New York: Barnes & Noble, Inc., 1964.

Williams, Jay. *The World of Titian.* New York: Time-Life Books, 1968.

*Available in a paperback edition.

11 | Paradise Lost
Michelangelo

Michelangelo: *Giuliano de' Medici*

The word "portrait" in the caption of figure 43 is in quotation marks, because the artist did not do this statue from life. Both Giuliano (Italian for Julian) and Lorenzo de' Medici were dead long before the artist carved their tombs in the family church of S. Lorenzo between the years 1524 and 1534. Even if we did not know this, we might wonder whether any living being could have been so handsome in face, so powerful in body, so graceful in his pose. The artist was obviously trying to do more than copy the dead man's features. To judge from the agitated surface of the stone, the swirling locks of hair, the complications of the armor, the swelling of the muscles on the arms, hands, knees, and chest, the artist wanted to give a sense of excitement and activity to the figure. The twist in the body—head turned one way, shoulders another, and legs shifting in an asymmetric position—adds to this sense of drama. Yet the face is expressionless, as impassive as that of the ancient Zeus from Artemision discussed in Chapter 1. Actually, the body is relaxed despite the twisting pull of opposing forces. The hands, too, are at rest. Yet the cutting of the stone (the agitated surface planes mentioned above and the dark shadows thrown by the many pierced and undercut concavities) suggests an energy inside the figure which is momentarily at rest but which might burst forth at any instant.

Modern art critics like to use the word "plane" to indicate a flat, or relatively flat, area in a work of art. The planes in the Dogon statue are relatively simple but sharply contrasted with one another. The planes in the Zeus are more complicated but gentler in their transition. The planes in Michelangelo's statue are both complicated (note the intricacy of the rib cage) and violent (highly lighted areas are close to extremely dark ones). Of all the statues we have seen so far, this one gives us the greatest sense of movement, although the figure, as has been said, is actually at rest.

Psychologically Giuliano is isolated from us. He does not look at us, and his eyes, when we walk around to look at them, have no focus, for the pupils are not carved into the eyeballs. He is lost in thought. He is unaware of us. Below him two nude figures (see fig. 44) recline on a sarcophagus which, we are to believe, holds the dead man's corpse. The female figure, a symbol of Night, is asleep with her head resting on her hand; a mask, the symbol of dreams, is at her side with an owl, the bird of night. The male statue, a symbol of Day, looks over his shoulder at us, his face not completely carved by the artist. Both figures are contorted in their poses and precariously poised on the lid of the sarcophagus. Both they and their counterparts across the room (figures of Dawn and Dusk accompany the statue of Giuliano's nephew, Lorenzo) contribute to the feeling of mystery and strangeness about these tombs that has fascinated people for four centuries.

This strangeness is heightened by several other characteristics in the statue of Giuliano: the proportions of the body, for example. His head seems small, his neck too long. His arms, especially his upper arms, are unusually long, and the muscles of his forearms, like those of his chest, are exaggerated to an almost grotesque degree. Compared to his head and feet, moreover, his hands seem abnormally large. This strangeness reaches the point of the bizarre in the grimacing face that decorates the breastplate of his armor and in the grinning masks on the straps that come over his shoulders. As we stand before the Medici tombs, we feel that Michelangelo was trying to say something by means of these exaggerations, distortions, and bizarre touches, but what it is he was trying to say, we cannot tell. This deliberate effort to puzzle, bewilder, and shock is something that was adopted and developed by artists as the sixteenth century progressed in the style we call Mannerism.

Michelangelo   1475–1564

The colossal figure of Michelangelo Buonarroti marks the end of one era and the beginning of another. Born in 1475, about the time Filippo Lippi painted the Madonna in colorplate 4, Michelangelo was trained in the Renaissance tradition of reproducing faithfully what his eyes told him he saw. But he soon stopped listening exclusively to his eyes. As he grew older he paid more attention to an inner voice urging him to express certain ideas and feelings which transcended rational experience. And as he did so he began doing things no other artist had done before. Combining a restless invention, a strongly introspective, brooding, and mystical temperament with a tireless energy that allowed him to attempt projects that would exhaust ten other men, Michelangelo achieved a

series of triumphs in sculpture, painting, and architecture that changed the direction of art in the Western world and dwarfed the achievements of most artists for centuries after he died.

His range of interests in painting and sculpture was actually quite narrow: the human body, principally the male figure. But Michelangelo evolved a line of thought that made the human body expressive of everything in the relationship between God and man. In the nude male figure he saw the reflection of the divine element in man, his spirit. At the same time the body, made of clay, vile and unclean, was a prison for that divine spirit which ever aspired to be reunited with God. This is why all the figures Michelangelo created, in both paintings and sculpture, turn and twist themselves into complicated, sometimes uncomfortable looking or even impossible poses. They appear to be wrestling with the soul inside them which, in turn, is struggling to escape. The more powerfully developed and physically virile the figure is, the more sublime seems this conflict between the body and the spirit.

Michelangelo's work has been much written about in the light of philosophical ideas of his time and of letters and poetry which he himself wrote. But such literary considerations are secondary to the expressiveness of the work as sculpture. If we cannot feel Michelangelo's power without reading about Neoplatonism, then we are reacting to philosophy, not to the visual ideas which Michelangelo has carved in stone. He himself would have been the first to insist that we must feel his ideas embodied in the carved surfaces, not read about them in a book.

This does not mean that we should refuse to read anything at all about a work of art, or to examine the artist's letters or theoretical writings. To read about historical events or trends in religion and philosophy cannot help but add to our understanding of that work, as long as these considerations remain peripheral and the object we are looking at central. The danger lies in letting these extra-artistic data come between us and the object. If we do, we are treating the object not as a work of art but as a visual document to clarify history or philosophy. We are enjoying it not for artistic reasons but for literary or biographical reasons. By such an approach we could elevate any superficial or run-of-the-mill picture to the realm of art, because it illustrates the spirit of the Counter Reformation, let us say, or artistic movements like Neoclassicism or Mannerism. We may even like the works of a first-rate artist for the wrong reasons, as many

Figure 43 | MICHELANGELO. *"Portrait" of Giuliano de' Medici*, Duke of Nemours. c. 1533. Marble, 5'8" high. From the Medici Tombs in the New Sacristy of the Church of San Lorenzo, Florence

people rave about the paintings of Vincent van Gogh because they sympathize with his tragic life, his self-mutilation, and his suicide. The same people will ignore a picture by Paul Cézanne because he was an ordinary hard-working painter, a dutiful husband and father, with little drama or adventure in his life. The irony, of course, is that if these people appreciated van Gogh's paintings for artistic rather than extra-artistic reasons, they would also respond to Cézanne's. The elements of painting—line, light, color, mass, rhythm, movement, etc.—are used in a powerful (though quite different) way by both men.

And so, after examining Michelangelo's sculpture, after responding to the visual ideas which Michelangelo is communicating through his carved surfaces, we can add a great deal of enjoyment to our response by reading about the artist, his career, his friends, his personality, and his ideas. Many of Michelangelo's letters and some of the poetry which he wrote have been preserved. We may even study the tenets of the Neoplatonists, for example Marsilio Ficino, their leading spokesman. After a description of the entire Tomb of Giuliano de' Medici, we will quote a passage from Ficino that expresses in words certain ideas that parallel what Michelangelo has said in stone. But the power of Michelangelo's statement resides in the volumes of his sculpture, not in a printed idea or information outside our experience of that sculpture.

Among the other bits of peripheral information which undoubtedly affects but should not dominate our reaction to the tomb is the fact that the Medici sponsored a sort of academy devoted to the discussion of Plato's ideas, a circle of intellectuals who gathered at the Medici court and expounded and readapted the ideas of this Greek philosopher whose writings had been relatively unknown in western Europe until then. Marsilio Ficino was the center of this learned circle.

Briefly stated, Ficino's philosophy, as applicable to the art of Michelangelo, involves the idea that man, separated from God in a previous existence, could return to God by purifying his soul here on earth. He could even effect a temporary reunion during moments of *ecstasy,* which literally means to "stand outside one's self." Since beauty was identified with creation and with the Creator, the awareness of beauty was innate in every human being, vaguely remembered from a previous existence where everything was beautiful. The longing for beauty, then, was closely identified with the religious impulse, and the recognition of true beauty slumbered in the breast of every human. In the breast of the artist, however, this sense of beauty was most developed. Whatever he did, therefore, intuitively and spontaneously, was beautiful. We see the result of such a philosophy in Michelangelo's highly original, strongly personal, and completely arbitrary concept of beauty: strange proportions, unusual poses, and the transformation of certain traditional details into seemingly inexplicable forms.

We might also learn that the Neoplatonic concept of man's soul involved a polarity between the active and contemplative temperaments. It was Michelangelo's purpose to personify the active life in the figure of Giuliano, erect, hand on his sword, and money in his fingers (the active type being generous and outgoing). Lorenzo, opposite him, has his chin cupped in his hand, his face shaded by his helmet, his other hand holding a money box. He is the contemplative mode of man to whom Dawn and Dusk are kin as Day and Night are to his active counterpart. (The Lorenzo of the sculptured tomb is not Lorenzo the Magnificent, but his grandson, the Duke of Urbino, who was born in 1492—the very year the older man died. Giuliano, the Duke of Nemours, was one of Lorenzo the Magnificent's sons and therefore the younger Lorenzo's uncle.)

We might also read about Michelangelo's own temperament: solitary, suspicious, given to mysticism, and influenced by the hell-fire preaching of men like Savonarola, whose sermons in Florence moved women to strip bracelets from their arms and throw them into bonfires along with books and works of art which the priest branded as works of the devil.

Other incidental information about the Medici Tombs includes the fact that Giuliano is shown wearing a Roman armor that resembles that worn by Augustus Caesar in a well-known standing portrait now in the Vatican Museum in Rome. Michelangelo was also fascinated by late Greek art which often emphasized muscular bodies in twisting poses. He was particularly influenced by the famous *Laocoon Group* of about 25 B.C., which was dug up in the ruins of Nero's palace in 1505, and by the *Belvedere Torso,* both now in the Vatican. We can go on to find more information about the tombs themselves. They were never finished. Michelangelo had planned to place two reclining river gods on the floor, thus forming the base of two triangles in which the portraits of the dead men would have been the apexes. He also planned additional statues, and fresco paintings on the walls above the tombs. We know that the tombs are unfinished, but opinion is divided as to whether the unfinished faces on two of the reclining figures were meant to be left that way. We can read volumes on the subject, weigh the arguments of various art historians, look at the sketches which Michelangelo made to see how many times he himself changed his mind about the design of the tombs. There is virtually no limit to the amount of research we can do into the background of this work. In his four volumes on Michelangelo, Charles de Tolnay devotes one whole volume of two hundred seventy-five pages to the Medici Tombs. The question arises: how much has this extraneous information

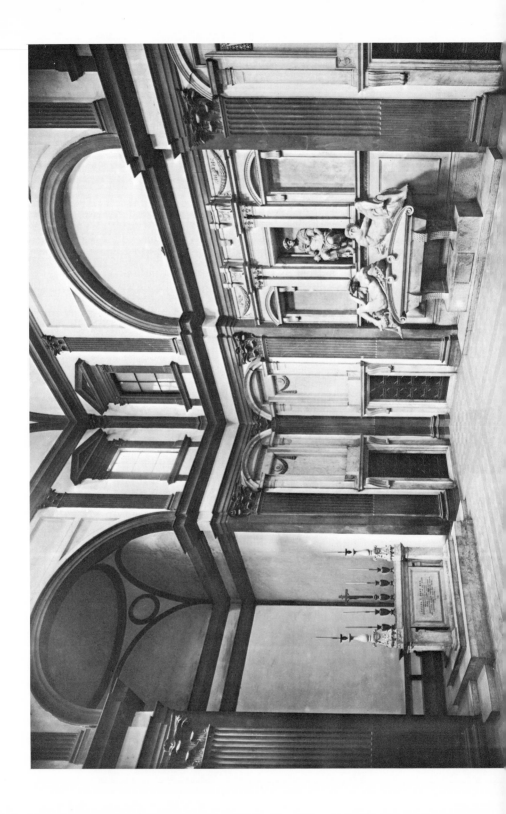

contributed to our esthetic response to the work? Let us turn back and look at the portrait of Giuliano in figure 43. How much more do we see now that we have read the above facts? What percentage of the impact of this statue comes from its form, and how much from this extraneous information? Would the work be less powerful if all of Michelangelo's letters and poems, all of Ficino's writings and those of other Neoplatonists had been destroyed when Florence was taken by French troops in 1494? Does the perusal of all this literary material raise the caliber of the sculpture done, say, by Baccio Bandinelli, a contemporary and rival of Michelangelo? No, the power of Michelangelo's art lies in his work itself.

Michelangelo: Tomb of Giuliano de' Medici

Michelangelo's architecture is even more strange than his sculpture. Although he used the classical vocabulary—round arches, triangular pediments, Corinthian pilasters, and the architrave-frieze-cornice combination—he did unusual and puzzling things with them. Like the architects of ancient Rome, he used pilasters, entablatures, and arched moldings to divide the wall into articulated and related sections. And like several of his Florentine predecessors, he used gray stone for what might be called the visual supports, creamy white stucco for the wall, and white marble for the tombs. But the big pilasters that flank each of the tombs do not end their sections of the wall. There is an added corner, recessed slightly, on one side of each pilaster, as if the pilaster were being forced out of the way by a newer and as yet not fluted and capitaled pilaster. The entablature also makes a double corner when it comes to one of the recessed spaces. This multiplication of elements becomes a favorite device among Mannerist and later Baroque architects.

Unlike his Florentine predecessors, Michelangelo did not make all the carved detail gray. A whole series of pilasters, niches, and moldings is white, and it forms a third category, we might say, which belongs to the wall in its color and to the visual supports in its forms. The area surrounding the statue of Giuliano consists of three rectangular niches which are separated by two pairs of Corinthian pilasters and which, in turn, support an attic story decorated with four balusters, two garlands of leaves, and, right in the center, a single console or scroll-shaped form. All this is good Roman detail, even in the way a section of the entablature

Figure 44 | MICHELANGELO. Tomb of Giuliano de' Medici. 1524–1534. Marble. New Sacristy, San Lorenzo, Florence

projects just above each Corinthian pilaster. But why does the entablature project again just before it reaches the gray pilasters at each side? And why are the pediments jammed in between the pilasters so tightly that it almost seems that their curve is the result of their being squeezed together from each side? Was Michelangelo trying to infuse his architecture with some sort of dynamic energy? Why else do elements cut across each other? (Notice the molding that peeps out between the paired pilasters.) Why else does the whole section of wall move in a bewildering series of strata in and out of space? (The ins and outs across the area with the niches are even more bewildering.)

Was Michelangelo trying to perplex and astonish the spectator, then? It certainly seems that way. Take the niches on the far left and right. The curved pediments have been broken at the bottom by the rectangular niches which have thrust themselves into the pediments' spaces and even spread out sideways in them. Again, forms cut across each other and push each other around as if some invisible forces were imbedded in the wall and were seeking its destruction. Everywhere stability is set against instability. These niches, with their heavy pediments, pilasters, and moldings rest upon small consoles, whose curved shapes and isolated position on the wall accentuate their incompetence (visually, of course) as solid supports. The gaping black voids of the doors under these niches add to the unsubstantial feeling, as does the fact that the ledges upon which the niches sit do not line up with those of the three central niches, but drop slightly below it, as if they were collapsing before our eyes.

One can find more examples of this perverse desire to make things look unstable and precarious. The windows at the upper left and right, with their unnecessarily heavy pediments, rest on insignificant bases that just touch the cornices above and below them as if they were teetering in space. The fact that the frieze is white while the architrave and cornice are gray makes the top half of the room look as if it were floating above the bottom half. And if one wishes to see evidence of Michelangelo's fascination with what is weird and shocking, one need only look closely at the carved details: leering faces with open mouths and empty eye sockets look down at one from the centers of several Corinthian capitals, from the tops of some of the pediments, and from various details of the sculptured groups. And when Michelangelo reworks a well-known Greco-Roman type of molding in which egg shapes alternate with dart shapes, he turns the eggs into grimacing human heads.

Here a quotation from Marsilio Ficino might help explain Michelangelo's motivation, might put into words what Michelangelo gives us in visual symbols, but can neither add a great deal nor detract from the work itself:

As long as our sublime soul is condemned to exist in this base body, our mind is convulsed with constant anxiety. Sometimes our mind is numb from sheer exhaustion, and at all times it is insane, so that movements, actions and emotions are like the dizziness of sick people, the dreams of sleepers, the ravings of madmen.

Projects

1. Select a single figure from Michelangelo's frescoes on the ceiling of the Sistine Chapel and compare it with the statue of Giuliano with regard to conception and style of execution.
2. One of the great portraits of ancient Rome is the statue of Augustus from Prima Porta. In what ways does this resemble the statue of Giuliano? In what ways is it different?
3. Point out some Mannerist characteristics in Michelangelo's stairway to the Laurentian Library in the church of San Lorenzo in Florence.
4. Examine five paintings by Raphael. How do their stylistic traits relate to the works of Filippo Lippi, Titian, and Michelangelo discussed in this book?

Suggested Reading

Ackerman, James S. *The Architecture of Michelangelo.* Vol. 1. New York: The Viking Press, Inc., 1961.

Buonarroti, Michelangelo, *Michelangelo: Paintings, Sculptures, Architecture,* ed. Ludwig Goldscheider. New York: Phaidon Art Books. 1963.

Clements, Robert J. *Michelangelo's Theory of Art.* New York: New York University Press, Inc., 1961.

Coughlan, Robert. *The World of Michelangelo.* New York: Time-Life Books, 1968.

De Tolnay, Charles. *Michelangelo.* Vol. 3: *The Medici Chapel.* Princeton, New Jersey: Princeton University Press, 1948.

Hartt, Frederick. *Michelangelo: The Complete Sculpture.* New York: Harry N. Abrams, Inc., 1969.

12 | Art for a New Patron
Paintings by Rembrandt and de Hooch and a Persian Miniature

In the art of the seventeenth and early eighteenth centuries, the art we call Baroque, we find three major tendencies: a swirling energy and theatrical spirit derived from Mannerism primarily in the Catholic countries with the exception of France; a restrained neo-Renaissance classicism in Protestant Europe and in France; a strongly realistic tendency which appears in Baroque art everywhere, but which produced particularly fine results in the Netherlands, or as it is usually called, Holland.

Once a part of the Spanish Empire along with Flanders, its southern neighbor, Holland gained its independence, adopted Calvinism, and embarked on a path of commercial expansion which produced a strong middle-class society. Unlike his aristocratic contemporary in Flanders, the hard working Dutch burgher lacked the leisure to acquire the learning and sophistication needed for the enjoyment of pictures with mythological, allegorical, or literary subjects. He preferred paintings he could understand at a glance, landscapes, pictures of inanimate nature such as bowls of fruit, or dead game, and scenes of everyday life, such as people eating, women sewing, or children playing games. If he bought paintings with literary subjects they were usually based on biblical narrative, for he knew that book well. Such pictures were for his house, not for his church, because the Second Commandment was literally interpreted by most Protestant reformers, and churches were left undecorated. But what he liked best of all was to see his own face and that of his wife in paint, detailed and exact, not idealized and made too glamorous—so real, as a matter of fact, that all his neighbors would be struck by the exact resemblance and impressed with his sagacity and good taste in choosing an artist capable of making such an exact likeness. These were the conditions that produced Rembrandt van Rijn.

Rembrandt 1606-1669

Compared to the lives of many artists, Rembrandt's was singularly prosaic. The son of a prosperous miller, Rembrandt Harmensz van Rijn was born in Leiden and attended the famous university there before he determined to pursue a career in art. After working for a succession of masters, he set up his shop in Amsterdam at the age of twenty-five and lived there until he died at the age of sixty-three.

In Amsterdam he was successful as a portraitist, as a painter of religious subjects, and as an etcher. Two crises in his life, the death of his wife and bankruptcy brought on by careless management and his own penchant for collecting works of art and curios, helped transform Rembrandt into a recluse who lived in a poor section of town, saw only a few of his friends, and lived in poverty until his death in 1669. His fall from public favor was not due to the failure of the group portrait popularly called *The Night Watch*, as is so often said, but rather to his refusal to follow the changing taste of his time in art. The loneliness and tragedy of his later years seemed to deepen his sensitivity as an artist so that his late paintings rank among the finest of his works and among the masterpieces of all time.

Unlike the countless portrait painters who plied their trade in seventeenth-century Holland and who carefully reproduced their clients' features (being especially diligent in rendering the costumes of their sitters with great exactitude, on the theory that clothes make the man), Rembrandt often ignored details of costume and jewelry, and even some of the facial features of the people he painted. He frequently cast shadows over ears, necks, hair, and other parts of his subjects' physiognomy, and concentrated instead on those features which he felt revealed most fully the inner rather than the outer life of his sitters. This passion to fathom the human spirit must explain why he painted dozens of portraits of himself. He certainly was not handsome; nor did he try to flatter himself, as we can see from the self-portrait in colorplate 7.

Although his etchings and his drawings show Rembrandt to have been a powerful draftsman—his line is vigorous, expressive, and subtle—he did not rely very heavily on line as an element in his paintings. The most prominent element in Rembrandt's pictures is light. Now, as we saw in the Ravenna mosaic, the mere placement of light and dark colors on a painted object does not make that object appear to be three-dimensional. The tones of light and dark must be related in a certain way in order to produce the illusion of mass or volume. In a simple cylinder one side is generally lighter than the other, provided that the source of light comes from one direction. As the surface of the cylinder curves away from the light, it becomes gradually less light and more shaded. Any irregularity in this graduated movement from light to dark would indicate some unevenness in the cylinder, a depression or a protrusion on its surface. The human figure is such a cylinder with irregularities on its surface—arms, shoulders, muscles, and so on. The task of reproducing the light and dark patterns that will give a convincing illusion of the human body is therefore a complicated one. The artist must retain the light-to-dark sequence of the basic cylinder and add to it such areas of light and dark as result from the protrusions and indentations that appear upon a particular body in a given light. If any of these departures from the pure cylindrical effect is not properly rendered, the believability of that figure as a human body will be impaired.

Add to this the interaction of light and dark with differences due to color and the possibility of more than one source of illumination, and the technical problems of making an accurate transcription of what the eye sees are enormous. Needless to say, artists like Giotto and Memling, who achieved their effects of light and dark purely by guesswork, never solved these problems completely. It took the artists of the Renaissance a full century to formulate rules to govern what they called *chiaroscuro,* a word composed of the Italian words for light and dark. Leonardo da Vinci not only studied the relationship of light to dark in his usual scientific way, but also noticed that in objects in nature the shaded sides often merge with adjoining dark areas and therefore lose their hard edges. By allowing the darks in his pictures to flow from the surface of one object to the surface of another object, Leonardo not only approached closer to the actual appearance of things in nature, but also imposed a greater unity—a visual unity, that is—upon his pictures. Instead of being stopped by every new volume in the picture and being forced to hurdle the sharp contour that divides one volume from another, our eyes can move gracefully through the picture. Leonardo called this effect *sfumato,* which is Italian for "smoky," because objects appear as if enveloped in smoke or mist. A comparison of the light in Lippi's *Madonna* and that in Titian's *Venus* will reveal how artists after Leonardo's time were quick to utilize his discoveries. Rembrandt carried this *sfumato* effect even further, as we shall see when we examine his self-portrait.

Rembrandt: *Self-Portrait*   Colorplate 7

More than most artists' pictures, Rembrandt's suffer when reproduced. What looks like dull black in reproduction is, in the actual painting, a warm brown color, which, because of Rembrandt's system of glazing, seems to be lit from within. The brown surface of the canvas, moreover, is subtly varied—blacker in one area, lighter in another—so that it is not like an opaque brown curtain behind the sitter but rather a warm haze from which the figure emerges to our view. Even good color reproductions, since they are merely pieces of paper with colored ink on them, cannot do justice to painters like Memling, Titian, El Greco, and Rembrandt who achieved much of their effects by means of glazes of color.

The volume of Rembrandt's figure in the self-portrait is ill defined as to contours, but we feel its bulk and solidity, because the relationship of light to dark is such that a convincing, three-dimensional body is suggested without being completely revealed. Most of it, as a matter of fact, is left to our imagination. The vagueness of the contours endows the image with a sense of mystery which is absent in, say, the Lippi *Madonna,* where forms are crystal clear to our eyes, like those of a piece of sculpture in broad daylight. Rembrandt's head is sculptural, too, but its volume turns from the light into the darkness before our eyes can reach its edges. We feel its volume continuing on in the gloom, but our eyes cannot follow our imagination. This suggestion of things beyond the limits of our experience, of an existence of objects beyond our knowledge, is no doubt one reason why people have for centuries been fascinated by Rembrandt's paintings, despite the fact that they are not what we would call pretty or charming to look at. As opposed to Lippi's forms which are clear-cut and easily grasped, and El Greco's which are restless and bewildering, Rembrandt's forms, though they are comparatively simple and naturalistic, are shrouded in a vibrant atmosphere that endows them with mystery.

The role of chiaroscuro in Rembrandt's picture is not only to conceal the irrelevant and the mundane, however. By means of the narrow beam of light with which the artist lights his figure, he illuminates those details which reveal to us most fully the personality of the sitter. Even these few details he has pared down to a minimum. Nothing has been included that might distract us from this analysis of character. Clothing is merely suggested: a line of light paint serves to show that the coat has a collar projecting over Rembrandt's chin; a dark silhouette suffices to describe the beret he wears; and a few dots of light paint depict the ribbon or metallic thread of the hat band. Such austerity in the rendering of details serves to augment the power of what Rembrandt describes with great care, the face.

Yet not even all of the face is depicted, but only those features which will best reveal the kind of man Rembrandt was. Like Giotto, Rembrandt understood the importance of the eyes and the mouth in communicating emotion, and in this self-portrait we are especially conscious of the searching glance of Rembrandt's eyes—a concentrated glance, troubled but kindly—and of the compressed mouth which is lined, like the eyes, by deep furrows. In human terms, the face expresses suffering along with a patient firmness that implies a determined struggle against adversity, the quiet heroism of a humble, middle-class workman.

But human values and textural appeal are not all that gives this picture the power that moves us when we look at it. It is also a forceful piece of design, all the more striking because there are so few shapes in it. The largest of these shapes, the light-colored area of the face, is set just to the right of the picture's vertical axis, a position which establishes tensions between the head, the nearby frame on the right, and the distant frame on the left. Its position above the horizontal axis of the painting compresses the space above it as it makes the large expanse of space below it seem even larger. The double asymmetry of this large, relatively complicated form and the tensions which this arrangement engenders are successfully resolved by the faint spot of flesh color at the lower left: the almost imperceptible form of the artist's folded hands at the lower left, a pale, amorphous spot of color, not important enough to detract from the preeminence of the face, but vital to the organization of the picture's space.

In this respect, and in several others as well, Rembrandt's picture is kin to the Chinese landscape by Yen-Tzu Yu. In both we have a search for the essential aspects of things through the elimination of all that is extraneous and distracting, and through the accentuation by minimal means of what is most significant. In both pictures the artists made conscious efforts to express their innermost thoughts and feelings, and both artists embodied these feelings in a formal arrangement in which the organization of space, particularly the juxtaposition of volumes against large areas of empty space, plays a prominent role.

Next to portraiture, the most popular form of art in Baroque Holland was landscape painting, but unlike their Chinese counterparts, Dutch landscapes were frankly realistic representations of nature in which man often occupied a prominent position. The Dutch middle-class patron delighted in a painted reproduction of what he could see right outside his window, or at least on the outskirts of the town he lived in: the ever-changing light of the cloud-strewn Dutch skies, or perhaps young saplings beside gnarled old oaks reflected in the water of a pond or a canal. Pictures of grazing cows, seated shepherds, or mounted travelers traversing green meadows or resting in shaded woods were easy to sell. So also were *still life paintings* of fruits and vegetables; pots and pans in the kitchen; dead rabbits and pheasants waiting for the cook; or a half-filled glass of wine, a dish of grapes, and a lemon, half-peeled, with an ivory-handled knife lying on the table beside it. *Genre painting,* scenes of families at dinner, of men playing cards and perhaps brawling in a tavern, or of ladies reading letters, sewing, or cooking dinner, were calculated to show the artist's skill in observation and in transcribing what he saw just as it appeared to his eye.

Pieter de Hooch   1629-c. 1684

One of these genre painters, Pieter de Hooch (best pronounced *Hoke*), was born in Rotterdam, the son of either a butcher or a mason. We know little about him except that he lived in Delft, where he did his finest work, and in Amsterdam, where his career went into decline. It is for this reason that we do not know when he died, but the last date that can be attached to one of his paintings with certainty is 1684.

He gained early fame for his gambling scenes and pictures of soldier life, but he eventually turned to depicting the domestic life of the upper middle class. Most of his pictures are of neat interiors with square floor tiles, exposed roof beams, and large double windows whose lines he utilizes in creating the illusion of space. Open doors often provide vistas into adjoining rooms or onto a landscape. He paints details with loving care and envelops them in a clear, warm light that sometimes comes from more than one source. The figures in his paintings are never in the midst of vigorous movement but are engaged in some quiet activity that matches the general tranquility of his pictures. The painting in colorplate 8, though it depicts an outdoor scene, incorporates many of these effects of light and space.

Pieter de Hooch: *A Dutch Courtyard*   Colorplate 8

If the Renaissance artists depicted man and nature in their most exalted aspects, it took the Dutch Baroque painters to discover the charm of ordinary people doing everyday things in a nature that looks old, well-worn, and lived-in. The water-stained wall and the warped cobblestone pavement in *The Dutch Courtyard* immediately establish a relationship between the painting and us. Instead of grandeur and idealistic perfection, we have here a feeling of informality and familiarity which we enjoy and with which we can identify. Although the unfamiliar costumes may remove the scene from our immediate experience—and even endow it with the glamor of a theatrical performance or a historical movie—the activities of the characters as they drink, talk, and smoke fall within the daily experience of each of us. But not all the appeal of this picture is due to the artist's close observation of illustrative detail. Much of it is due to the picture's formal characteristics: its design.

The picture is divided vertically through the middle by the tallest of the trees, the figure of the woman, and the door; it is divided horizontally by the top of the fence and the lintel above the door, not exactly, of course—that would be dull and mechanical—but in a subtle, scarcely perceptible, and highly varied way. The four quarters formed by this division have a distinct relationship to each other. Those on the upper left and lower right involve an empty space with one isolated, vertical accent in each: the girl in one and the belfry in the other. The remaining two quarters are spatially more complicated, yet there is a distinct balance of similar but unequal things: the random grouping of limbs and branches at the upper center echoes the informal grouping of the people around the table, and the fence at the lower left with its strict perspective lines is almost a mirror image of the casement window at the upper right.

Spatially the picture reveals a quiet but lively arrangement, although the space composition is static compared, say, with El Greco's. Take the lower right section of the picture, for example. The volume of the little girl is set dramatically into the space of the corner of the courtyard. We feel this spatial contrast especially, because the artist has placed the light bonnet against the dark wall, and the dark skirt against the light pavement. There are similar contrasts in the figures around the table, and even in the table itself. Light is used not only as chiaroscuro, to make volumes look round, but also to help place things in space. The exactitude of this arrangement of volumes is reinforced by the perspective in the picture, not only by the correctness of the perspective but by its measured quality as well. Through its perspective, the picture invites us to come in and stroll around.

First we enter the large space defined by the perspective of the cobblestones, but we can go only so far. We are stopped by the brick wall and the wooden fence, though only for a moment, for the door is left invitingly open, and we can wander into the cool garden, up the shaded steps, and on out of sight. On the left, once our eyes climb over the fence, they can move on to the belfry, and then past it into infinity. Although the vanishing point of the linear perspective is located at the very center of the picture, we are not pulled into the painting as into a tunnel. We follow a zigzag path. Our stroll through the picture is slow and leisurely. We stop first with the object closest to our eyes, the girl. Then we move left to the table, then right to the door, then left into the sky. To this leisurely, strolling movement de Hooch has added another feature that adds to the intimacy of the scene. He has enclosed us inside the limited space of the courtyard, but teases us by hinting at things we cannot see. The projecting steeple suggests what lies behind that tantalizing fence—undoubtedly a city street with shops and people, horses and carriages, and so on, all of which we may not look at. And what is the cool, shady garden like? All we can see are the steps leading into an area which promises us delights that we cannot enjoy. Likewise, one shutter on the window is open, but from this angle we cannot look into the house.

The brightest color in the picture is the brilliant orange red of the woman's skirt, set right up against both the apron which is the brightest blue in the picture and the yellow blouse which is one of the highest-keyed colors in the composition. Clearly, de Hooch wanted our eyes to return frequently to the very center of the canvas. The other colors, the reds of the open shutter, the brick wall, and the distant tile roof and the blues of the sky, the girl's clothes, and the closed shutter, are more subdued in key. The equilibrium achieved between these few intense colors and the more somber ones, by the nearly equal proportion of light and dark tones, and by the static nature of the various forms in the picture reinforces the mood of tranquil enjoyment which the picture evokes in us.

One more thing must be pointed out with regard to the de Hooch painting. Composition involves not only the arrangement of shapes on the two-dimensional surface of the canvas, or picture plane as it is sometimes called, but includes the placement of objects in the pictorial space. Part of the pleasure evoked by the de Hooch painting lies, as we noted, in the fact that it allows us to enter into the courtyard, around each person, into the garden, and on into the sky. But we also enjoy the sensation of space *per se,* because space, like light, color, and texture, is one of the many ways in which we experience the world around us. The pleasure we feel in crossing an open meadow, for example, or penetrating into a dense forest, or traversing a pass through the mountains comes in part from our response to the different kinds of spatial relationships. The measured precision of the space suggested by the de Hooch painting, therefore, has much to do with the tranquility which the picture communicates, just as the drama of El Greco's painting is in large measure due to the ambiguities of its spatial composition.

A Persian Manuscript Illustration   Colorplate 9

In the Persian manuscript illustration in colorplate 9, the artist seems to have done everything he could to thwart the illusion of three-dimensional space. The courtyard or patio in the lower right corner of the picture seems to tilt up, its pavement stones suggesting the masonry of an upright wall. The garden at the rear of the patio resembles a flat screen and the pavilion under which the two central figures are sitting merges with the vegetation instead of standing in front of it. What the artist has done is to combine two viewpoints simultaneously. The pool of water at the center of the patio—very much like the pool in the portico of the Alhambra Palace in figure 38—is seen as if we were up in the air looking down at the courtyard, and the trough into which the excess water runs off extends straight down as if it were the stem of a flower. The ducks swimming in the pool, however, like the people throughout the picture, are depicted as if we were viewing them from a normal eye level.

Unnatural as this combination of viewpoints may seem to us, we must admit that it enhances the picture as a piece of decoration. Painted in the manner of de Hooch, the figures would have overlapped and hidden one another. As it is, they become parts of a richly patterned two-dimensional composition, the flatness of the composition reinforced by the fact that the figures at the bottom of the picture, which should be the largest because they are closest to our eye, are actually among the smallest. Even when the artist resorts to what might pass for linear perspective, he negates the third dimension, as for example in the furniture in the patio and in the steps that lead to the front door of the palace on the lower left.

If we try to figure out the architecture of the palace we note that it consists of two parts, one at the rear of the court and one near this end of the court; yet the two are not distinguished in terms of linear perspective. Instead, they form flat areas of varied and elegant colored patterns. Particularly charming is the rendering of the two balconies which extend, like two boxes, from the second story of the palace: we see the one at the left as if from above, and the one in the center of the picture as if from below.

Yet what the artist has sacrificed in verisimilitude he more than made up for by transforming the visible world into a marvelously patterned and gorgeously colored work of two-dimensional decoration. Everywhere our eyes stop in the composition we encounter richly developed ornament. We might expect this riot of colored patterns to result in monotony, but the Persian artist offers us great variety within this narrow range of expression. The patterns in the picture fall basically into two categories: strict, repetitive geometric patterns and free-flowing, irregular asymmetrical shapes. There are places where these patterns involve strong contrasts: the flowers against the background, for example, or the pool of water against the patio's pavement. There are other places where the contrast of patterns is barely evident, as in the pavement of the patio. The opposition of rectilinear shapes with curves, geometric patterns with random ones, concentrated areas and relatively empty ones, dark accents and light, bright colors and pale offer our eyes a veritable feast of two-dimensional movement and flow.

The shapes in the picture, as a matter of fact, flow right over the "frame" onto the page beyond it: the trees in the top of the picture, for example, and the figures at the lower left. The world in which the action of the illustration is taking place, therefore, breaks through the boundary that separates picture and text and physically unites the painted pages with the intervening written ones.

Whereas the colors in the de Hooch, the brightest of which are in the red skirt and blue apron, impel our eyes to keep returning to the center of the composition—the same point where the lines of perspective converge—the colors in the Persian painting, like its "perspective," invite our eyes to wander over the flat, decorated surface. A variety of blues dominate the composition, appearing particularly often on the clothing and in the architecture. In terms of actual quantity, however, gold paint appears most frequently—in the sky, in much of the architecture, and in the patterns on almost all of the costumes. There are also numerous greens and tans, as well as lavenders and grays. Particularly bright, though used sparingly, is a brilliant yellowish red which serves to pull our eyes to various parts of the composition. Needless to say, the colors are applied with a minimum of gradation from light to dark, for the employment of chiaroscuro would, of course, have violated the intentional flatness of the picture.

Thus far we have been considering the painting's design without referring to its specific subject matter. Actually, the picture depicts Solomon and the Queen of Sheba, although the various episodes depicted here—an angel talking to Solomon, an old woman at the palace door, and so on—illustrate a poem by Jami written about 1480. This manuscript was produced and (we can presume) illustrated in about 1560. Although the name of the scribe is given, the name of the painter is not. An interesting feature of the picture is that Solomon is represented as Mohammed often is, with his face covered by a veil and his head surrounded by golden flames. Despite its subject matter, this is not religious art in the true sense of the word—an image made to assist the worshipper in his devotions—but it is merely an illustration of a biblical story, for the fear of idolatry was strong in the Moslem world, even in Persia where the human figure was a favorite motif in manuscript illustration.

Today called Iran, Persia lies on a land corridor between the Far East and the Arab world, and has at various times been influenced by each. During the century before the Parthenon was built, Cyrus, Darius, and Xerxes extended the boundaries of the Persian Empire from Egypt to India, and would have penetrated into Europe but for the resistance of the Greeks at Marathon, Thermopylae, and Salamis. In 641 A.D. the Arabs, in their expansion over North Africa and Spain, conquered Persia, introduced the Moslem faith, the Arab alphabet, and their highly decorative and generally nonfigurative art and architecture. Persian artists raised the

Arab style of manuscript illustration to new heights, adding to it certain features from Chinese art, particularly from Sung dynasty painting. An example of the latter in colorplate 9 is the strange clouds that resemble bundles of knotted rope.

When, in the sixteenth century, the Moslem Moguls conquered most of India, they brought with them many Persian artists, and there resulted a style of manuscript painting that combined Persian with indigenous Indian and some European characteristics. Meanwhile, in Persia, the introduction of Western perspective and chiaroscuro ended the distinctiveness and charm of Persian miniature painting.

Projects

1. Find a good color reproduction of another portrait by Rembrandt. Consider first the human values conveyed by the picture, and then the impact of the painting in terms of design.
2. Vermeer was one of the great masters of genre painting. Compare his treatment of minute detail with Memling's, Titian's, and Rembrandt's. Which of these artists do you consider the greatest realist, and why?
3. Peter Paul Rubens and Rembrandt both lived in the seventeenth century. Select a painting by Rubens which includes two or more full-length figures, preferably in a color reproduction. Does the artist's style owe anything to Titian, Michelangelo, El Greco, or Rembrandt? Cite specific details in your answer.
4. Examine one of Rembrandt's pen and ink drawings. How has the artist used line to (1) depict details of costume, (2) suggest volume by indicating areas of shadow, (3) describe the mechanics of the body without diagramming it, and (4) indicate human relationships without depicting facial expression in detail?

Suggested Reading

Benesch, Otto. *Rembrandt as a Draughtsman.* New York: Phaidon Art Books, 1960.

Dupont, Jacques, and François Mathey. *The Seventeenth Century.* New York: Skira, Inc., Publishers, 1951.

Gray, Basil. *Persian Painting.* New York: Skira, Inc., Publishers, 1961.

Leymarie, Jean. *Dutch Painting,* trans. Stuart Gilbert. New York: Skira, Inc., Publishers, 1956.

Redeker, Hans. *Rembrandt,* trans. by Albert J. Fransella. New York: Barnes & Noble, Inc. 1965.

Rembrandt van Rijn. *Drawings,* ed. Seymour Slive. 2 vols. New York: Dover Publications, Inc., 1965.

Rembrandt van Rijn. *Paintings by Rembrandt,* ed. A. Bredius and H. Gerson. New York: Phaidon Art Books, 1968.

Rembrandt van Rijn. *Paintings, Drawings, and Etchings,* ed. Ludwig Gold-
  scheider. Greenwich, Connecticut: New York Graphic Society, 1964.
Rosenberg, Jakob, Seymour Slive, and E. H. Ter Kuile. *Dutch Art and Architec-
  ture, 1600-1800.* Baltimore: Penguin Books, Inc., 1966.
Wallace, Robert. *The World of Rembrandt.* New York: Time-Life Books, 1968.
Weigert, Hans. *Rembrandt.* Folio Art Books. New York: Crown Publishers, Inc.,
  1967.
White, Christopher. *Rembrandt and His World.* New York: The Viking Press,
  Inc., 1964.

*Available in a paperback edition.

13 | Palaces and Stairs
Versailles, the Spanish Steps,
and the Palace at Würzburg

If we would fix on one characteristic that is part of all Baroque architecture, sacred and secular, Protestant and Catholic, it is that buildings were calculated to make a strong impression upon the spectator. It was during the Baroque era that theater and stage design blossomed and new dramatic forms such as opera, the oratorio, and the ballet were born. It is no exaggeration to say that palaces like that at Versailles were conceived as theatrical backgrounds for the rulers who lived in them and that the Baroque church might be called a stage set for worship. Whole cities were dramatized by means of geometrically shaped public squares, by sculptured fountains, and by landscaped gardens.

The Palace of Versailles, located some eleven miles outside of Paris, was built mainly in three stages. First, a modest brick and stone hunting lodge was erected by Louis XIII in 1624. This was then surrounded on three sides by a larger palace which Le Vau designed for Louis XIV in 1668. And finally, from 1678 on this palace was nearly tripled in size with the addition of two wings. Jules Hardouin-Mansart (grandnephew of the great architect François Mansart) designed these additions; he continued Le Vau's façade system, enclosed the long balcony which is now known as the Hall of Mirrors, and supervised the decoration of much of the interior.

Just as he imposed his royal will on the people of France, so did Louis XIV stamp the architecture of his palace and, indeed, the landscape that surrounds it with a master plan. Not only the palace, but barracks, coach houses, stables, kennels, and the gardens with their fountains are arranged on each side of a major axis. Besides 250 acres of carefully landscaped gardens (perpetually trimmed and tended, of course) Versailles also included the Petit Parc, 4000 acres which contained the Lac des Suisses and a Grand Canal for which Louis imported nine gondoliers and their families from Venice so that he could have excursions in gondolas. Elsewhere on the grounds were a small zoo and an *orangerie* where orange trees were grown for Louis' pleasure. Also connected with

Versailles was the Grand Parc, a forest of 15,000 acres where the King and his party might hunt. This hunting preserve had an enclosing wall twenty-six miles long with twenty-two gates of entry.

It has been estimated that it took 36,000 men and 6000 horses 50 years to complete Versailles to the King's satisfaction. An army of architects, sculptors, painters, wood-carvers, carpenters, and decorators was required to do the work. So many tapestries were required to cover the walls that Louis kept the famous Gobelin factory busy weaving them, as well as producing furniture, metalwork, jewelry, and textiles for the palace. Some 50,000 people lived at Versailles in its heyday, including 1500 domestics connected with the kitchen, the pantry, and the butlery and 9000 soldiers and guards. The palace façade measures nearly a half mile in length and the roofs cover thirty acres.

Figure 45 | LOUIS LE VAU, JULES HARDOUIN-MANSART, and others. The Palace at Versailles, France, aerial view of the garden façade. 1669-1685. Total length of the palace façade: 1903 . Gardens by André Le Nôtre

The gardens that front the palace on one side, which were laid out by André Le Nôtre, are more than a decorative setting for the palace. They are an extension of the architecture itself. Their various sections, like rooms open to the sky, are embellished with statues and fountains, avenues of trees, and beds of colored flowers and shrubs. There were once more than 6000 fountains with an estimated 14,000 jets of water. So much water was required for these fountains that only those in part of the grounds could be turned on at one time. It was in various areas of the garden that the King often served his guests at banquets or entertained them with ballets in which he himself occasionally took part, appearing in the part of Apollo, the sun god. Lully wrote music for outdoor concerts and some of Molière's plays were written to be performed against a background of trees and shrubs.

The aerial view of Versailles allows us to grasp the geometric concept which has been imposed upon both the works of man and nature. Symmetry is almost inviolate: everything on one side of the main axis is reproduced with scarcely any deviation on the other—not only the shapes but the colors—for we must remember that the flower beds as well as the borders are made of variously colored flowers and shrubbery. Even the trees were once trimmed so that they would conform to the all-encompassing geometry of this vast complex. It is as if a gigantic color-filled mold had been impressed upon 250 acres of land, mostly vermilion, with areas of green blue, lavender blue, and white surrounded by dark green hedges of clipped boxwood.

One can imagine the battalions of workmen, divided into various regiments, subduing its sector of the terrain; and the supervisory staff, like lieutenants and captains, majors and colonels, following the orders given to the general staff—the architects in charge—by the commander-in-chief, the Sun King himself—Louis XIV. For he was the absolute ruler of the architecture just as he was of the nation. Everything that happened in either realm was at his bidding. The military analogy may be carried still one step further, for it seems as though every shrub were lined up in some complicated formation, as though every flower were taking part in an elaborate drill maneuver, and as though every column in the façade were standing at attention before the eye of the all-powerful monarch.

The gardens of Versailles were meant to be experienced by walking through them along paths, down steps, from terrace to terrace, looking this way and that, past fountains and flowers, statues and sheltered nooks bordered by carefully trimmed shrubbery and trees. Only in this way could one feel the vastness of this design, the regularity of its plan, the rigor of its exactitude, and the magnificence of it as an idea—a world made over to the desire of one man, subjected to his will, and created purely for the delight of his senses—one man and, of course, the privileged few who were invited by the king to live at court.

In contrast to the garden, whose separate shapes are compounded of curves as well as horizontals and verticals and therefore seem to expand and contract toward and away from each other, the façade of the palace which faces the garden seems rigid and immovable. Like the Farnese Palace, it radiates power and monumentality in its blocklike symmetrical regularity. But unlike its Italian prototype, it is ornamented with carved architectural detail and sculpture. Predominantly rectangular, it stretches relentlessly to the left and to the right of the central axis, its rigor broken only by a few projections. Most vigorous of these projections is the central block, which was designed by Le Vau. This block divides the garden side of the palace into three major units, each of which is in turn subdivided by three projecting pavilions. (See figs. 45 and 46.) In LeVau's central block, the middle pavilion is larger than the flanking two, and contains three openings in the basement story while the other two porticos contain one each. The pavilions in Hardouin-Mansart's wings, on the other hand, are all identical with each other, each having three openings on the basement level.

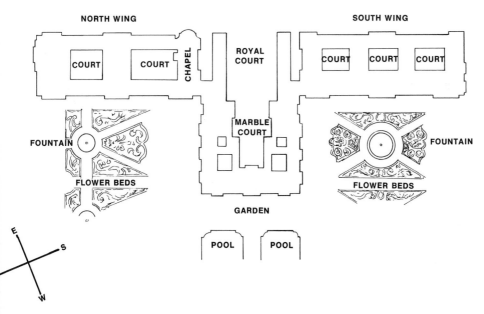

Figure 46 | Plan of the Palace at Versailles

The number "three" figures prominently in the building's design, the façade's three major units being subdivided by the three projecting pavilions, each of which contains three windows. Horizontally, too, the façade divides itself into three levels: the arcaded basement story, the colonnaded main story, and the smaller attic story just below the roof. The insistent repetition of elements—arches, windows, and columns—strengthens the impression of a military review and the feeling of unlimited power and dominion. This identical, almost mechanistic repetition is interrupted by the projecting pavilions and by the subtle variations in these pavilions (large and small with two or three windows) and by the rhythmic alternation of columns and pilasters which save the façade from monotony.

Many more variations upon the main theme may be observed if one studies the façade. In the central section the windows are grouped by threes, whereas in the wings there is no grouping but rather a continuous flow, interrupted only by the three projecting pavilions. The roof is masked by a balustrade from which sculptured forms, one between each window, rise against the sky. There are two motifs, sculptured urns and "trophies" (collections of weapons, helmets, and other articles of antique warfare). The sequence established by these two sculptured motifs is a, a, b, b, a, a, b, b, etc., except at the corners where an extra large trophy stresses the end of the sequence. Over the pavilions stand statues, larger than life, of various subjects.

The Spanish Steps in Rome

Not only did the Palace of Versailles become an ideal model for the residence of princes and petty rulers throughout Europe, but the grandiose concept of architecture and landscape united in one gigantic, ordered organization influenced the design of cities or parts of cities. Portions of Rome and Paris, as well as of Washington, D.C. (designed, significantly enough, by a Frenchman, Pierre L'Enfant), reflect this geometric tendency in Baroque architecture. A prime example of this space organization, and one that involves four elements—a city square, a fountain, a grand stairway, and a church—is the Piazza di Spagna in Rome, and the great stairway known to the English-speaking world as the Spanish Steps.

Figure 47 | FRANCESCO DE' SANTIS. The Piazza di Spagna and the Spanish Steps, Rome. c. 1725. As depicted in an engraving of about 1750 by Giambattista Piranesi

Veduta di Piazza di Spagna.

1. Fontana detta la Barcaccia, Architettura del Cav. Bernino. 2. Scalinata, 3. Chiesa della SS. Trinità de' monti, 4. Strada

Piazza Barberini a Strada Felice nel palazzo X––nata vicino alla Trinità de' monti. A paoli due a mezzo

Presso l'Autore a Strada Felice nel palazzo X––nata vicino alla Trinità de' monti. A paoli due a mezzo

Piranesi Architetto

Located in what was once the Spanish quarter in Rome, it is now an Anglo-American neighborhood, with the American Express offices near the steps and an English tea room across the street. John Keats lived in the house on the right as one looks at figure 47.

The so-called Spanish Steps, as they rise from the Piazza di Spagna to the church of la Santissima Trinità de' Monti, consist of three major sections, not counting the broad area above the sidewalk which is not a part of the street nor yet a part of the stairway proper (see fig. 48a). It is, however, marked off from the street by six little turrets of stone that seem to guard the steps like sentinels. The first actual climb we take is up three flights, each consisting of twelve steps. These thirty-six steps which comprise section one are divided into three tiers horizontally. They are also divided into three vertical avenues by two step-shaped walls. The central avenue is in turn divided into three vertical parts, although these parts are not separated by walls but are merely set at slight angles to each other. (See figs. 47 and 48.)

This first portion of the staircase gets narrower as it rises, forming a trapezoid as a whole. The stairs on the far left and far right, however, do not diminish in size and therefore do not form trapezoids. They are not rectangular either, but form parallelograms which seem to push in toward the central avenue of steps. The feeling of compression is sustained by the fact that this central avenue, like section one as a whole, is a trapezoid in shape getting narrower as it rises. But the outer flights of the central avenue are not trapezoidal in shape, nor are they parallelograms: they are rectangles that seem to be thrust directly into the central flights, thereby squeezing these into trapezoids. The illusion of this inwardly crushing movement is heightened by the fact that the three flights of steps in the central avenue seem to be buckling under the pressure and breaking outward toward the street.

As we begin our ascent of section one, we have first of all a choice of taking one of these five avenues which vary in shape: trapezoid, rectangle, or parallelogram. Secondly, we feel the constricting character of the space: the walls come closer to us as we rise and the centermost steps get narrower. But soon we reach the first plateau (fig. 48b), a place to pause, catch our breath, and take our bearings. Below us, the steps seem to expand and to embrace the fountain in the middle of the street. Above us, we see another expanding space, section two, and the pleasant prospect of green foliage, flowers, and perhaps (we cannot see it yet) some statuary or a fountain. And so we mount the next flight eagerly, making our choice between climbing the central flight (whose concave lines are a direct contrast to the outward bulging stairs we have just passed) or ascending the flights at the sides.

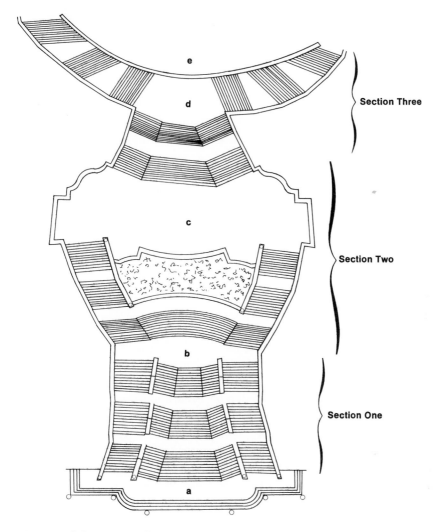

Figure 48 | Plan of the Spanish Steps

If we choose the central flight we come to the charming landscaped garden, but we cannot continue our ascent that way. We are obliged to turn left or right to go on. As we suffer this inconvenience, however, we have the pleasure of seeing the garden from the side and of looking at the people on the stairs across the garden from us. We may also see people's faces looking down at us from the balustrade above us. Eventually, we reach this balustrade ourselves and enter the second plateau—actually a small *piazza* whose pavement forms a very complicated and dynamic shape (fig. 48c). No one, unless he is in a great hurry, can resist walking toward the center of this landing and looking over the balustrade to see what can be seen. This balustrade, incidentally, has a very complicated plan which includes one large and sweeping convex curve and two smaller concave curves, connected by abrupt right angles, all shapes that add to the excitement of the space.

As we lean on this balustrade to rest, we can see—besides the garden, the steps, and the people—the street far below us and the fountain now framed by houses on either side. The next leg of our journey, section three of the staircase, forms another constricting space, again trapezoidal, but this time consisting of only three vertical divisions arranged like the central ones in section one. When we reach the next plateau, we find ourselves in the least interesting space of all (d). Small in size and ill-defined in shape, this plateau has the character of leftover space. It is dwarfed, moreover, by the high wall of the next plateau, and its view is blocked by the broad plateau below it. It is clearly no place to linger, and so we move on, obliged to turn left or right to ascend the final portion of the staircase. This portion is particularly frustrating because it takes us far out of our way and offers us panoramas which are much inferior to what we have just enjoyed. As we labor up the strangely shaped flight of steps (again three) our excitement wanes as our breath grows shorter.

It must not be thought that these stairs are more exhausting to climb than other stairways of comparable length. Actually, the rate ascent is moderate: each step is less than six inches high, and three times as deep as it is high. Still, climbing stairs is always arduous, and each of the plateaus serves to break the monotony of the climb and provides a resting place. The fourth plateau, the highest and the broadest of the four (e), is the most rewarding of them all. Physically and psychologically, we are ready for a well-earned rest. It is precisely then that we are in the proper mood to lean over the final balustrade and enjoy the sight that now delights our eyes: not only the street, the fountain, the stairs, and the people, but a panorama of the city's rooftops, the spires of churches, the facades of palaces, the broad avenues, the winding Tiber, and on the other side of the river, the massive Castel Sant' Angelo and Michelangelo's majestic dome of St. Peter's. Behind us, at the center of this spectacular staircase and heralded by the repeated rhythms of the number three, is the Baroque façade of the church dedicated to the Trinity.

During most of the history of architecture, stairs were merely means for getting from one level to another. In medieval churches and castles stairs were often of the spiral kind, arranged around a central support and enclosed in a cylindrical tower which was removed from the main space of the building, sometimes even set against the outer side of the external wall (see fig. 32). In the early Renaissance the Italian architect and theorist, Alberti, wrote: "The fewer stairs there are in a building and the less space they take up, the better." The stairway in the Farnese Palace, as we have seen, conforms to this dictum. It is tucked away so as to be almost impossible to find, and it could not take up less space and still serve its purpose. It consists of five steps that lead to a landing (see figs. 42 and 49a) and then one long flight of steps that is enclosed between solid walls so that as we ascend we can look at nothing but where we are going.

Although this staircase in the Farnese Palace was built in 1530, several people in the late fifteenth century had thought of making stairs a positive rather than a negative element in architecture. Among these were Leonardo da Vinci and Francesco di Giorgio, but neither ever saw his ideas actually constructed. Italy in the sixteenth century was in decline but Spain was at her peak, her ships plowing every sea and her explorers extending her empire on several continents. It must have been the resultant spirit of power and magnificence that gave form to the idea of the grand staircase as a structure which makes a ceremony out of climbing or descending from one level to another.

It was in Toledo, about sixty years before El Greco came there, that the first of these monumental staircases was constructed. It is one of several types called the square newel staircase, which consists of three or four flights of stairs separated by landings and built around a square or rectangular area of empty space called a stairwell which dramatizes the entire complex by allowing those who are ascending to look across at those who are ahead of them or up and down into the central well of space. (See fig. 49b.)

The delight produced by such shifting spaces and changing views led to another, more spectacular arrangement of stairs called the T-plan staircase. Here, we mount a central flight of steps, and when we reach the first landing, we encounter a blank wall and are forced to make a choice of turning 90° to the left or to the right (fig. 49c). Whereas the square newel staircase leads us back to a place just above where we began, the T-plan staircase takes us out of our way no matter which way we turn. In such a staircase we have the feeling of being a pawn in the hand of the architect, forced to follow the path he has laid out for us, puzzled about which way to turn, inconvenienced, perhaps, by the fact that we have turned the wrong way to get where we want to be, confused by the fact that we are now facing in a direction at right angles to the one we wanted to take, and irritated by the fact that we have ended up not immediately above the point where we started but about as far away from that point as the stairs could possibly have led us. On the other hand, we are delighted by the novelty of our journey, by the surprise at moving in a perpendicular direction from the way we intended to go, and by the pleasure of being able to look not only down at the flight below us, but out at the hall that inevitably fronts such a staircase. We can scan that space from our elevated vantage point as a ship's captain might scan the horizon from the bridge of his vessel.

It seems quite fitting, when one thinks about it, that the grand staircase became popular in an age of powerful and often totalitarian principalities, when the individual—even the aristocratic courtier—was a pawn in the prince's power, when ceremony and ostentation were ways of life, and when the ruling prince, like the architect of the staircase, offered his faithful followers innumerable delights in exchange for complete submission to his will. It is significant in this connection to note that both of these types of staircases and a third type, the imperial staircase, were drawn in sketches by Italians, but were built for the first time in Spain, whose government was more centralized and autocratic than those of the various Italian city-states. It is significant, too, that these stairways are still being used in government buildings, public libraries, museums, and concert halls, all of them buildings whose appearance is calculated to impress the spectator with the power and magnificence of the organizations that built them.

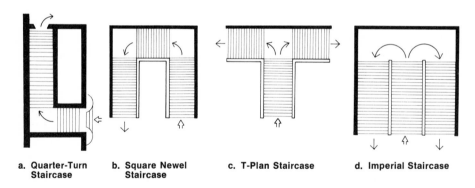

a. Quarter-Turn   b. Square Newel   c. T-Plan Staircase   d. Imperial Staircase
   Staircase   Staircase

Figure 49 | Four types of staircases

Most spectacular of all, the imperial staircase was first built in the Escorial, the colossal monastery-palace erected by the despotic and fanatic Philip II. The epitome of royal grandeur, this staircase was imitated in a variety of forms by petty princes and wealthy churchmen in various parts of Europe. In its basic form it consists of three flights of steps, two of which turn at $180°$ angles to the third (fig. 49d).

Staircase in the Bishop's Palace at Würzburg

Just as the rulers of Europe's myriad princedoms all tried to display their power and good taste by constructing luxurious palaces and gardens inspired by Versailles, so also did the princes of the Church. The palace at Würzburg was the residence of the Prince-Bishop of Speyer, who employed one of Germany's most famous architects, Balthasar Neumann, and one of Europe's most celebrated mural painters, Giovanni Battista Tiepolo, to create for him an entrance to his palace that would impress every visitor.

The staircase begins at an open and well-lighted underpass into which carriages could drive from a spacious cobblestone courtyard to discharge their passengers at the foot of the stairs. This entrance space, brightly lit by sunlight during the day and by torchlight at night, contrasts dramatically with the dark stairway that initiates the ascent. After a dozen or so steps, we come to an unexpected landing at the darkest point of the entire staircase. Here we may pause to get our breath and look about us. Ahead of us we see another flight of stairs which is just like the one we have mounted. Above us, to the left and to the right, we see the balustrades of the stairs that are still before us. Through the arches which support these stairs, we get glimpses into the spaces below, lit with various degrees of illumination and divided by the measured rhythms of the supporting columns. High above we see the brightly lit ceiling with its multicolored paintings and its central portion painted to simulate open sky. After another dozen steps we come to a second landing and a blank wall of stone. We have now reached the halfway mark of the staircase and its most spectacular point.

Here we must turn around in a full $180°$ angle, and a whole new vista greets our eyes. Below we see the gloomy stairs which we have just climbed, with the lighter entrance hall beyond them. Above us we see the brilliant space decorated with sculpture, architectural ornament, and paintings. The opulence of this decor proclaims immediately the power, wealth, and good taste of the master of the house. As in the T-plan staircase, we must now make a decision whether to turn right or left to continue our ascent. And as we begin the second half of our journey, we begin to see more and more, to feel more keenly the shifting of elements, some of which sink below us, some of which come nearer as we rise. As we ascend, we can look down on people, just as a moment earlier others had looked down at us. What is more, we are being looked at ourselves. As we rise on the staircase, we become aware of the impression we are making on others. Our elevation on physical terms is matched by our rise in self-esteem and psychological elation. If we were eighteenth-century

Figure 50 | BALTHASAR NEUMANN. Staircase at the Bishop's Palace in Würz-
burg, Germany. 1719–1744. Ceiling by Giovanni Battista Tiepolo.
1765–1775

Würzburgers, we would feel pride in our new fur-trimmed long coat and frizzed wig and our partner's latest fashions as we mounted the glittering stairs.

As in church architecture during the Baroque era, all the visual arts—architecture, sculpture, and painting—have here combined to produce a maximal impact. As in most Baroque interiors, moreover, the painter has made a point of obliterating the boundary line between his and other arts. Here Tiepolo has painted architectural details above the entablature that separates the wall from the ceiling. And on this painted architecture he has disposed his painted figures so that they appear to be real people sitting or standing above us, looking down at us just as we look down on the people who are coming up the steps below us. The ceiling has been painted away, so to speak, and our eyes follow the figures into the distance, where we see city walls and temples. And directly above our heads, instead of a plaster ceiling, we see a bright blue sky full of billowing clouds and flying mythological beings.

Projects

1. Examine a Baroque church façade from seventeenth- or eighteenth-century Spain, Mexico, or South America. Can you find any vestige of the classical orders? How would you characterize the emotional effect this façade produces on you?
2. Find photographs and plans of one of the following churches: San Carlo alle Quattro Fontane in Rome, Sant' Andrea della Valle in Rome, the Pilgrimage church of the Vierzehnheiligen (the Fourteen Saints) in Germany, or the Wieskirche, the church in Wies, Germany. Describe its general form and outstanding characteristics.
3. Study the plan of one of the great examples of city squares, for example Michelangelo's Capitoline Hill in Rome, Bernini's square in front of St. Peter's in Rome, or Gabriel's Place de la Concorde in Paris. Notice the size and relationship of the various buildings and spaces, and point out some of the sensations that you might experience while walking through these squares.
4. Choose a building or other architectural complex in your vicinity. Describe the sensation it gives you and try to explain it in terms of the arrangement of the space. Notice particularly your response to any symmetry or axial arrangement, changes from one level to another, color schemes, and textures.

Suggested Reading

Busch, Harald, and Bernd Lohse. *Baroque Europe,* trans. Peter Gorge. New York: The Macmillan Co., 1962.

Kelemen, Pal. *Baroque and Rococo in Latin America.* * 2 vols. New York: The Macmillan Co., 1951; Dover Publications, Inc., 1966.

Kitson, Michael. *The Age of the Baroque.* New York: McGraw-Hill Book Co., 1966.

Kubler, George, and Martin Soria. *Art and Architecture in Spain and Portugal and Their American Dominions, 1500-1800.* Baltimore: Pelican Penguin Books, Inc., 1950.

Millon, Henry A. *Baroque and Rococo Architecture.* *New York: George Braziller, Inc., 1961.

Tapie, Victor L. *The Age of Grandeur: Baroque Art and Architecture.* *New York: Frederick A. Praeger, Inc., 1966.

Wolfflin, Heinrich. *Renaissance and Baroque,* trans. Kathrin Simon. Ithaca, New York: Cornell University Press, 1966.

*Available in a paperback edition.

14 | Form and Content
Goya and Monet

Our reaction to any work of art depends on the work's expressive power, and this power may be said to exist on three levels of experience. There is what might be called a formal level on which we respond to the object as a physical thing—to its colors and their relationship, to its texture, scale, flatness, or three-dimensionality. These are qualities which make up the object's *form* as opposed to its *content* and are therefore referred to as its *formal characteristics.* This level of appreciation is purely sensuous. It involves, besides our sense of sight, our sense of touch as well and also a certain amount of what is called empathy, a muscular and psychological reaction on our part to what we see. When our eyes follow curves, we tend to follow them vicariously with our bodies. To acute angles or zigzags we react quite differently, because we feel these changes of direction as if we were actually moving along their path.

These formal characteristics comprise the vocabulary of the worker in the visual arts, and by putting these characteristics together, as the poet puts words together, the artist expresses ideas. But the ideas we are talking about now are primarily visual ideas, not intellectual ideas. They reach us directly through our eyes and optic nervous system rather than through our intellect. Two lines which meet each other at a right angle communicate certain visual ideas regardless of what this right angle happens to describe in the subject or content of the picture. Perpendiculars, as a rule, can suggest ideas of strength, solidity, restfulness, formality, and a lack of movement or struggle. Acute angles, on the other hand, imply movement, aggressiveness, or an expanding, sideward pushing force. Angles which approach but are not perfect 45°, 90°, 135°, or 180° angles convey ideas of conflict, tension, and instability, because our eye wants to push them toward those four simpler and more satisfying relationships.

Almost invariably, diagonals suggest movement. Conversely, horizontal lines suggest solidity and restfulness almost without exception. Verticals are less placid but still convey feelings of solid strength or poised equilibrium. When we add curves to this vocabulary, colors, textures, spatial effects, and so on, we develop something quite as complicated as the vocabulary of our speech; it is more complicated, actually, because there is no Webster's Dictionary for this language, and no precise definitions can be given for the artist's "words." They are not definable in a spoken language because they are nonliteral: they affect our optic nerves directly, not through the medium of words. But to confront a painting without understanding this vocabulary is like seeing a play by Molière done in French without knowing a word of that language: we may enjoy watching as the handsome hero courts the demure heroine behind her pompous father's back and, at the end, forces the old man to yield his daughter's hand in marriage, but we cannot say that we understand the play unless we can understand the words with which Molière has achieved this sequence of events.

It often happens that a person who is very fond of a particular picture cannot understand why it is not considered a great work of art. It is a picture, he says, depicting a cool mountain stream nestled among shady trees with mountains in the distance and a clear blue sky. What he is doing, of course, is what we did with Molière's play. He is enjoying the subject matter or plot of the picture, but the way the painter has presented his subject is as much a mystery to him as Molière's language is to the non-French-speaking playgoer. Anyone with moderate talent can learn to paint streams and trees, and anyone who is literate can write a play about a boy, a girl, and a pompous father. An artist's greatness, like that of a great playwright, lies not only in the subjects he can present to us, but in the power he can generate by means of his particular language; it lies in the syntax or orderly arrangement of elements that we have previously called design.

If we look at the mosaic from Ravenna on this formal level and try to react only to its formal characteristics (this is a highly artificial thing to do, because we normally react on every level simultaneously), we will be struck immediately by the beauty of its color and texture. We derive sensuous pleasure from the glittering sheen of the glass cubes out of which the picture is made, especially the rich gold of the sky. The blue green of the water is also pleasant to look at. We are also aware of the few and sharply isolated forms in the picture, particularly the strong vertical form of Jesus, echoed more faintly by the disciple behind him. We also feel the diagonal line of the boat and its passengers. Spatially the picture is flat and relies for its power on the strong contrast of the major patterns and on the rhythmic interplay of their subdivisions: the folds of drapery, the faces and hands, the waves of the sea, the lines of the net, the parts of the boat, and so forth.

If, however, we begin to respond to the human bodies as people—two men in a boat, two men on land, fish in the net, and so on—then we are entering another level of experience, a secondary level in terms of complexity, the level of recognition which we shall call the cognitive level. Many types of art rely heavily on this level of experience, for example a still life painting of a vase of flowers, or a bowl of fruit. Landscape painting, too, depends for its effect chiefly on the pleasure we get from looking at the painted trees, farmhouse, cloudy sky, and perhaps grazing cattle. The cognitive appeal is also strong in what is called genre painting, a group of people flying a kite, for example, or two men on horseback.

The third of the three levels of appreciation, the most complicated and variable of the three, is what we shall call the associative level. On this level the work of art refers to something which lies outside the work itself, to literature, history, religion, or some other realm with which the artist associates his work by means of some clue within the work or merely by a title attached to but outside the work. What we know about the artist's life, the period in which he lived, the art style in which he worked, all these factors also lie on the associative level of appreciation.

This level of experience is quite variable, because one viewer may know a great deal about, say, the historical incident to which the work refers. Another may know little about it. If in the picture of the man flying the kite, we recognize Benjamin Franklin, the picture immediately gains a new dimension; it becomes associated in our minds with a great American: a statesman; the inventor of the lightning rod, bifocal lenses, and the Franklin stove; the publisher of *Poor Richard's Almanac,* the signer of the Declaration of Independence, the author of the *Autobiography,* etc. If in the picture of the two men on horseback we recognize Don Quixote and Sancho Panza, the picture will acquire a totally different meaning on the associative level, even though it has not changed in the formal or cognitive aspects. If we have never read Cervantes' book, we may still know what these characters stand for. On the other hand, if we are Spaniards we will have certain feelings about the picture which no American can quite match. The reverse is true with the picture of Franklin. A foreigner may know much about Benjamin Franklin but cannot possibly equal an American's feelings of direct kinship with him. This variability and complexity is especially notable in religious pictures which depend on the knowledge and emotional commitment of a member of one religion or sect. No Protestant can feel what a Catholic feels before a picture of the Assumption of the Virgin. And a Buddhist may read all about it, but he can sense this associative aspect of the picture only vicariously.

Obviously, there is the danger of letting this associative level dominate our reaction to a picture, of letting our enthusiasm for some book we have read, some political ideal about which we feel strongly, or some religious thought which we consider very important outweigh artistic consideration. It would be foolish to suggest that we eliminate these associations. First of all, we cannot do this (if we admire Benjamin Franklin we cannot for a moment pretend that we do not); and secondly, we should not, because these associative values are valid and highly desirable attributes of some works of art. It is not a matter of either the formal characteristics or the associative values. It is a matter of proportion. As a work of art, a picture or a statue must in addition to its cognitive or associative values have a power of its own in artistic terms, in the language and logic of art. If it conveys literary ideas or religious thoughts without communicating visual ideas, then it may have value as an illustration of a poem or a biblical event, but it is not a work of visual art.

The question naturally arises: are the formal characteristics of a work bound up with or independent of its cognitive or associative characteristics? Sometimes they are independent. A picture of a bowl of fruit may be done in predominantly graceful curves or in harsh angles, in gentle contrasts of color or in violent ones. The vocabulary of art is not necessarily bound to the subject matter. Sometimes, however, the various levels of expression are closely connected one with the others, and the formal elements of a picture, its visual ideas and design will augment its cognitive and associative ideas. The integration of these three expressive levels is what distinguishes the great illustrator from the ordinary illustrator. A case in point is the etching by Francisco Goya in figure 51, one of a series that condemns the atrocities committed by Napoleon's troops in their invasion of Spain. Before we examine this picture, however, let us discuss the process of etching, what its virtues are and how it differs from other print mediums.

The Technique of Etching

In the etching process, which was discovered sometime in the early 1500's, a polished metal plate, usually copper, is covered with a coat of acid-resistant substance. The design is then scratched onto the plate with a needlelike stylus. The point of the needle need not cut the metal, but merely penetrate the acid-resistant ground so that when the plate is immersed in a nitric acid bath, the metal will be eaten away wherever it is exposed. Before immersion, the back and edges must also be protected from the acid. While the plate is immersed, bubbles form along the scratched lines and show that the acid is working. From time to time, the artist may remove the plate and examine the lines under a magnifying glass to check their depth. Certain lines may be "stopped out" to keep them from being etched more deeply when the plate is returned to the acid. And of course, new lines may be scratched in.

As a result of these processes, etchings acquire certain characteristics which distinguish them from other kinds of prints and give them certain expressive possibilities which a particular artist might find challenging. For one thing, the etched line tends to be of a uniform thickness because it is scratched with a needle-shaped point and is eaten uniformly by the acid. This distinguishes it strongly from an engraving, whose lines are actually cut into the metal and therefore go from thick to thin according to the pressure of the artist's hand. There may be heavy lines and lighter lines in an etching because, as we have seen, various lines may be etched for various lengths of time, but each group of lines tends to be of uniform width and blackness.

When the plate has been etched to the artist's satisfaction, the plate is washed and the varnish removed. The plate is covered with ink and then wiped clean. The areas which were never touched by the acid will not retain the ink and consequently will remain white when the plate is printed. The etched grooves, from which the ink cannot be wiped, will print black. The resulting impression will, naturally, be a mirror image of the original drawing, so that anything like an inscription must be done backwards in order to print right. Since etchings are printed on damp paper and under great pressure, the copper plate will sink slightly into the paper. Moreover, since the pressure forces the paper into the grooves, the inked lines of an etching will be slightly raised, although this may not be noticeable to the naked eye.

An aquatint is a kind of etching in which large areas of gray tones, sometimes perfectly even and sometimes graduated from light to dark, are added to and around the shapes done in the regular etching technique. In Goya's *Tampoco* (fig. 51), for example, the plate was probably etched first, after which the aquatint ground (often powdered resin) was sprinkled on the plate. When the plate was heated, the grains of resin melted, covering it at those points and leaving the metal exposed between the grains of resin. When the plate was reimmersed in the acid bath, the acid ate away the plate between the grains. But first, anything to be left white had to be "stopped out" with stopping varnish. The plate could, of course, be etched several more times, and each time other parts could be stopped out, thus producing different shades of gray.

Francisco Goya: *Tampoco*

The even black line so characteristic of etchings is used in Goya's *Tampoco* in several ways. It forms the outlines of objects such as a hand, boots, or features of the face. It suggests differences of color and texture by being placed in parallel strokes or other arrangements as in the officer's boots, his coat and hat, the bush, the bark of the gallows tree. It also functions as shading and shadow where needed. Besides the tones produced by the etched line there is a gray haze in the sky and on the ground, the result of the aquatint technique.

In composition, *Tampoco* is very simple, a triangle which is divided in the middle (and through the exact center of the picture) by the hanged man. This triangular arrangement should give the picture a feeling of stability and restfulness, and it does, despite the grimness of the subject. Yet there are conflicts within this large triangle: the heavy diagonal of the dark tree and the soldier leaning out of the triangle, the abrupt contrast of the lightest and the darkest areas in the very middle, and the roughness of the bush next to the smoothness of the dead man. Moreover, the triangle does not sit solidly. Its base slopes upward at the left, and it is interrupted by what looks like a rocky ledge on the right. As a matter of fact, this triangle is composed of very unstable elements.

So far we have been speaking of the picture's formal characteristics and its impact on us on the formal level of purely visual effects. The fact that we recognize a hanged man, one of many victims of a brutal mass execution, and another man, who is dressed differently and who is looking at the corpse with cold indifference or even sadistic pleasure, these things belong to another realm of experience which we have referred to as cognitive. Also part of this realm is the title of the print which, incidentally, was actually etched into the plate by the artist. A direct translation of *Tampoco* does not mean much by itself because this etching, one of a series, is meant to be looked at in sequence. The caption of No. 35, *"No se puede saber por que,"* means "No one can tell why (these things are happening)," to which No. 36 adds: *"Tampoco"*—"Nor this."

So far we have considered things which we can see with our eyes and recognize with our minds. The general theme of man's inhumanity to man

Figure 51 | FRANCISCO GOYA. *Tampoco.* Aquatint etching, 5 ½" high, 7 wide. No. 36 from *Los Desastros de la Guerra.* Begun in 1810, completed c. 1820, not published until 1865. Rosenwald Collection. National Gallery of Art, Washington, D.C.

pertains to the secondary level of cognition, but the specific instance of brutality, an episode in Napoleon's occupation of Spain, pertains to something outside the picture. The degree to which this association with a historical event enhances the picture for us depends directly on how much we know about political events of this time, of Goya's involvement in them, and of his attitude toward what happened. Such associative values must always be additional to the first two levels of meaning, or else only those who have studied history would be affected by Goya's *Desastros de la Guerra,* only those who understand Neoplatonism would react to Michelangelo's tomb of Giuliano, and so on. When we let associative values predominate, then the work of art becomes merely a document by means of which we can reconstruct the past. Then any picture about the Napoleonic invasion will do. In fact, it is almost axiomatic that the poorer a picture is as a work of art, the better it is as an illustration of a historical event, as a glance at any illustrated history book will amply prove.

The triangular composition, we have said, expresses stability, restfulness, and quiet. But Goya, as a brilliant satirist, knew how to evoke bitter laughter. Yes, there is peace and quiet here, because everybody is dead except the executioner. The struggle is finished; the dispute is ended. But not in the composition. There the struggle goes on. The vertical victim defies the diagonal created by the Frenchman and his gallows. The dead man is a solid form, black hair against the sky, light body against the dark shrubs, whereas the Hussar is a formless figure, broken up in lights and darks and nearly hidden by the shelf of rock. Who is right and who is wrong? The Spaniard is a positive form, solid and unbroken, whereas the Frenchman is cut up into sections and nearly swallowed up by the Spanish countryside. And who is the real victor? Perpendiculars, we said, suggest strength and solidity, and the dead man is both perpendicular and parallel to the frame of the picture. Only one portion of the dead man's body is not imbued with this defiance of his persecutor: his head. The line of the neck, which was broken by the rope, inclines at an angle identical with the angle at which the Frenchman leans back and gloats, as if only death could make the Spaniard bow to Napoleon's rule.

How do we know the artist did this on purpose? Actually, it does not matter whether he did or did not. What matters is that it is there, and if we can discover a visual idea that illuminates and sharpens one of our intellectual ideas, so much the better. Such discoveries are the essence of art appreciation; whatever is meaningful to us is legitimate, whether the artist put it there consciously, unconsciously, or just accidentally. Most great artists have intuitions about things they themselves do not understand, as the Freudian interpretation of *Hamlet* proves about Shakespeare.

The only requirement is that the associative idea be reinforced by the form of the work.

Let us allow our eyes to rove through the print in search of additional meaningful discoveries. Why did Goya put a bush behind the dead man, such an active, scribbly lined area? Was it to set the dead corpse against the liveliest area of the whole picture? He may not have meant to do so, but he did. Notice the strange horizontal-vertical shape of the rocky ledge at the right, a highly unnatural one, as a matter of fact. There is only one other horizontal-vertical angle in the picture: the dead man's unnaturally straight back and the bottom edge of his coat. Is Goya comparing the fortitude of the Spanish guerrilla fighter (it was in this struggle that the term *guerrilla* originated) to the very rocks of the earth? If so, what does that make the Frenchman? Moreover, the Frenchman's lower leg forms a diagonal of about the same angle as that of the gibbet and is modeled in the same way, by parallel and slightly curved lines. Did the artist do this on purpose to establish a kinship between the Frenchman and the gibbet, making him a sort of second cousin once removed? And is it a coincidence that the pronged top of the gibbet repeats exactly the angle which the two principal figures make with each other? Finally, the triangle of the composition, so solid looking at the top, sits on a foundation which slants slowly upward on the left and is strangely broken up at the right. This is a triangle which gets less solid as it reaches the ground until it teeters unstably like a rocking horse. Whether or not Goya intended this as a visual symbol of the shaky foundation upon which the French conquest was built is not important. If we discover it, then it is there, for a work of art is not only what the artist did but also what we make of it.

Francisco Goya   1746–1828

If the life of Rembrandt was relatively undramatic, the career of Francisco Goya y Lucientes was fraught with struggles, intrigues, adventure, and tragedy. Although the stories about his killing men in brawls, performing in bullrings, and engaging in continual amatory escapades are undocumented, he did tread a narrow path between conformity and rebellion in his life as in his art.

His portraits of Spain's royal family border on caricatures, yet he was a favorite at court, and though his rough manners betrayed his lowly origin, he moved in aristocratic circles. Even his liaison with the haughty Duchess of Alba was smiled on. A freethinker at one of Europe's most reactionary courts, he audaciously satirized political figures and the Church in his etchings, and when the Inquisition threatened him he presented the etching plates to the King.

During the Napoleonic occupation of Spain, Goya painted Joseph Bonaparte and his French generals. When the English liberated Spain he made portraits of the Duke of Wellington. Yet when Philip IV returned to the Spanish throne, Goya was forgiven and reinstated as court painter. When, however, he saw his friends disappear into prisons or exile, the old painter asked to go to France for his health and died there at the age of eighty-two. The great tragedies in his life were the deaths of all but one of his twenty children and a mysterious illness that struck him down at the age of forty-six and left him totally deaf and tormented by roaring noises in his ears for the rest of his life. It was undoubtedly his resultant isolation and anguish that led to the fantastic and nightmarish character of some of his late paintings and etchings.

Art in the Nineteenth Century

In art as in politics, the nineteenth century saw a sequence of conflicting ideas and ideals which, in politics, often erupted in bloodshed and, in art, sometimes led to hardship for the artist and a lifelong struggle for recognition. In France, where the conflict in both politics and art was most virulent, the crises in both activities were most significant for Western civilization. Several factors were responsible for the way art developed. First of all, the French Revolution of 1789 swept away a relationship between artist and patron which had existed since the early Renaissance; it eliminated the aristocracy whose wealth, leisure, and good taste had provided a healthy climate for art. True, the artist before that time was often treated like a household servant, a little higher in status than the gardener, the cook, and the fencing master, but he had security at least. Since then the artist has been freer, it is true, not subject to the whims of a capricious princeling perhaps. He is emancipated, free to paint or sculpt anything his heart desires, but he is also free to starve. In the nineteenth century his one hope lay in getting his work accepted by the judges of the gigantic exhibitions sponsored, in France, by the Académie des Beaux-Arts so that his work might become known and commissions, private and of government origin, might come his way. This exhibition was called the Salon and the judges, all professors at the government École des Beaux-Arts, approved only works which conformed to the style which was currently in vogue and in which, of course, the judges themselves painted. The result is that every artist whom we admire today was a rebel and an outcast. The pictures to which the academicians awarded all the prizes and ribbons now clutter up the storage rooms of the great museums of the world, and the word *academic* has come to symbolize everything old-fashioned, dull, and lifeless.

But even if a creative artist succeeded in exhibiting his work in the Salon and received some commissions, his patron would probably be some wealthy *bourgeois,* some self-made industrialist who had little understanding of what the artist was trying to do but merely wanted something pretty or diverting, if possible something that included a pretty girl. Such conditions produced the bohemian artist, the long-haired, unwashed genius who lives in a sixth floor walk-up apartment, paints pictures that no one but himself and his colleagues understand, and purposely does things to *épater les bourgeois,* to shock respectable people.

A second factor in the development of art in the nineteenth century was the opposing principles of certain styles. Neoclassicism was a concept that had originated in the second half of the previous century, partly because of the discovery of Pompeii and Herculaneum, two cities which had been buried under volcanic ashes since 79 A.D. Not only did the Neoclassicist go back to ancient literature and art for his inspiration, but he also admired the classic ideals of balance, stability, clarity, and the spirit of quiet heroism. Specifically, the Neoclassicist stressed the importance of line, the power of drawing, as the artist's chief means. A reaction set in during the early 1800's in literature and music as well as art which we call Romanticism. Most artists of this persuasion preferred the Middle Ages over antiquity because they were mysterious, colorful, and fraught with spiritual fervor. Instead of Homer and Horace, the inspiration for the Romantic artist was Dante and Shakespeare, and certain contemporaries like Byron and Sir Walter Scott who wrote so much about the Middle Ages. Whereas intellect was the touchstone of the Neoclassicist, emotion was at the heart of the Romantic's esthetics, and color, the rich color of Titian and Rubens, was his principal means. Both Neoclassicists and Romantics haunted libraries to find new subjects to paint and to research the costumes, armor, furniture, etc., of whatever period their prospective pictures concerned.

It was only a matter of time before a reaction set in against the Romantics' emotional excesses and their literary bent. By the middle of the century a number of artists voiced the opinion that the greatest historical painter was not he who painted scenes from history but rather from his own time. The movement called Realism, in literature as in art, emphasized the observation of people and activities in the artist's own environment. As Balzac, Flaubert, and Zola wrote about contemporary life in France, so Millet and Manet painted the peasants and the city life that they observed, and a group of landscapists near the village of Barbizon depicted the countryside there with equal fidelity. In the second half of the century a group of artists, all of whom admired the Realists in general and the Barbizon painters in particular, developed their own personal brand of Realism which came to be called Impressionism.

Monet: *Woman Seated Under the Willows*   Colorplate 10

If we look at this painting from a distance (or squint at it so as to blur the separateness of the brushstrokes), we might easily mistake it for a color photograph or even a real view out of a window. The chief reason for this is the quality of its color. The painting as a whole is very high in value, that is, closer to white than to black. As a matter of fact, there is no black here at all: the darkest colors in the picture are blue and violet. All of the colors, moreover, have been mixed with white before they were applied to the canvas to heighten their value.

In this respect, the picture is very different from the outdoor scene by de Hooch, in which many of the colors approach black, and even the lightest colors are not as light as the majority of the colors in the Monet. With respect to colors, the Monet is much closer to natural appearances than the de Hooch, but what about detail? In the Dutch painting we can tell what everything is, down to the buttons on the gentlemen's coats. In the Monet, on the contrary, details are so blurred that we cannot even see the features of the woman's face.

We recognize details in the paintings by de Hooch and van Eyck partly because they are sharply outlined and have colors which set them apart from other details. In the Monet, line is all but absent. Only the branches of the trees and some of the architecture is indicated by lines. All else is hinted at rather than defined, suggested rather than described. And whereas in Titian's painting details are discernible more through their textures than through their outlines or distinctive colors, in the Monet there is a sameness of texture throughout the picture. The woman's face is treated in almost the same way as her dress, the grass, the water, the sky, and the trees.

The character of the brushstrokes and the quality of the color are quite different from anything we have seen so far. Every portion of the picture contains several different colors. The grass, for example, is not merely green. It is covered with separate strokes of light and dark green, yellow green, and blue green, and even touches of yellow, orange, blue, and violet. The woman's white dress contains some of the very same colors, but in different proportions of course. The same is true of the trees, the distant buildings, and so on. Instead of separate areas of distinct color, we have here an interwoven fabric of brushstrokes and colors which pervade the entire canvas and sparkle with a brilliance that simulates the actual light of nature.

Monet's realism, then, lies in the total effect of the picture, not in the distinctness of separate parts. He is less interested in the woman, the trees, and the houses as entities in themselves than he is fascinated by the light effects which these objects achieve in this particular place, season of the year, time of day, kind of weather, and so on. Monet has captured an instant in time, a fleeting glimpse of a scene which will probably never again be just like this. He has not told us a story. He has not given us his feelings about the scene. He has not shown us the personality of the seated woman. He has simply set down for us the shapes and colors which struck the retina of his eye. He has given us an optical impression of the scene.

Claude Monet   1840–1926

The most significant aspect of Claude Monet's life was his courageous persistence in continuing to do what he believed despite public neglect, critical hostility, and recurrent financial crises, one of which drove him close to suicide. That he was able, with several pictures, to gain entrance to Salon exhibitions makes his determination to follow his own ideals even more heroic.

A man of abundant energy and strong convictions, Monet became the leader and chief theoretician of a group of painters who held their first exhibition together in 1874. It was Monet's painting, *Impression-Sunrise,* which made one critic deride these painters by calling them "Impressionists." His infatuation with light impelled him to paint more and more those subjects which were most affected by the changes in light: sky and water. Accordingly, he outfitted a medium-sized rowboat as a studio so as to be closer to his subject. Monet lived long enough to hear himself proclaimed as a great painter and to enjoy the admiration of younger painters.

The Theory of Impressionism

The work of the Impressionists was the final development of what we might call the Renaissance tradition—the practice of painting things as they appear to the eye, as if pictures were a mirror on a wall or a window through which one looked at nature. Impressionism also inaugurated certain tendencies which distinguish art in the twentieth century from that of the Renaissance. Primarily landscape painters, the Impressionists greatly admired the Dutch landscapists of the seventeenth century, except for one thing. Nature, they said, is not as dark, not so full of blacks and browns, as the Dutch landscapists had made her. Nature in the sunlight is full of brilliant color, and the way to approach this brilliance was to use less black and brown pigments. By the early 1870's Claude Monet, Camille Pissarro, and others had banished black from their palette entirely: it was not a color at all they said. More and more, too, they abandoned the old master practice of putting color on top of color, but laid each brushstroke directly on the white canvas. Monet's *Woman Under the Willows* is an exceptional picture in that it was painted on a canvas which was first tinted a light yellow orange.

Paints are made by grinding pigments of vegetable, mineral, or earth (bituminous) origin and mixing them with a vehicle: oil in the case of oil paint, egg yolk in the case of tempera, and water plus gum in the case of watercolor and fresco. These pigments are not simply blue or yellow or red. There are dozens of blue pigments, for example. Cerulean blue is more greenish than cobalt blue. Prussian blue, thallo blue, and ultramarine are three shades of deep blue, the last containing some red and therefore approaching violet. All these blues, being natural pigments, are at their greatest intensity unmixed. When they are mixed with other colors (other than white) certain properties of their hue are canceled out by certain properties of the pigment they are mixed with, and the luminosity of the mixture is reduced.

The Impressionists made this discovery intuitively and began painting more and more with pure pigments, mixing them only with white, which diluted the colors without darkening them. Instead of mixing colors on a palette as the old masters had done, the Impressionists put separate strokes of pure pigment next to each other, leaving the eye to make the mixture when the picture was looked at from some distance. At first they had to find an excuse for these daubs of bright color, for example flowers in a flower bed or leaves of various greens in a clump of bushes, but after awhile they found ways of using this "optical mixture," as they called it, throughout the picture, thus maintaining the maximum luminosity of which the colors were capable. Monet's *Woman Seated Under the Willows* is a good example of this. The only thing the Impressionists mixed with their paints was white pigment in order to simulate the object to be painted. Pure Cerulean blue, for example, would be too deep for painting a sky. The addition of white would produce the proper color without, of course, reducing the brightness of that blue.

As a rule, artists do not read scientific treatises. Whether the Impressionists did so, received secondhand information, or discovered it intuitively, they began to do something in their pictures which scientists at that time had begun to observe in laboratories. By putting various shades of green in the representation of a tree, plus touches of yellow and orange in the lighted parts and blue, violet, and purple in the shadows, they were denying the "local color" of that tree. They, like the scientists, were saying that an object in nature does not possess its color inherently but derives it from the light that it reflects. A green leaf, for example, absorbs all the rays of the spectrum except those which give it its green color. These it reflects. If it is yellow green, then some yellow rays are reflected along with the green. If, on the other hand, the light that shines on this leaf changes, its color changes as well. We have all noticed how different a person looks under fluorescent lights, for example.

As they sat at their easels in a field or on a river bank, often side by side, the Impressionists observed how the color of objects changed as the sun rose or set or hid behind clouds. They also saw how colors reflected on one another, the red of a tile roof on the whitewashed wall of an adjoining house, the yellow green of a sunlit meadow on the side of a dark green oak. Shadows especially were shot through with reflected lights and sometimes generated their complementaries: an orange glow in an area of blue, yellow amid a patch of purple, or red in a shadow on green grass.

Eventually, as they worked, they came to realize something else which a French scientist named Chevreul had written about in 1839, the principle of simultaneous contrast, according to which two spots of different colors affect each other when placed next to each other. Each asserts its identity and consequently appears to our eye to be brighter than when it is seen by itself. The Impressionists' system of laying down colors in separate strokes of pure pigment, then, had three consequences: it produced an actual brightness because it utilized pure pigments; it generated an apparent brightness because of the simultaneous contrast; and it broke up the local color of an object into its spectral components. Moreover, the separate touches of paint, not unlike the glass cubes of the Ravenna mosaic, animated the surface of the painting and greatly contributed to the power of the picture to suggest the sparkling and transitory effects of sunlight and atmosphere. Finally, the use of multicolored brushstrokes in every part of the picture provided a unifying factor throughout the composition.

Otherwise, the composition in Impressionist paintings was often loose and random, as indeed it had to be if the painters followed their own precept of rendering faithfully what their eye observed. Nevertheless, the very choice of one spot of a river bank rather than another, of one view of this spot rather than another, involved criteria even if the artist insisted he was painting nature just as she was. These unconscious criteria were, of course, not those rules which the Academy taught and against which the Impressionists were rebelling. There were, however, two factors which did affect the composition of the Impressionists' paintings: photography and Japanese prints. Photography, first perfected by Daguerre in 1839, made a strong impression on artists of all persuasions. It allowed the academic artist to invest his Neoclassical compositions with an even greater verisimilitude in anatomy, perspective, and chiaroscuro. The Impressionists were interested in photographs more because here was a direct, unemotional, and exact transcription of nature in black and white. The camera operated objectively without selecting, without stressing what was "beautiful" and eliminating what was "ugly." And as for composition, the camera simply recorded what it saw when it was pointed in a given direction, the very ideal which the Impressionists asserted.

Japanese prints first came into Europe, incredible as it may seem, as wrapping paper for porcelain which was popular in Europe. They must have seemed quite incomprehensible to people whose idea of art was conditioned by the Renaissance realism and the shallow dexterity of academic art; their colors were gaudy by academic standards, their drawing "incorrect," their perspective childish, and their composition simply nonexistent by Western standards. One of Hokusai's prints, for example, depicts Mount Fuji on the right-hand side of the composition and nothing but sky and clouds on the left. A favorite device that the Japanese printmakers employed was to cut the composition at one corner with a fragmented form, as Hiroshige does with the boats in colorplate 11. And, of course, the Japanese artist's delight in atmospheric effects found an enthusiastic response among the Impressionists.

These characteristics elicited anything but enthusiasm among the academician or the average art lover of the time, and when the Impressionists began to employ some of these devices, the general public laughed at their pictures, the critics were bitter in their disapproval, and the officials of the art world regarded these young artists as subversives and anarchists. Naturally, their work was not accepted in the Salon exhibitions, which were full of mythological and historical scenes (generously garnished with nudes), pastoral scenes of grazing cows in the seventeenth-century Dutch manner, sentimental scenes of parents watching their daughter being courted or a cuddly dog looking very proud because he is wearing a new collar.

It is hard to account for the hostility with which the Impressionists' pictures were greeted year after year. To us they are so pleasant and picturesque. They remind us of travel posters. Today's avant-garde artists consider them old-fashioned, a little "corny," or, of all things, academic! Actually, the outrage with which they were met in the 1870's and 80's has its counterpart in many people's anger at much art done today. Because they do not understand it, they feel left out or actually threatened. "There must be something wrong with a person who does something that makes no sense to me," is their reasoning. A few years ago a U.S. senator recommended an investigation of modern artists. His thesis was that modern art was part of the worldwide Communist conspiracy to over-throw Christianity and weaken the Western world. When it was pointed out to him that the Soviet government has branded modern art as a product of decadent capitalism and banned it in the Soviet Union, the senator replied that this just proved his point: Russia knows how dangerous modern art is; that is why it bans it at home and encourages it elsewhere. Perhaps in the next century our great-grandchildren will see the art of the 1960's as clearly and as pleasurably as we do the art of the 1870's. And perhaps they will be puzzled by the vehemence of people who attack "modern art" today.

Year after year the Impressionists struggled for recognition and finan-cial reward. Occasionally one or two of them got a picture into the Salon, but in 1869 Monet's belongings, including his paintings, were seized by his creditors, and he was unable to work for lack of paints and canvas. In 1874 the group, exasperated by the Salon juries' prejudice, rented a photographer's studio and held an exhibition of their own. The critics were hostile and the public laughed at the paintings. Someone said that the artists had painted these pictures by loading a special gun with tubes of paint and then firing it at their canvases. One critic wrote a humorous piece about escorting an imaginary friend through the exhibition and stopping before a landscape by Pissarro:

> At the sight of this astounding landscape, the good man thought the lenses of his spectacles were dirty. . . . "By Michelon!" he cried. "What on earth is that?"

The critic pretends to be on the artists' side and explains to his friend that it is a ploughed field covered with frost.

> "Those furrows?! That frost?! But they are palette-scrapings placed uniformly on a dirty canvas. It has neither head nor tail, neither top nor bottom, neither front nor back."
> "Perhaps. . . but the impression is there."
> "Well, it's a funny impression! . . ." [1]

The vast variety of art through the ages proves that men in each era and culture are conditioned to see things in a particular way. Any other way is incomprehensible to them. Academic taste in the nineteenth century was governed by an idea which had grown up in the eighteenth, the idea that

1. Louis Leroy, "L'exposition des impressionnistes," Charivari (April 25, 1874), quoted by John Rewald, The History of Impressionism (New York, 1946), p. 256.

certain types of art were more exalted than others. The highest form of painting was called historical painting, although this term actually meant a narrative type of painting whose subject matter and method of rendering were calculated to illustrate the noblest and most heroic aspects of mankind. One of the reasons this form of painting was rated most highly was that the artist had to be at once an intellectual to read the great works of history and literature, a philosopher to select a significant incident to paint and fathom its deepest meanings, a scholar to make his costumes and background setting historically accurate, and a great craftsman to represent his figures and setting realistically. Originality consisted mostly in finding a new subject which would lend itself to teaching virtue and heroism.

Portraiture was on a lower level because it was more a matter of merely copying what the artist saw before him, and the only thing that saved painting from being regarded as a mere craft was the fact that the painter could, by making the landscape dramatic and sublime, suggest the hand of the Creator in nature. Genre and still life painting, though popular among the untutored lovers of art, was deprecated by the connoisseur as too trivial to be great art. The artists of the past most admired by the academician were Raphael, Michelangelo, and many lesser late-Renaissance painters. Rembrandt was ignored because he painted people as they looked rather than idealizing them to inspire the viewer with noble thoughts. Dutch genre paintings were called coarse and vulgar because they often depicted people drinking in taverns, playing cards and brawling, or just doing uninspiring things like paring apples or cooking supper, and Dutch landscapes were not admired because it was felt that the artists depicted merely what they saw.

It was bad enough, according to academic dogma, to paint landscapes at all (without putting the ruins of a Greek or Roman temple in them, or a reclining Venus or nymph so that the landscape might trigger exalted thoughts in the viewer's mind), but to paint pictures of one's ordinary environment and to deliberately eliminate such details as might hint at something beyond just what the eye beheld—this was infuriating to those conditioned by academic doctrine. They must have felt very much like the man in the street today who looks at a Cubist or Surrealist painting and cannot imagine why the artist could not have painted things the way they look.

Not only did the Impressionists believe in painting what they saw before them (the Realists were doing that), but they came more and more to believe that the entire picture must be painted at one time and on the spot. Landscape painters of the past had all made sketches out of doors, sketches that they could later use to paint landscapes in their studios.

The resulting pictures consisted, therefore, of details which had been sketched one at a time, perhaps at different times and in different places, all reassembled in the indoor light of the studio. In order to capture the essence of a scene, particularly the constantly changing effects of light and atmosphere, the Impressionists set up their easels out of doors directly in front of what they wanted to paint so that they could record what they saw, their retinal impression, as quickly as possible. As a result, their pictures revealed a sketchiness that added to the spontaneity and in-stantaneousness of their scenes.

Actually, painters from the Renaissance on had made quick sketches or studies, brushing in colors and forms loosely to establish relationships without taking time to develop detail; but they called these studies sketches, not finished paintings. It was only after working on the sketch for days or weeks, either on a new canvas or over the sketch itself, that they considered the picture to be finished. Yet the great number of oil sketches left behind by painters like Rubens and Constable would indicate that those artists liked these studies well enough to preserve them, that they appreciated the freshness and spontaneity of their sketches which was lost when details were carefully developed. One has the feeling that these artists would like to have painted that way but would never have found buyers.

But if the Impressionists painted in rough daubs of color and left details vague or blurred, how can we call them realists? The answer to this question is that realism is not an absolute but a relative term. Art can never be completely realistic. It can only suggest reality. It can give the spectator only the illusion of reality. And it can do this in a variety of ways. Memling and other fifteenth-century Flemings achieved an illusion of reality through the abundance and exactitude of the details in their paintings. Filippo Lippi and other Renaissance Italians did it through their knowledge of anatomy and perspective; Titian created a reality of texture; Rembrandt chose a few significant details. Each artist had to sacrifice certain aspects of reality in order to stress the particular ones he desired. So also the Impressionists. They chose to capture the sunlight on their canvases, to make the spectator feel as if he were surrounded by and immersed in the air and light that floods through their pictures, and so they sacrificed the many other facets of reality.

Projects

1. Find sharp, clear reproductions of three etchings, one by Rembrandt, one by Goya other than *Tampoco,* and one by the nineteenth-century American artist James McNeill Whistler. Compare the "handwriting" of these artists, and describe how the lines in each case produce different effects.

2. Compare Goya's *Tampoco* with an engraving by Hogarth, preferably one of the *Rake's Progress, Harlot's Progress,* or *Marriage à-la-Mode* series. How do they differ with regard to (1) the character of the line, (2) the dramatic impact, and (3) the relative emphasis on cognitive and associative levels of expression?

3. Look for a good color reproduction of a landscape by Monet. How many different colors and shades of color can you discern? Do one or two colors predominate? How many different kinds of brushstrokes did the artist use? Justify the use of these colors and brushstrokes from the standpoint of (1) the cognitive level and (2) the formal level of expression.

4. Select a color reproduction of a painting by Edgar Degas, preferably one of his ballet dancers. What arguments can you find to prove that he belongs with the Impressionist group? In what ways does he differ from Impressionist theories and practices?

Suggested Reading

Canaday, John. *Mainstreams of Modern Art.* New York: Holt, Rinehart and Winston, 1966.

De Salas, Xavier. *Goya.** New York: Barnes & Noble, Inc., 1962.

Goya, Francisco. *The Disasters of War.** New York: Dover Publications, Inc., 1966.

Goya, Francisco. *Goya,** ed. Gaston Diehl. New York: Crown Publishers, Inc., 1966.

Goya, Francisco. *Goya: His Complete Etchings, Aquatints, and Lithographs,* ed. Enrique L. Ferrari. New York: Harry N. Abrams, Inc., 1962.

Holland, Vyvyan. *Goya: A Pictorial Biography.* New York: The Viking Press, Inc., 1961.

Pool, Phoebe. *Impressionism.** New York: Frederick A. Praeger, Inc., 1967.

Raynal, Maurice. *The History of Modern Painting,* trans. Stuart Gilbert. Vol. 1. New York: Skira, Inc., Publishers, 1956.

Raynal, Maurice. *The Nineteenth Century,* trans. James Emmons. New York: Skira, Inc., Publishers, 1951.

Rewald, John. *The History of Impressionism.* New York: Museum of Modern Art, 1962.

Schickel, Richard. *The World of Goya.* New York: Time-Life Books, 1968.

Seitz, William C. *Claude Monet.* New York: Harry N. Abrams, Inc., 1960.

*Available in a paperback edition.

15 | New Directions
Hiroshige, Cézanne, van Gogh, and Picasso

In Japan, as in the West, the print was a popular art form, mass-produced, and calculated to appeal to a middle-class buyer. Favorite subjects for these prints were the actors of the Kabuki theater, wrestlers, beauty queens, and famous geishas. Landscape in Japan, as in the West, was a later development. In the eighteenth and nineteenth centuries, these prints attained a perfection which amazes Westerners. The technique involved a team of four separate individuals. First, a publisher commissioned a print or series of prints. Then a designer, the real artist of the work, made his design on a transparent sheet of paper. The third member of the team, the cutter of the woodblock, then pasted this design face down on a block of cherry wood and, by cutting through the paper, gouged out the wood in between the lines of the drawing and achieved a block similar to Dürer's but with fewer lines.

After a number of proofs had been printed from this key block, the designer proceeded to work out the color scheme of his picture, painting one color on each of the proofs. From these, in the same way as he cut the first block, the cutter made one block for each color. It was now the task of the fourth member of the team, the printer, to make the finished picture by printing each of the blocks on a piece of paper so that the colors combined to produce the print as the designer had originally envisioned it. Contrary to the Western system of applying the ink evenly on the block with a roller, the Japanese printer brushed the color onto the block, often blending the color so as to produce gradations from light to dark or transitions from one color to another. Moreover, the printing was not done by a press, as in the West, but by laying the paper on the wooden block and gently rubbing the back of the paper with a pad made of bamboo leaves. Since the printer's part of the process required great skill and sensitivity, different impressions of the same print may vary greatly in quality. Not all Japanese prints that one sees framed, therefore, are outstanding examples of that art.

Hiroshige   1797-1858

Ando Hiroshige was the last of the great Japanese printmakers. He was extremely popular during his lifetime, being praised for his rendering of atmospheric effects, especially mists, rain, wind, and moonlight. Though primarily a landscapist, Hiroshige included people in his pictures and emphasized anecdote. Although he tended to caricature the people in his prints, his humor was gentle rather than caustic. In about 1833 he began a series of fifty-three prints, each of which described one of the post towns or stopping places along the three-hundred-mile Tokaido, a pilgrimage road that ran between Tokyo and Kyoto. Since the road wound around precipitous mountains, over streams, across valleys, and along the picturesque eastern coast of Japan, Hiroshige had much variety of subject matter to choose from. The pilgrims he depicted varied from the wealthy lord surrounded by retainers and borne in a litter by coolies, to the foot-weary pedestrian being accosted by the representatives of competing roadside inns.

Hiroshige: *Mitsuke* from the *Tokaido Road* Series   Colorplate 11

Because of the way it is made, this picture contains only about six colors, and they are repeated in several parts of the composition. The water at the lower left is dark blue and becomes lighter as it approaches the golden tan of the sandbar. Blue appears again on the other side of the bar, in the sky at the top of the print, and in the clothing of the two ferrymen in the center. A darker tan color is used for the shadows in the sand and in the mist that envelops the tops of the trees. The standing ferryman's hat is yellow, as are the boats. The shadows on the boats are tan, and a final color, pink, appears on the legs and arms of the ferrymen and in the publisher's mark at the upper right.

Mitsuke is the twenty-ninth print in the series called *The Fifty-Three Stations of the Tokaido Road,* and depicts two ferryboats pulled up on a large sandbar which runs down the center of a river. A group of pilgrims have crossed the bar and are about to board another ferry to take them the rest of the way. Compared to Goya's etching, with its tightly constructed, triangular composition, this woodcut is diffuse in its arrangement. Almost everything in Goya's etching is completely contained within the frame; here forms run beyond the frame. Goya has given us a selective, unified, and self-sufficient scene. Hiroshige implies that this is only a fragment of a larger unit, that there is something previous to this and something subsequent. Where Goya's aquatint exudes a formality which has its roots in the art of Renaissance Italy, Hiroshige's print suggests an informal randomness, and a mood that is intimate rather than monumental.

The primary reason for this is that the Japanese work is strongly asymmetrical. Secondly, it is seemingly random in its arrangement; the frame cuts off the boats at the right and the hills at the left in a casual way. We feel that the frame could be moved further to one side or another without substantially changing the picture. We could never do this with the Goya etching. But the randomness of this woodcut is deceptive. Hiroshige's design is carefully worked out. The two boats at the right thrust their pointed forms into the picture in a gentle but positive diagonal direction, gentle in that the angle of the boats is not an abrupt 45 , for example, but more like a 15° angle, and positive in that the tan-colored boats are seen against the dark blue water on the far right, and their dark prows are set against the light sand further on. The thrust of the two boats is countered by the strong line that marks the edge of the sandbar and by the cluster of boats and people at the left.

The predominance of diagonals in the picture—not vehement diagonals but free-flowing, curving lines just slightly at variance with the horizontal limits of the picture—communicates a looseness and a floating sensation which is appropriate to both the misty atmosphere and the subject of ferryboats. And as our eyes follow the undulating lines, we feel the sensation of free, independently moving forms in space, so unlike the tightly constructed arrangement of the post-Renaissance art we have seen, except, of course, the Monet landscape.

Only two details are parallel to the sides of the picture, and they are mere whispers of verticality: the almost imperceptible masts of the two distant boats and the inscription at the upper right. The number "two," incidentally, figures prominently in the composition. There are two boats, two boatmen, two bodies of water, two lines of trees, and so on.

As in the painting from the Sung dynasty, space here is ambiguous. Intellectually, we understand that the small figures and boats are in the distance, but from our sensuous perception of the picture, they are not. The sharpness with which the distant people, the trees, and the edge of the sandbar are outlined tends to bring them forward. The dots on the sand in the foreground, moreover, do not seem to recede into space but insist on piling up on a vertical plane. This effect of spacelessness will become more apparent if we look at the print upside down and thereby eliminate the cognitive aspects of the picture. Looked at in this way some of the forms which seemed to be close to our eye a moment before appear to be no closer than the "distant" ones. The diagonal pole which one of the boatmen is holding seems actually to be touching the sky, the distant edge of the sandbar, as well as the nearby boat.

Looking at the print right side up again, we must remark on the expressiveness of Hiroshige's drawing. The shape of the standing ferryman, for example, his relaxed stance, the clasped hands, the curved inclination of his body, and the tilt of his head, are caught with only a few lines and some areas of flat, unmodulated color. Without seeing his face or the expression on it, we sense the casual interest with which he watches the progress of his erstwhile customers. At the same time, the varied silhouette of his shirt, the shape of his hat, and the projecting pipe are interesting to us as shapes apart from their descriptive function.

Also on the formal level, the arched form of the standing boatman serves as a visual bridge that connects the oblique lines of the boats with the counter-tilted lines in the upper part of the print, a function for which the second boatman and the tilted pole he holds provide a marvelous directional counterpoint.

Even a superficial comparison of the Hiroshige print with the Monet landscape will show that the Impressionists did not copy the style of the Japanese but merely found in this art certain qualities which they missed in the academic art of their time. It was the freshness and vigor of the prints that fascinated them, the clear, bright colors, the poetic rendition of nature, especially of atmospheric effects, and the unusual, non-Renaissance manner in which the various shapes in the pictures were arranged and related to each other. The art of the Salon exhibitions, on the other hand, had none of these characteristics. Instead, its chief aims were to reproduce natural appearances as closely as possible and to communicate ideas which were either morally uplifting, melodramatically exciting, wistfully sentimental, or amusing.

Jean Léon Gérôme   1824–1904

Outstanding among the academicians of the second half of the nineteenth century was Jean Léon Gérôme, whose works won numerous prizes in Salon exhibitions. He was decorated with the Legion of Honor in 1855, was made a member of the Institute in 1865, became a professor at the École des Beaux-Arts in the same year, and was singled out for additional honors at the Universal Exposition of 1867 with a special exhibition of his most famous paintings.

Figure 52 | JEAN LÉON GÉRÔME. *Pollice Verso (Thumbs Down).* 1859. Oil on canvas, 69" x 40". Phoenix Art Museum, Phoenix, Arizona

Gérôme's popularity rested on his paintings of antique subjects and scenes of the Near East which Europeans were finding particularly fascinating at the time. His style of painting was, of course, technically perfect and meticulously realistic. Needless to say, he was the implacable enemy of Impressionism and, as a member of the Salon exhibition jury, he voted against the works of any artist who did not conform to his idea of what art should be.

Gérôme: *Pollice Verso (Thumbs Down)*

One of Gerome's most popular paintings, this picture depicts the tense moment in the ancient Roman gladiatorial combat when the victor looks to the vestal virgins for their verdict as to whether he should spare or kill his opponent. In all respects the painting shows the artist's technical proficiency and careful research on the architecture, costumes, and armor of ancient Rome.

Dramatically, the scene is nicely unified, with the protagonist set in a prominent position and the psychological relationship between the victor, the victim, and the judges clearly indicated. But the excitement in the picture is generated entirely by the gestures, not by the artist's use of painterly means. The figure of the standing gladiator, for example, is alive only on a cognitive level; we know that when a foot is in this position and a hand is in that position, that the body is engaged in such and such a motion. As a piece of design, however, the figure is a dead collection of separately rendered shapes without any sequence or relationship that is meaningful or interesting on a pictorial level. Even the lights and shadows on the figure merely describe it but have no independent vitality of their own. How much more expressive is Hiroshige's boatman, done with only four colors and a few lines.

What is true of the single figure is true also of the painting as a whole. The relationship between the gladiators and the architecture has no meaning in terms of design. One feels that they could be moved further to one side or another without changing the structure of the painting. The two columns at the upper right begin a vertical movement which leads nowhere and accomplishes nothing. The oriental rugs are handsome in color and pattern, but they, too, do not play any role in sustaining rhythms or supplying contrasting accents. They simply describe themselves.

Like his drawing, Gérôme's color is illustrative rather than organic in the composition. Wherever our eye lands, we follow shapes and colors which lead nowhere, fail to combine, to build, or to lead on to something more intense. They are like the descriptive passages in an undistinguished novel, interesting in themselves but inconsequential with regard to the rest of the work.

With all his loving depiction of tiny details, Hans Memling never weakened the power of his forms, and despite his fidelity to natural appearance, Pieter de Hooch retained the structure of his composition and made every detail function in the total design of his painting. It is not the quantity of detail, then, nor the degree of faithfulness to natural appearances that make Gérôme's painting an unsatisfactory visual experience. It is rather the lack of power in the painting's design, the feebleness of relationships, and the failure of the various details to do more than merely describe themselves.

The Postimpressionist Painters

The term Postimpressionism, unlike Impressionism, does not refer to a style or philosophy of art but rather to a period of time during the late 1880's and 90's when a number of artists departed from Impressionist practices in order to explore other directions. Since each of these artists struck out on a path of his own, it is wrong to speak of a Postimpressionist style. Two of these artists, Cézanne and Renoir, were part of the original Impressionist group. Two others were younger men and joined the Impressionist group only briefly before striking out on their own. One of the latter, Paul Gauguin, eventually spent years in Tahiti and other South Pacific islands. The other, the Dutchman Vincent van Gogh, did his best work during the year and few months he lived in Arles in southern France. Monet, on the other hand, remained an Impressionist until his death at the age of eighty-six in 1926.

Monet's fascination with light to the exclusion of all else led him on several occasions to paint the same subject over and over at different times of the day or seasons of the year. There are, for example, fifteen pictures of a haystack under different sorts of light. His twenty-six pictures of the façade of Rouen Cathedral say nothing about the church or man's relationship to it as a piece of architecture or as the house of God. Each picture is a piece of canvas filled with a thick crust of paint—rough strokes which, even when one backs away from the picture, reveal nothing of the marvelous sculpture that covers the façade or of the stained glass rose window; it is not a painting of the church but of light striking the church. The Postimpressionists felt that art should have a goal more profound than this.

What Paul Cézanne missed in the Impressionists' pictures was the sense of order, organization, and structure which he felt in the art of the old masters. Even as an Impressionist Cézanne drew his shapes more precisely than his colleagues and tried to work out the relationship of one part of his picture to the other. As he matured, Cézanne continued these tendencies, adopting the Impressionists' bright palette and painting out of doors as they did, but also doing several things they did not. Most noticeable among the differences is his use of a sharp outline around the objects he painted. Outline serves to limit an area, to hold it in. The Impressionists de-emphasized outline as much as possible, because, of course, they saw no outlines around things in nature. An outline is merely an artistic convention to which we have become so accustomed that we do not see anything unnatural about it in a picture. But as a means of stressing the shape of things, outline is ideal, and it was the shape of things and the relationship of shapes in space that interested Cézanne more than their visual appearance.

Paul Cézanne   1839-1906

Like Monet, Cézanne persisted in his way of working despite public indifference and critical hostility. He was a good friend of the Impressionists Monet, Pissarro, Renoir, Degas, and others, and he participated in the first Impressionist exhibition of 1874. But soon thereafter, his work began to differ so radically from the accepted canons of art that his colleagues asked him not to exhibit his paintings with theirs. Fortunately, he was financially self-sufficient during his mature years so he could go on painting as he pleased without having to sell his pictures.

Compared to the gregarious Monet, Cézanne was introverted, suspicious, and solitary. Except for several stays in and around Paris, he lived and worked mostly in his native Aix-en-Provence in the south of France, where he tramped around the countryside, his easel and his paints strapped to his back, looking for "motifs" for his pictures. He often painted the same mountain, stone quarry, or farmhouse over and over. He did many portraits of himself, his wife, and a few close friends, and he often used the same pieces of cloth, pitchers, and bottles in his still life paintings.

Needless to say, he painted for his own satisfaction rather than for public sale. He seemed, as a matter of fact, to regard his painting as research, and what he was doing as a new discovery in art. His work continued to arouse controversy, and as late as 1902 he was refused the Legion of Honor. In 1904, however, a whole room at the Salon d'Automne, an exhibition grudgingly sponsored by the government, was devoted to his work, and by the time he died two years later, he was receiving the admiration of many younger artists.

Cézanne: *Still Life*   Colorplate 12

If we were to test this painting, as Leonardo recommended artists should do, by comparing it with a mirror's reflection of the objects depicted—bottle, carafe, glass, apples, tablecloth—we would find several "mistakes" in the picture. Water carafes are invariably symmetrical; this one is lopsided. Apples are round; these are flattened out. The tablecloth refuses to lie down properly and seems to be made of stiff cardboard or sheet metal. A talented teenager could have done better than this at making things look believable. It is clear, therefore, what Cézanne did *not* try to do. The question to ask is: what *was* he trying to do?

Consider the white piece of cloth. The sharp edges of its upper and lower contours have something in common with the curved edges of the carafe. In its smaller convolutions the cloth is related to the mouth of the carafe, as well as to the curves on the wine bottle next to it, the fruit, and the pattern on the blue tablecloth. One may argue that any wrinkled piece of white cloth would do the same thing, but a photograph would show that a wrinkled cloth would also be full of random shapes that have no relationship to each other. This is why Cézanne's cloth does not look as real as a photograph; he has eliminated all but the most significant forms, that is, he has stressed forms that mean something when they are combined with each other. The patterns in Gérôme's oriental rugs, on the contrary, though they are charming to look at, are actually a disruptive factor in the total effect of his painting.

Cézanne not only eliminated all that is unnecessary to his design, he also exaggerated and distorted some of the details to suit his purpose. The pattern on the blue cloth, for example, does not seem to lie on the surface of the cloth but to exist all by itself. It seems hardly plausible, moreover, that part of that pattern on the far left should duplicate almost exactly the neck and shoulders of the carafe, that the stripes at the lower center should repeat the stripes on the wall, or that the numerous circular patterns made by all the cloths should so obviously echo the shape of the fruit, bottle, carafe, etc. Cézanne is guilty here of deliberately falsifying natural appearance, as he did in making the carafe asymmetrical. Notice also the opposition to the curved shapes offered by the straight lines of the table leg and the background wall, as well as by the neck of the bottle, the shadow on the carafe's neck, and the parallel stripes of the cloth at the lower center. As far as color goes, the apples, especially the lower four, contrast abruptly with the otherwise monochrome blue green color scheme. One of these apples is red, one is yellow, and the other two, again for the sake of contrast, contain both colors.

But the effectiveness of Cézanne's painting is not due to the number of repetitions and contrasts of shapes. A numerical quantity of attributes never made any work of art effective, any more than a large vocabulary makes a man a significant writer. It is the quality of the attributes rather than their quantity that counts—what an artist or writer says with his vocabulary. Of course, we cannot convey in words the feelings that Cézanne communicates by means of his design, because the language of painting is visual rather than verbal. Nevertheless, as our eyes move over the painted surface, we can feel the energy of its lines, forms, and colors as they oppose or attract one another. This energy is not unbridled, but held down by a rigorous geometry. Each form is firmly anchored in space, immovable and monumental. We are not charmed by the beauty of the apples as fruit, delighted by the contrasting texture of glass and cloth, or attracted by the graceful rhythms of line or pattern. If we like Cézanne's picture, it is because we feel the power with which he invests his forms, the quiet drama of these harsh, roughhewn, almost clumsy forms, in the same way that we feel the rugged grandeur of a mountain cliff.

Unlike his Impressionist contemporaries, Cézanne paid little attention to light effects in this picture. We cannot even tell from what direction the light is coming. In their few still life paintings, the Impressionists surrounded the painted objects with a vibrant atmosphere that dissolved their contours. And, as usual, they represented these objects as they appeared from one specific angle at one particular instant in time. Cézanne, on the other hand, outlines his forms with clear-cut precision. He arranged them almost as if each object were observed at a different time and then put next to the other in the painting, and there is nothing evanescent or mutable about these objects; each one has its hard-edged, preordained place in space, and in its immutability seems to transcend the limits of time.

There is, moreover, little textural variety in this picture. Everything has virtually the same texture. Painters of still life in seventeenth-century Holland depicted glasses so as to make us want to pick them up and drink out of them, cloth that we would like to handle, apples whose shiny skins would stimulate our appetites. And there is a charm in these pictures, a random, slightly cluttered informality, that reminds us of tabletops we all have seen. Not so with Cézanne. Whether he painted apples, mountains, or people he treated each as an element of his total structure, as part of an architectonic, monumental construction. We have arrived, therefore, at an art in which not only the associative values are almost absent, but where cognitive appeal has yielded almost completely to pure form.

Vincent van Gogh   1853–1890

Through his many articulate letters and through the testimony of his friends we get a vivid picture of the short, tragic life and volatile personality of Vincent van Gogh. Always full of enthusiasm and alternating between self-doubt and confidence that someday the world would understand what he was trying to say with his art, van Gogh was overly intense about everything he did.

Born into a strict Calvinist family in southern Holland, van Gogh did not start drawing until he was twenty-seven years old. Unsuccessful as a schoolteacher, a clerk in an art gallery, a minister, and an evangelist, he poured his passionate feelings into his pictures, and in eight feverish years produced the several hundred paintings upon which his reputation rests. Since his art was unconventional even by Impressionist standards, he had no financial or critical success. Other than his brother and a few friends, no one wanted his pictures. Not until the year of his death was one of his paintings sold at a public exhibition. Tormented by a series of mental breakdowns and troubled about his continued financial dependence on his brother, he committed suicide at the age of thirty-seven.

Van Gogh: *The Olive Orchard*   Colorplate 13

Painting directly from nature was less important to Vincent van Gogh than to Claude Monet, yet he usually did so, and we have stories about his painting through windstorms by tying his easel down to keep it from blowing away. Actually, van Gogh was interested in nature chiefly as a point of departure, as a catalyst to his emotional reaction to things. The touches of his brush were not prompted so much by what he saw as by what he felt at the moment he was painting. Sometimes his brushstrokes are almost independent of what they depict. Certainly the strokes on the furrowed field in the foreground of this painting do not describe the field so much as they animate that part of the composition. And the colors he chose were not intended to represent the light on the ground but rather to heighten the picture's dramatic impact as we look at it.

The colors in this picture are unusually subdued for van Gogh, who generally used brilliant hues in his work. As a whole, the painting is pervaded by a dry tan color which is characteristic of the arid countryside around St. Rémy in southern France where the artist was living in 1889. Over this tan tonality, van Gogh has painted many other colors. The lower part of the picture, for example, includes touches of various browns, as well as gray, dark blue, and straw yellow. All of these colors are applied to the canvas in rough, angular, and isolated strokes that animate this area. Some of these brushstrokes are a half inch long, and in their agitated path across the canvas, they suggest hordes of crawling organisms or magnetized particles all lined up in obedience to some unseen force. The application and organization of these ribbon-shaped strokes sets up a pulsating movement that flows from the lower right to the upper left.

A horizontal band of yellow stops this diagonal movement temporarily, but in the green area of the olive trees' foliage, the brushstrokes increase the angle of their ascent and leap upward like green flames. Among these leaves we find several shades of green, as well as blue, brown, and some touches of white. The sky above the trees is not a placid blue but an agitated curtain of diverse but closely related hues, predominantly yellow green and tan, but flecked with strokes of pale green, yellow, and rose. The paint here is applied so thickly that some of the brushstrokes actually stand out in relief, as if they had been applied with a tiny trowel. In their direction, these strokes continue the pull toward the upper left, but less vehemently than those of the other two strata.

Reduced to its simplest terms, then, this painting consists of three horizontal zones, the lowest alive with brushstrokes that seem to leap this way and that toward the upper left; the next zone swarming with curved and more vertically oriented strokes; and the third, paler and plainer than the other two, still vibrating with the energy induced from below but dispersed and dissolving. Across the two lower zones, as a counterpoint to their individual rhythmic patterns, the gnarled trunks of several trees leap upward as if alive. With their unnaturally strong outlines, they suggest snakes, whips, or spiralling flames, as the ground suggests a raging torrent of water and the trees, wind-tossed flames. Such metaphorical transformations of one thing into another are typical of van Gogh's paintings and are one source of their remarkable power.

In the midst of this image of a convulsed nature, the straight lines of the ladder and the simplified shapes of the three women provide a new and surprising contrast. The undulating, overly emphatic outlines of the three figures make them kin to the landscape they inhabit, but in the flatness of their color and in the lack of brushstrokes within their contours, they assert their independence. Compared to the photographic exactness of Gérôme's gladiators, these figures are anatomically unarticulated and clumsy. But each of them consists of strong patterns whose vigorous contours relate them forcibly to the other elements of the composition. Gérôme would undoubtedly have given us a picture of olive gatherers in southern France that might better have satisfied our antiquarian interests, but van Gogh has created an image the power of whose forms and the impact of whose design transcend both its time and its subject matter.

It is wrong, of course, to say that van Gogh's paintings have an emotional content and that Cézanne's do not. All art must appeal to our emotions, not only the visual arts but the literary and the performing arts as well. It is actually a matter of degree. The emotional content of van Gogh's picture is tempestous and unbridled. Like the swirl of a raging torrent or the convulsions of an earthquake, it tends to overwhelm the spectator with its violence. Cézanne's, on the contrary, is restrained and tightly controlled; the objects in his picture sit unmoving and immovable in their places, but they exert a tension on one another and generate an excitement which is felt quietly, like the towering peaks of a mountain range.

The Properties of Color

White light, we all know, is made of all the colors of the rainbow or spectrum. In pigment, however, if all the hues of the rainbow were mixed together in proper proportions, we would, theoretically at least, get black. Actually, we get a neutral, brownish gray. For the sake of convenience, we speak of colors in terms of three properties: hue, value, and saturation. We call hue that quality which allows us to distinguish one color from another. For example, red, orange, and blue green are all hues. We call red, yellow, and blue primary hues, because it is possible to produce any hue of the spectrum by mixing these three in various proportions. Two primaries mixed together in proper amounts will produce the secondary hues. Red and yellow make orange; yellow and blue, green; blue and red, violet. Primaries mixed with their related secondaries produce the six tertiary hues, red orange and yellow orange, yellow green and blue green, blue violet and red violet. In between these secondary and tertiary hues lie innumerable intermediate hues. Since each secondary hue is a mixture of two primaries, it complements the third primary. Red is therefore known as the complementary hue of green; yellow of violet, and blue of orange. Combining any two complementaries will consequently mingle all three primaries and therefore produce the theoretical black. Even a slight admixture of green to a red pigment will make that red darker and duller than it was when unmixed. On the other hand, setting a patch of red next to a patch of green or juxtaposing any other complementary hues will make each seem more intense than it was separately, because each contains elements which the other lacks.

The second property of color is value (sometimes called *tone* or *key*). This term designates the degree to which a color approaches black or white. Pink, for example, is a red hue with a high value. A brick red may be of the same hue of red but of much lower value, closer, in other words, to black. A painter may heighten the value of a hue by adding white pigment, as the Impressionists did to make their pictures look bright and sunlit, or he may lower the value by adding black, or any color which contains its complementary or whose value is lower than its own.

But the addition of a complementary to a hue also does something else. It reduces the saturation of that hue, that is, the purity or vividness of that hue, for example, the amount of red pigment in a red hue. On certain days, we know, the sky is bluer than on other days, so that we might say that its saturation varies. There is a given point, theoretically speaking, when any hue is at its maximum saturation point. The addition of white to this hue will raise its value but reduce its saturation. The addition of black or any complementary will lower both its saturation and its value. A pink carnation and a brick may, therefore, have the same saturation of red, but vary greatly in value. An apple and a tomato, on the other hand, may be equal in value, but they obviously vary in their saturation of red. *Intensity* and *chroma* are sometimes used as synonyms for *saturation.*

At their maximum saturation point, all hues are not of equal value, however. Bright yellow is closer to white than even the most saturated red, and that same red is closer to white than the purest blue. In order to give a red and a yellow equal value, therefore, we must raise the value of the red by adding white, or reduce the value of the yellow by adding black or some other hue that will bring its value down. We must not forget, finally, that red, blue, and yellow, as they have been discussed here, are only theoretical concepts. Actual pigments, as we noted in Chapter 14, are made of mineral and vegetable dyes and do not come in simple red, green, or yellow orange. Red, for example, may be alizarin crimson, cadmium red, rose madder, vermillion, or another pigment, each of them loosely called "red" but tending toward yellow or blue in various degrees.

Looking at three of the paintings discussed in Chapters 14 and 15, we note that as far as hues go, the painting by Monet ranges through only a small part of the spectrum. Various shades of green and blue dominate the color scheme, with the pervasive light orange tonality serving to bind the composition together. Since much white has been mixed with the pigments and no black at all, the value of the painting is very high. A comparison of the Monet with the de Hooch will demonstrate how much the addition of black to the pigments in the Dutch painting has reduced the value as well as the saturation of the colors in the latter. The admixture of white to the pigments in the Monet, however, has also reduced the saturation of most of the colors, but a close examination of the painting will reveal many isolated strokes of relatively highly saturated colors, strokes whose simultaneous contrast with each other further heightens the brilliance of the color scheme and thereby simulates the effect of sunlight. In the lower sector of the painting, for example, we can discern curved strokes of bright dark green, lemon yellow, and sky blue.

In the Cézanne *Still Life* the range of hues is also very narrow. As a matter of fact, it is virtually a blue green painting with a few areas of red, yellow, and white. Moreover, each color is laid down in a solid and relatively flat area. That is, brushstrokes are discernible, but they do not contrast with one another as they do in Impressionist paintings. Whereas the trees in the Monet picture contain, in addition to green, touches of yellow, orange, violet, and blue, the tablecloth in the Cézanne comprises only various shades of blue. Thus the identity of each volume in the still life is preserved by the character of its color as well as by its sharp outline. Each volume functions as a unit in the geometry of the total design, whereas in the Monet one volume merges with its neighbors in an all-enveloping atmosphere of air and sunlight. The forms of the apples in the still life are given added emphasis by their abrupt contrast with the surrounding blue, especially since they are close to being complementaries, that is, orange and blue. Since Cézanne, like the Impressionists, banished black from his palette, the values of his colors tend also to be high—closer to white than to black—but only relatively so, for the absolute value of the Monet is much higher. The contrasts of values, on the other hand, are much more pronounced in the Cézanne; there is a greater difference, for example, in value between the blue cloth and the pattern on that cloth than in any two adjacent areas in the landscape. As a result, our eyes move easily through the Monet painting from one part of the landscape to another while in the still life we are made aware of each separate form, even of the patterns on a piece of cloth. The saturation of the colors in the Cézanne is, on the whole, much greater than in the Monet.

The colors in most of van Gogh's paintings are highly saturated. *The Olive Orchard* is therefore unusual in its subdued color scheme: mostly greens, blues, and browns of low saturation and low value. In the sky the value is high, but the saturation is still low. The picture differs from the Monet and the Cézanne chiefly in the abrupt contrasts of values in large areas—the sky, for example, next to the darker trees—contrasts which enhance the dramatic impact of the picture. As with the other two painters, the characteristics of van Gogh's color help to fulfill the artist's expressive purpose. Set against each other in sudden juxtaposition, and animated by swirling or choppy brushstrokes, van Gogh's colors serve him in his attempt to dramatize his landscape and to offer the viewer a heightened visual experience of nature.

Painting in the Twentieth Century

Van Gogh's approach to art was the antithesis of Cézanne's. Where the latter was controlled and methodical in his painting, the former abandoned himself to his impulses and emotions. Where one worked slowly, almost painfully (sometimes scraping out a section of a picture to rework it again and again), the other painted in the heat of excitement, applying the paint so fast that brushes were sometimes too cumbersome and he actually squeezed the pigment onto the canvas directly from the tube. One of the four main currents of art in our century, Expressionism, is based on this hyperemotional approach to art.

About 1905, several groups of artists in Paris and in Germany began to carry the ideas of van Gogh and his contemporary, Paul Gauguin, even further. Colors became more saturated and sometimes departed from natural appearance: skies might be painted red, trees blue, and the ground various shades of orange and lavender. Color combinations were often discordant, and slashing, explosive brushstrokes heightened the violent impact of the paintings.

By about 1908, a number of artists in Paris revolted against this emotional approach to painting and produced pictures inspired by Cézanne's ideal of geometrizing nature. The objects depicted in these paintings had sharp edges and mostly straight lines or simple curves, characteristics which impelled one of the critics to dub this movement Cubism. Although it has undergone many transformations, this is still a prominent movement in art today, both in painting and in sculpture. It is interesting to note here that both the Expressionists and the Cubists were intrigued by the art of primitive peoples, of the black Africans, and the various inhabitants of the Pacific Islands, which had not up to that time been considered art but merely objects of ethnological curiosity.

The third of the four major movements in modern art began during World War I and reflected the frustration and anger of certain artists at what was happening in supposedly civilized Europe. Partly an attempt to commit artistic suicide, and partly an excuse for unbridled fun and horseplay, this movement, which was christened Dada, seems to have erupted nearly simultaneously in Switzerland, Germany, Paris, and New York. There were poetry readings at which several poems were read simultaneously, plays in which the performers wore preposterous costumes and said ridiculous things, and made music by ringing electric bells and beating on various objects. Most of these spectacles ended in riots and the arrival of the police. In the visual arts, the Dadaists mocked esthetic values. Marcel Duchamp exhibited the "ready-made," a store-bought object such as a bottle rack or a snow shovel which he mounted on pedestals and declared to be a work of art. To one exhibition he sent a reproduction of Leonardo's *Mona Lisa* with mustaches painted on her face; to another he sent a urinal which he entitled *Fountain.*

The Cubists had made pictures into whose design they had incorporated pieces of paper for the sake of textural variety, newspaper or wallpaper that often imitated wood grain or marble. Such pictures are called collages, from the French *coller,* to glue. The Dadaists used this technique for different ends, combining torn theater tickets, and cigarette labels, but mostly fragments of photographs assembled in surprising and absurd relationships. They also made sculpture by nailing together odd pieces of wood, metal objects, and anything that would shock and outrage the viewer. Visitors to one Dada exhibition in Cologne were provided with hatchets so that they could chop up anything they did not like. By 1921 Dada was dead, but its spirit has returned in recent years. We see it in the sculpture made of rusty metal scraps (an idiom facilitated by the invention of the acetylene torch), in pictures to which not only paper but all sorts of materials and objects have been glued, nailed, or stapled, and in Happenings, those performances that involve sound, sight, and sometimes touch when the audience is brought into the action.

From the ashes of Dada rose the fourth of the major movements in art today, Surrealism, an artistic and literary movement which originated in Paris in the early 1920's. The aim of the Surrealist is to exploit the irrationality which had been the keystone of Dada, and to explore the world that lies below the level of consciousness. Strongly affected by the ideas of Sigmund Freud and his successors, Surrealist art has taken many diverse forms: from the photographic realism of Salvador Dali to the childlike drawings of Paul Klee (which also resemble drawings made by the insane), and the lines, dots, and amoeba-shapes of Joan Miró which suggests the magic patterns of primitive peoples, at once whimsical and frightening.

But to summarize the major movements of art is merely to understand what happened. Understanding may be requisite to experiencing something, but it is not synonymous with that experience. Art must be felt, or else we are like the museum-goer in the *New Yorker* cartoon, referred to in the preface of this book, who knew all about art but did not know what he liked. When we confront a painting whose style is radically different from what is familiar to us, whose subject matter and manner of execution baffle or even infuriate us, it helps very little to be told that it is a Cubist painting with certain Surrealistic overtones. We should first of all remind ourselves that this picture was made by an artist in order to communicate an emotional experience. If the picture does not communicate, however, it may be that we are letting our ideas of what art should or should not be interfere with our response. It might be well, therefore, to look at the picture in the three steps outlined in Chapter 14, attempting to experience the picture first on the formal level of its design, then to examine its subject matter on a cognitive level, and finally to see what associations the design and the subject matter together arouse in our minds.

We should always keep in mind the fact that there is no reason why we should like every modern painting, any more than we should like every modern novel or poem or piece of music. We should realize, too, that the more time we spend looking at the visual arts, the more acute our powers of observation will become and the more easily we will be able to convert these visual stimuli into emotional responses. Just as we cannot understand calculus until we have mastered algebra, so we cannot feel what a painter like Mondrian is trying to communicate until we have sharpened our visual responses with "easier" kinds of painting such as the Cubist pictures of Picasso, Braque, and Gris.

One thing that makes it difficult to experience certain modern works is that the artists themselves sometimes act as if they do not care whether the general public understands them or not. They seem, as a matter of fact, to try intentionally to shock, baffle, and infuriate their audience, even more so than the nineteenth-century rebels who wished to bait the bourgeoisie. There are painters who drip paint on their canvases and smear the pigments together. There are sculptors who make constructions that move, light up, and even make noise. Pop Art takes its inspiration from such things as comic books, labels from canned goods, or food on cafeteria trays (*popular* objects). Op Art involves patterns that produce *optical* illusions: lines that seem to wiggle when we look at them, colors that make our eyes vibrate. It seems almost as though modern artists, like the Mannerists of the sixteenth century, are desperately trying to find something to do that has not been done by their predecessors.

Some of these things will no doubt prove to be mere fads and their authors basking in the publicity they receive, but there are also serious artists working in these styles, artists who are exploring the processes of vision and searching for new styles and trying new materials. Why, we may ask, do they have to keep looking for new things? Why can they not continue in the styles of the past which are pleasant to look at and uncomplicated? The answer is that no creative artist has ever worked in the style of his predecessor, not now and not in the past. The difference between Giotto's innovations and Picasso's is chiefly one of degree; the change is just more abrupt today than it was in the past. But this is as true in science and technology as it is in art. More has happened in the last five decades than in the past five centuries in all areas of our lives, and the creative artist would no more paint like Rembrandt or Cézanne than we would travel by ox cart or dress like our grandfathers.

The arts in the twentieth century have undergone a revolution as violent as the one that transformed the Greco-Roman world into the medieval era. Both revolutions, incidentally, led from a realistic art style to a more abstract idiom which better expressed the ideals of the new era. And just as Latin, the universal language of the Western world, was transformed into the various Romance languages, so has what we might call the Renaissance idiom—one-point perspective, chiaroscuro, anatomical accuracy, atmospheric effects, and so on—given way to a Babel of separate artistic languages, each with its own vocabulary and syntax. Yet all these new visual languages have certain basic roots in the art of the past. Picasso, no less than de Hooch, Memling, and the anonymous designer of the mosaics in Ravenna, speaks to us in terms of design, in the rhythms of lines and volumes, in the tensions created and resolved by volumes in space, in the interaction of light and dark tones, in intense and pale colors, and in that most mysterious of all elements, harmonious proportions.

Pablo Picasso   1881–

The man who has most contributed to the proliferation of styles in our era, an astoundingly prolific and inventive artist and a man of magnetic personality, is Pablo Picasso, who was born in Málaga in southern Spain. The son of an academic painter and art teacher, Picasso is said to have begun to draw before he could talk. At fourteen he entered the Academy of Fine Arts in Barcelona, whose entrance examinations, which normally took a month to complete, he finished in one day.

In 1900 he made his first trip to Paris, which for half a century had been the center of Western art. He returned four years later and has made France his home ever since. In 1908 he and Georges Braque evolved the style which has come to be called Cubism, and in the 1920's he became fascinated by the theories of the Surrealists.

Due to his prodigious facility, the technical problems which worry other artists have never been his primary concern. Instead he has been intrigued with the idiom or language of expression. Often inspired by the styles of past art but never imitating them outright, he has worked in a bewildering number of manners that range from fairly realistic to various degrees of abstraction. Nevertheless, everything he does bears the strong imprint of his personality.

Pablo Picasso: *Girl Before a Mirror* Colorplate 14

Our first reaction to this painting may be one of abhorrence. The color scheme seems garish and discordant, the drawing brutal in its distortion and careless in its execution, and the subject matter may seem to some viewers to be weird, or even disgusting. Yet no one would deny that the picture makes a strong impact on the spectator. It is a powerful image whether we happen to like that image or not. But wherein does the power of the image lie?

On the formal or purely sensuous level of experience, the colors strike us because of their high saturation. That is, most of the hues—particularly the reds, blues, and oranges—have not been diluted by the addition of white in the Impressionist manner but have been applied full strength. Nor have they been put on in the Impressionists' small dots or in the methodical strokes of Cézanne or in the snaky streaks of van Gogh. The colors in this picture have been laid down in flat, unmodulated areas which form two-dimensional planes like cutout pieces of colored paper. Each of these areas has a definite shape surrounded by a black line. Consequently each of these precisely shaped areas functions as a distinct part of the total design. Note also that only a few hues have been used—vermillion (an orange red), blue, yellow, green, black, and various shades of lavender—and that these hues are repeated in many parts of the picture. That is, although their range goes from one end of the spectrum to the other, from red at one end to violet at the other, the actual number of hues is small, and three of them are primary hues.

If Monet's landscape resembles a mosaic, the Picasso is like a stained glass window. Each color area in the Picasso contrasts abruptly with its neighbor, and each seems to project or recede according to its hue, tone, and saturation, warmth or coldness. If we run our eyes across any part of the central portion of the painting, we will feel that certain forms seem to move in front of others. Instead of traveling gently over forms that are modulated by means of color and light and shadow (as in the Giotto for example), our eyes follow flat planes and are forced to jump from one to the other, in and out of abruptly stratified spaces. The resulting rhythm is staccato, irregular, and full of unexpected syncopation. Its analogy in sound would be a jangled, dissonant, and strongly rhythmic piece of dance music played by shrill and rather loud instruments, perhaps a Dixieland band of the kind, incidentally, which was popular at the time that this picture was painted. If we follow any of these color areas, our eyes are forced also to cross barriers of black lines, parallel stripes, and grid patterns.

Despite the bewildering effect of this picture, there does appear to be some principle of order. Our eyes are propelled by the curved forms from one area to another. We sense a kinship between the various forms, because the human eye tends to relate forms of similar shape. Thus the preponderance of curved forms unifies the central area of the picture. So do the repetitious striped patterns even though their colors vary (red here, black there, and green elsewhere). In deliberate contrast to the curved character of the central forms, the "background" consists of straight lines that cross each other to form a grid of diamond shapes. Still, there is a kinship between this grid and the curved forms because certain colors are common to both. Moreover, each diamond shape contains a circular form which ties it to similar forms in the "foreground."

The words "foreground" and "background" are put in quotation marks, because there is actually no illusion of realistic space in the picture. In fact, there is deliberate ambiguity. Intense colors, we have noted elsewhere, seem to advance toward us, and neutral colors to recede. The colors of the grid, therefore, seem closer to our eyes than the girl's pale face, for example. It is only our cognitive impulse which tells us that the girl's head is "in front" of the grid. Such surprising spatial paradoxes are a favorite device of the artist in our time, and contribute to the feeling of tension and restlessness which is typical of contemporary art.

Much more could be said about the purely sensuous aspect of this picture. Like most artists of the twentieth century, Picasso relies more on the formal level than on the cognitive level of expression. We do, however, recognize a human face and figure (however much transformed) at the left, and we do, after an instant or two (especially if we know the title of the painting), see a mirror and a reflection of a face at the right. Quite obviously, though, it is not the artist's aim to make us enjoy the mere recognition of a girl and a mirror. Thus we tend to ask ourselves: "Did the artist have any purpose in transforming nature in this way other than to create a compelling pattern of shapes and colors?" Now, Picasso is unusually reticent among modern artists. He refuses to explain his pictures, maintaining that his work should be felt, not talked about. Still, the unusual and surprising imagery in this picture seems to demand some interpretation, and certain associative ideas do come to mind. The fact that the girl at the left has two faces, one in profile and one full face, suggests the multiplicity of the human personality, something we all know and sometimes vaguely feel about ourselves and others, but which is here dramatized by colors and shapes. Picasso, like most artists today, is fascinated by the ideas of Freud and his successors, but it would be futile to seek literal correspondences between psychologists' postulations concerning the ego and the id, for example, and the free inventions of a painter like Picasso. The artist formulates intuitive rather than scientific truths, and we must realize this when we seek to experience his work, yet these intuitions may be felt by others.

When we think of our body, for example, we may visualize it in its external appearance to which we have become accustomed by looking at it, or in its internal makeup as we remember it from scientific charts and diagrams we have seen. But we also have an awareness of our body which is based not on what we know but on what we sense when we feel our body as a mysterious network of nerve endings, tubes and organs, chemical processes, and cyclical changes. This is actually our most intimate and deeply felt consciousness of our body. It is also highly irrational, for it is based on subjective sensations rather than objective facts, but if it were possible to resolve this visceral consciousness into colors and shapes, it might involve transparencies, simplifications, and transformations such as Picasso has invented in this picture. At any rate, Picasso has given us neither the visual, external view, nor the scientific, physiological view of the female body. He has created a symbol rather than depicted a representation of femininity, and by having the girl look into the mirror, moreover, he has injected the idea of self-contemplation and introspection. Not only does the girl who has two faces to begin with, feel her own femaleness, but she also sees herself in the mirror as still another person.

Pictures of women looking into mirrors abound in the history of art, but in all of them the mirror reflects the person who looks into it. In *Venus with a Mirror,* Titian has represented the physical, material, and external aspects of a woman, an image full of sensuousness, delicacy, and grace, but in a limited way: we see her and we remain within the bounds of physical reality; and when she looks into her mirror, she sees the same woman we see. Picasso's girl, on the contrary, sees in the mirror not the external features of a woman, nor the strange, x-rayed image of burgeoning fecundity, but a third person, an even stranger being whose shapes and colors are more startling and removed from reality. More than a striking image on the primary or sensuous level, therefore, Picasso's painting is rich in associative values. It is full of surprising and suggestive imagery which we can pursue through as many levels as we have the ability to penetrate.

Projects

1. Choose a color reproduction of a painting by Monet, Cézanne, van Gogh, and Gauguin and discuss how the brushstroke for each picture suits the expressive purpose of its artist.

2. Select a color reproduction of a picture by Paul Klee, Joan Miró, Henri Matisse, or Georges Rouault. Analyze it on the formal, the cognitive, and the associative level of expression.

3. Examine a color reproduction of a woodcut print by one of the German Expressionists. In what ways does it differ from the woodcut of Hiroshige in style and in the feeling it projects? How can you account for these differences?

4. Select a color reproduction of a painting in the Cubist idiom by a painter of your choice. Describe the spatial sensations you feel as you look at it and try to account for these sensations in the painting's formal characteristics.

Suggested Reading

Apollonio, Umbro. *Picasso.** Folio Art Books. New York: Crown Publishers, Inc., 1967.

Arnason, Harvard H. *History of Modern Art.* New York: Prentice-Hall, Inc. and Harry N. Abrams, Inc., 1968.

Barr, Alfred H. *Picasso: Fifty Years of His Art.* New York: Museum of Modern Art, 1946.

Daix, Pierre. *Picasso.** New York: Frederick A. Praeger, Inc., 1965.

Gore, Frederick, ed. *Abstract Art.** Movements in Modern Art Series. New York: Crown Publishers, Inc., 1967.

Hiroshige. *Down the Emperor's Road with Hiroshige,* ed. Reiko Chiba. New York: Charles E. Tuttle Co., 1965.

Hiroshige. *The Fifty-Three Stages of the Tokaido,* ed. Ichitarō Kondō. Honolulu: East West Center Press, 1966.

Hoffman, Edith. *Expressionism.** Movements in Modern Art Series. New York: Crown Publishers, Inc., 1967.

Jedding, H. *Van Gogh.** Folio Art Books. New York: Crown Publishers, Inc., 1967.

Knuttel, Gerard. *Van Gogh.** New York: Barnes & Noble, Inc., 1962.

Murphy, Richard. *The World of Cézanne.* New York: Time-Life Books, 1968.

Penrose, Roland. *The Eye of Picasso.** New York: New American Library, 1966.

Raynal, Maurice. *The History of Modern Painting.* New York: Skira, Inc., Publishers, 1949-1950.

Rewald, John. *Post-Impressionism.* New York: Museum of Modern Art, 1956.

Schapiro, Meyer. *Paul Cézanne.* New York: Harry N. Abrams, Inc., 1952.

Schapiro, Meyer. *Vincent van Gogh.** New York: Harry N. Abrams, Inc., 1950.

Schmeller, Alfred. *Cubism.** Movements in Modern Art Series. New York: Crown Publishers, Inc., 1967.

Schmeller, Alfred. *Surrealism.** Movements in Modern Art Series. New York: Crown Publishers, Inc., 1967

Wertenbaker, Lael. *The World of Picasso.* New York: Time-Life Books, 1968.

*Available in a paperback edition.

16 | The New Language in Architecture
Frank Lloyd Wright and Le Corbusier

Except for the invention of the Gothic flying buttress, very little that is new in structural methods occurred in architecture between Roman times and comparatively recent times. Except for Michelangelo's great dome over St. Peter's in Rome and the new manipulation of space in the Baroque era, architecture changed principally in terms of decoration. Its expressive impact is therefore skin-deep, so to speak.

To be sure, the round arch and simple planes of Renaissance architecture recalled the imposing dignity of ancient Rome; the broken pediments and surprising curves of the seventeenth-century Baroque style shouted with religious ecstasy; and the precious curves of the eighteenth-century Rococo style whispered with aristocratic elegance. But after that, design was divorced completely from structure and utility, and style became chiefly a matter of ornamenting the wall surface, of adopting and adapting the classical orders, Gothic details, and the inventions of creative architects of the past such as Michelangelo.

This revival of "styles" achieved an especially superficial level in the nineteenth century, which has thereby acquired the name the Age of Revivals. Churches, banks, and government buildings were modeled on the Parthenon; libraries and courthouses on the Pantheon; other churches, city halls, and university buildings on a variety of Gothic styles. Romanesque, Renaissance, Baroque, and other kinds of ornament were also revived. Egyptian, Persian, Chinese, and Moorish motifs were incorporated into public as well as private buildings. An architect might do a house in the Lombard Romanesque style one day and a Venetian Gothic building the next, and it was not unusual for a patron to ask for a house in the Tudor style with a drawing room employing Turkish motifs, a small Greek temple out in the garden, and a carriage house with Gothic trim. Absurd as this may sound to us, we do almost the same thing today when we build a fluorescent-lighted, air-conditioned supermarket in the "Colonial style," or live in a "Georgian" house whose kitchen has all the latest push-button appliances. As we have seen, a style is created to fulfill the needs of a given era, both practical and spiritual needs; but style is also closely connected with techniques and materials. If the Greeks had not had abundant stone and had been forced to use brick, their architecture would undoubtedly have been different in style and structure, expressing the same values, no doubt, but in different ways. We know that the Greeks actually knew the principle of the arch but evidently found it unsuited to express the feelings they wanted their buildings to convey.

The technical changes brought about by the Industrial Revolution in the late eighteenth and nineteenth centuries were tremendous, but the general public and most architects failed to realize their possibilities. The same old forms were simply produced by new means: for instance, cast-iron Corinthian columns and entablatures. But even more crucial to the development of architecture were changes in building techniques. In the past, all the parts of a building were fashioned at the construction site. This meant that the carpenter who made a window built it for a particular spot on a particular house, proportioning its cornice and its sill so as to make that window harmonious with the stonemason's and the roofer's part of the project. Such a house became a created thing, unique and different at least in some degree from every other house ever built. Today, the various parts of a house are ordered by the contractor from a factory. The men who make them, largely by machinery, have no concern for the destiny of their work. Moreover, these parts will have a certain uniformity which is one of the virtues of the factory system but which compares poorly with the individualism and subtlety of handmade objects. Our reaction to this state of affairs, however, should not be like that of William Morris, who yearned to return to the great era of handmade art, the Middle Ages, but rather like that of Frank Lloyd Wright, who as early as 1901 saw the machine as a boon to the architect who had the vision to design for it. The machine makes good standard parts, identical and economical, but ornament of a traditional kind very poorly and at great cost. Good modern architecture, therefore, has little ornament of the applied type such as cornices and fluted pilasters, a lack which is made up in other respects, however.

The repetition of mass-produced units and variations within that repetition actually constitute a form of decoration (as we saw in the columns of the Parthenon and in the arches of the Colosseum). The contrast of materials has always been a source of ornamentation (see the Pantheon in figure 18 with its veneer of polished marbles). Today's new materials—plate glass, aluminum, stainless steel, plastics, and a host of aggregates or artificially produced stone—expand the possibilities of such decoration. Finally, new construction methods, which will be discussed later, have left the architect free to use the parts of a building themselves in a decorative way. Windows, for example, once were restricted as to size by the width of the lintel or arch that supported the wall above them. Today, with the use of steel beams, the whole side of a building may be one big window and thus function as a part of the building's ornamentation.

The Steel Skeleton

The simplicity and precision of machine-made forms have replaced the complexity and diversity which is the hallmark of traditional ornament. We may regret the change, but to produce hand-wrought ornament by machine methods is not only esthetically dishonest but actually not satisfying. To produce it by hand is extravagant by today's pay scale and also unsatisfying, because we no longer have the specialized craftsman who has devoted his entire life to perfecting his skill in producing just one style of detail. But the loss in one direction is more than made up for in another. Improved methods of steel production have made steel beams inexpensive enough to be generally used, and have thus introduced the first real structural change since the twelfth century: the elimination of the wall as a weight-bearing element. In a building with a steel skeleton, the walls are merely curtains that separate interior from exterior and keep rain and wind out. In a tall building, the steel skeleton actually supports the walls. In fact, walls may be omitted at any point, hence many buildings look as if they are raised on stilts but are merely steel skeletal structures whose walls have been left off on the ground floor. Many buildings today, done in what is called the International Style, consist of boxlike steel skeletons with large expanses of glass.

Because a thin strip of steel bends in the direction of its broader side, steel beams are shaped so that thin sides and broad sides oppose one another; that is, their cross sections are generally T-shaped or I-shaped. Quite obviously, such a beam will span a greater distance between two supports than will a stone beam. Nor need the steel beam stop when it reaches those supports; it may go right on for a considerable distance beyond those supports. Thus the floors in a building constructed of steel sometimes project beyond their supports on all sides, a feature which is called a cantilever, and a building so constructed is said to be cantilevered.

Frank Lloyd Wright   1869–1959

A genius, Frank Lloyd Wright once wrote, is a man who understands what others only know about. Throughout his long life, Wright inspired adulation in a few and aversion in many, because he was convinced that he was a genius and that he understood what the rest of us only know about. Only time will prove him right or wrong. All we can do so soon after his death is to marvel at the originality of his buildings and the fertility of his imagination. Comparatively late in life, in 1908, Wright designed a series of houses that revolutionized architecture throughout the world, the so-called Prairie Houses. There had been rumblings of new ideas in Europe, but as far as we know, Wright worked his problems out in his midwestern isolation. Up to then, a room had been a box whose walls were pierced with windows to let in light and with doors to let in people. A house had been a collection of boxes which, when fitted together, constituted a bigger box or series of boxes covered by a roof. The shapes and sizes of the rooms in the Farnese Palace, for example, were determined, or at least limited, by the preconceived shape of the building as a whole (see fig. 42). The architect worked from the outside in; he decided what shape his building should have, and then he determined where in that shape he should put the kitchen, the bedrooms, etc. Wright reversed that process: he began with the living room, its hearth and its chimney, and then placed not rooms but living-spaces around it. Instead of using doors, he often allowed one space to flow into the next, the one interlocked with the other and presenting to the viewer a series of constantly shifting spaces and panoramas. This Wright called *organic architecture,* implying a growth and a development similar to that of a living organism. Except for kitchens, bedrooms, and bathrooms, of course, there was an openness in Wright's houses that made space not a static factor, contained within closed walls, but a dynamic experience, which was heightened and dramatized by constant surprises: a low ceiling after a high one, an unexpected placement of a window, an abrupt confrontation with the landscape seen through glass.

In its tendency to merge internal and external space, and in many other respects, Wright's houses have much in common with Japanese architecture. Perhaps the outstanding difference between architecture in Japan and the West is the fact that the Japanese house consists of wooden supports arranged in a horizontal-vertical system that makes a framework or skeleton from which the walls, floors, and ceilings are hung. Despite the frigid Japanese winters, houses tend to be open, with windows often extending from ceiling to floor and from post to post, and the building materials are often quite fragile: paper, cardboard, straw, and reeds. The walls on the north and west, where the winter rains and snows come from, are solid, whereas those on the east and south are actually removable screens. Movable walls inside the house, moreover, allow the space of one room to merge with that of another. The eaves of the roof extend far out all around the house to shield it from the noonday sun. Except during periods of Chinese influence, Japanese architecture has favored asymmetrical arrangements, a grouping of spaces in an unexpected way and in a way that relates to the landscape. The openness of the Japanese house, moreover, focusses attention outward from the interior rather than vice versa, and the gardening skill of the Japanese is no doubt a consequence, or at least a concomitant, of this openness.

Combined with a great sense for function and utility is the Japanese respect for esthetic values that borders on a religious attitude. No piece of wood in the traditional Japanese house is covered with paint, though it might be stained and rubbed to bring out the beauty of its texture and grain. Interiors are planned with an eye to a harmonious color scheme of natural materials, various tans and greens of straw and reeds and different tones of wood such as cypress, bamboo, and Japanese cedar. Most amazing is the fact that all parts of this house are prefabricated, so to speak, before the house is begun. All parts are cut and fitted together, numbered, and stacked in their proper order, and an entire house can sometimes be put together in the space of a single day.

Although he staunchly denied the influence of Japanese architecture on his work, Wright was loud in his admiration of it. He insisted on the idea that a house must grow out of the landscape in which it stands, that natural forms and man-made forms should harmonize, that materials be used for their inherent beauty of color and structural possibilities, and that there should be no sharp boundary between interior and exterior space: in all these he was voicing Japanese ideals. Reminiscent of Japanese buildings, too, are Wright's long, low-floating roofs, the interlocking rectangular volumes, the sweeping horizontals, and the large, flat areas of a single, unbroken color (usually white) trimmed with or framed by black horizontal and vertical borders.

Frank Lloyd Wright: The Robie House   Colorplate 15

Two features above all others dominate the exterior view of this house: the long roof that sweeps over the building from one end to the other and appears to hover over the ground, and the less insistent vertical forms that seem to pin the roof down and keep it from floating away. This horizontal-vertical relationship is echoed all through the building, the horizontal members jutting out unexpectedly above and below the big roof, and the vertical ones asserting their presence by their clean-cut edges and the dramatic play of light and shadow.

Horizontals clearly dominate the structure, reminding us of the flat terrain upon which it stands, the level midwestern landscape which gave

Wright's Prairie Houses their name. Notice how the shadows cast by the limestone topping on the brick walls serve to multiply this horizontality. The feeling of suspension, of floating above the ground, is insistent, partly because each of the roofs extends into space seemingly without support (they are cantilevered, of course, by means of steel beams), and partly because the roofs do not conform to the shape of the floors below them (they either extend beyond the floor or fall short of its edges). The pitch of the gabled roofs, incidentally, is so slight that in colorplate 15 the roofs appear to be perfectly flat.

In its emphasis on horizontals and verticals, the Robie House has something in common with the Farnese Palace (fig. 40) whose façade is dominated by repeated horizontal bands and the smaller verticals of the thirty-eight windows. Yet what different effects these two pieces of domestic architecture produce! The inviolate symmetry of the Italian palace, its flat, blocklike surface, and its inflexible repetitiveness of forms give it the forbidding formality and aloofness of a fortress. Wright's building is deliberately asymmetrical so as to set it as far as possible from that grandiose regimentation of forms which was once the hallmark of aristocrats' houses but later became customary for public libraries, government buildings, and banks. If we walk past the Farnese Palace, the façade will not change; it will retain its regular, rhythmic monumentality, and we can be sure that if we walk around to one of its sides, we will encounter another flat façade with more repetitive windows and pediments. Not so the Robie House. With every step we take, we get a new glimpse of the building; we discover fresh vistas over, under, and around its various parts because Wright's house forms a dynamic composition. Its walls move inward and outward in space as one's eyes travel over the building. Levels also shift: the terraces and roof-lines rise and fall in different strata. Despite this fluidity in its design, the house stands solidly in an equilibrium produced by the sharply defined volumes and the precision and logic of their arrangement.

The Robie House: Plan

The interior as well as the exterior of the Robie House is dominated by the chimney which marks the fireplace as the center of the house, as the hearth has always been the heart of domestic dwellings throughout the ages. If we look at the plan of the ground floor (which is actually located below the level of the sidewalk), we see this fireplace, a double fireplace, actually, quite near the entrance hall (see fig. 53) where it serves to divide the billiard room on the west from the children's playroom on the east. This is the only division between these rooms. There are no doors. On the

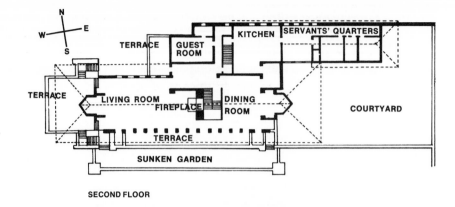

SECOND FLOOR

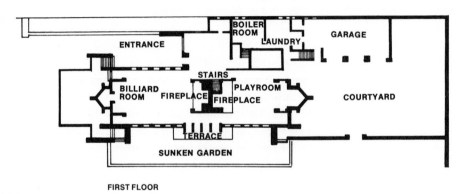

FIRST FLOOR

Figure 53 | The Robie House, plan of the first and second stories

south ten windows, arranged in two continuous ribbons of five each, let daylight in. Between them, four French doors open onto a terrace that overlooks a miniature garden, which is also sunk below the level of the sidewalk. This first floor is devoted to recreation and utility spaces. Behind it a garage opens onto an enclosed courtyard.

Alongside the pivotal chimney rises the stairwell that leads to the second floor (see fig. 53). Here the dining room and the living room rest on the walls of the rooms below them, and they are similarly separated by a fireplace and the stairway that leads to the third floor. Not only do the dining and living rooms form one continuous space without doors, but they share one continuous and uninterrupted wall between them. This wall, the south wall, consists entirely of windows, fourteen of them, with just enough brick showing between each window to remind one that this is a wall. This time twelve of these fourteen windows are French doors and lead onto a terrace that overlooks the sunken garden.

At the east and west ends of the living and dining area are two curious alcoves that contain bay windows, the only spaces whose lines do not make a 90° angle with the other walls in the house—a startling and dramatic touch. On each side of the western alcove, two doors and a few steps lead to a large terrace, part of which is sheltered by the cantilevered roof and part of which is open to the sky. (The dotted lines in fig. 53 mark the edges of the roofs). From this terrace two series of stairways lead down to the lower level, to the sunken garden on the south side and the entrance on the north. These stairways provide a series of landings from which one may enjoy viewing the house and its landscaped grounds. The kitchen sits directly over the boiler room and the servants' quarters rise above the laundry and the garage. The third floor consists entirely of bedrooms which are glassed in and which open onto terraces.

Besides formulating a new philosophy of architecture, Wright invented a host of specific devices and systems. He gathered several windows into one continuous ribbon (the ancestor of today's ubiquitous picture window) instead of spacing them singly, and he sometimes ran windows around a corner to stress the sense of openness. He pioneered indirect lighting, built-in furniture, and air conditioning, and he was the first to use carports instead of garages and heating pipes imbedded under the floor instead of radiators.

Personally, Wright was a controversial figure all of his life. Even as a young man he cultivated the "genius look," enhancing his lean, craggy features by letting his hair grow long and by wearing a flowing bow tie and a broad-brimmed hat. He spoke and wrote voluminously, giving out opinions on the art and life of his time and of the past. The ancient Greeks had no sense for materials, he declared, because they covered parts of their lovely marble with paint. Michelangelo was no architect, he argued, and an inferior painter, because he treated both of these arts like sculpture. Wright could wax as lyrical about things he loved as he could be scathing about the things he did not. "Early in life," he said a few years before he died, "I had to choose between honest arrogance and hypocritical humility. I chose honest arrogance, and have seen no occasion to change, even now."

Reinforced Concrete

After the structural use of steel, the most important development in the new architecture is the use of reinforced concrete. Concrete by itself, being an artificially made stone, has the same advantages and disadvantages as stone. It works well under compression but badly under tension.

That is, much weight can be piled on it if there is sufficient support, but it will tend to pull apart in places where it is not being held up directly (see fig. 10). Steel, on the contrary, has great tensile strength but limited compressive strength. It would take great power to pull a rod of steel apart, but only a small amount of weight to bend that rod. When concrete is poured around one or more such rods, however, the resulting "stone" combines the compressive strength of concrete with the tensile strength of steel to form a very fine building material, easy to make, economical, and versatile. Reinforced concrete can be made on the building site; only its ingredients need be transported; and it may be mixed and poured by relatively unskilled workmen. It may also be poured into molds that have forms other than the rectangular form which is most natural to steel construction. Among men who have made unusually creative use of reinforced concrete are the Italian engineer-architect Pier Luigi Nervi and the Swiss architect Le Corbusier.

Le Corbusier 1887–1965

Twenty years younger than Wright, Charles Édouard Jeanneret, who called himself Le Corbusier, was a painter as well as an architect, most of his pictures revealing a rather austere kind of Cubism, quite abstract and done in somber blues, browns, and grays. Like Wright and many other architects, he was philosophically inclined, but more practical than Wright. His love of mathematics and precision in general was oddly blended with flights of fantasy, especially with respect to life in the future. Like Wright, he drew plans for vast complexes of buildings whose form and structure were so radical that they never got built. Le Corbusier drew plans for rebuilding Paris, Antwerp, Algiers, Buenos Aires, Bogotá, and many other cities. Of these, only one has become a reality and that is still under construction—Chandigarh, the new capital of the Punjab in India.

Where Wright sought to harmonize each of his buildings with its particular setting and cultural environment wherever the building happened to be, Le Corbusier seems deliberately to have done the opposite. His buildings appear to ignore the characteristics of their location. Instead of hugging the ground, they rise defiantly from the earth, often raised on stilts to underscore their self-sufficiency. In 1914, Le Corbusier designed a house whose simplicity of design and capacity for prefabrication and mass production were intended to anticipate the postwar housing shortage. This Dom-Ino House consisted of a reinforced concrete skeleton of six columns and floor- and roof-slabs, a veritable cage of structural members, into which movable divisions could be set according to the anticipated needs of the tenants. Despite their ingenuity, economy, and logic (qualities which are constants in this architect's work), the Dom-Ino Houses were never built.

In one of the many books he wrote, Le Corbusier made his most quoted and much misinterpreted statement that a house is a machine for living. A machine, he explained, is primarily functional, but sometimes beautiful as well. When it has both of these qualities, he concluded, then its function and its beauty are inseparable. In good architecture, too, he asserted, functionalism and beauty should be inseparable.

But Le Corbusier's concept of beauty was based on more than his personal whim. Over a period of many years, he worked out a system of proportions, a module based on the human body whose dimensions he subdivided into various ratios. This Modulor, as he called it, is much more capable of variation than other previous systems of proportions as, for example, the age-old Golden Section (*a* is to *b* as *b* is to *a* plus *b*). And so, if Wright was a Romantic who relied on his personal sensibilities and the intuitions of his genius for his guides, then Le Corbusier was a Classicist who searched for perfect and provable systems for constructing his architecture. Each of Wright's structures is unique: each has its own personality, almost like a living creature. To duplicate such a house, to build a Robie House over again somewhere else, would violate everything it stands for. Le Corbusier's buildings, on the other hand, are more like beautiful machines, made to be reproduced and used anywhere in the world. But where most machines do not show the touch of their maker, Le Corbusier's structures reveal the imprint of his intellect and esthetic sensitivity. Architecture, he once wrote, goes beyond utilitarian needs. "It is human passion that can make drama out of lifeless stone."

City Planning

According to Wright, the country is man's natural habitat; cities are artificial, man-made evils. Not only that, but "ruralism as distinguished from urbanism is American and truly democratic." With a country as large as ours, he asked, "where there is so much idle land, why should it be parceled out by realtors in strips 25′ 50′ or 100′ wide? This imposition is a survival of feudal thinking, of the social economics practiced by and upon the serf. An acre to the family should be the democratic minimum if this machine of ours [the city, he means] is a success!" Wright's answer to the urban tangle was a separation of working and living areas connected by rapid transportation. The city would then be an "ideal machine . . . invaded at ten o'clock, abandoned at four, for three days a week. The other four days of the week would be devoted to the more or less joyful matter of living elsewhere under conditions natural to man."

Today, Wright's idea would work only in some sparsely populated region such as Arizona. The countryside around our large urban areas is disappearing with every year that passes, and unless some planning is done soon, whole sections of our nation—the Atlantic seaboard from Boston to Norfolk, for example—will become one vast urban sprawl. As an inhabitant of the more crowded Old World, Le Corbusier proposed another solution: a city which consists not only of office towers but apartment towers as well, the one in the business district of the city, the other in surrounding residential zones. Connecting the two would be high speed roads, either elevated or sunken so as to leave the landscape for the enjoyment of pedestrians. Outside this business-residential area, and separated from it by miles of green countryside, would be the factory and industrial district, also connected by expressways to the residential district.

Instead of sprawling over the countryside, as do our suburbs, Le Corbusier's residential area would consist of a few gigantic apartment houses, each one conceived as a complete housing development by itself. That is, each apartment in one of these buildings is designed as a complete house, or "villa," the French word for a country residence, but raised one above the other, with the corridors functioning as streets. Thus 1600 people inhabit the 337 villas in the apartment block at Marseille, but in a vertical instead of horizontal disposition. By concentrating his living units upwards, Le Corbusier has salvaged the land between each of the apartment blocks, land that can become parks and recreation areas for the residents, places to sit, stroll, and take children for walks, space for cafés and restaurants, shops, schools, and churches—all in a garden setting instead of an urban tangle.

Even the space *under* this vertical village is utilized, for the building is raised on stilts for the greater convenience of pedestrians, and the roof, instead of being wasted on utility spaces and shingles, contains playground, clubhouse, outdoor movie theater, children's swimming pool, gymnasium, and even a 1000-foot racetrack for runners.

Figure 54 | Le CORBUSIER. The Marseille Apartment Block, detail showing
         | Le Corbusier's Modulor

Such are the compensations for the lawns and shrubbery which the apartment dweller must do without. The only question is whether he prefers living in an apartment-villa, surrounded by public gardens and recreation spaces, or living in a separate house whose grounds he must maintain, whose repairs and other services he must furnish himself, and whose pleasures he can enjoy only after tedious hours of commuting from work to his residence. One such apartment block in Nantes, France, is built picturesquely over a stream and must be approached over a bridge. In other words, its nearly 2000 residents can enter their homes over a bridge six feet wide! A surburban housing development of that size would require miles of intersecting streets and "lanes." Since each tenant buys his apartment, just as he would his own separate house, the ultimate question is not: "Would you like to have your own house with an acre of ground around it?" but: "Can we, in view of an ever increasing population, continue to live in separate houses? Do we want to see the countryside between our cities disappear completely? Must we have to travel farther and farther between where we work and where we sleep?"

Le Corbusier: The Marseille Apartment Block   Colorplate 16

So far, Le Corbusier's alternative to the urban sprawl has not caught on. A section of Marseille was earmarked for such a project in 1946, but only one apartment block was built. There are seventeen stories in this building; two of them, the seventh and eighth, contain a shopping center—grocery store, drug store, beauty parlor, laundry, post office, doctor's and dentist's offices, restaurant, an eighteen-room hotel for visitors to the "village," and, of course, a café on a terrace overlooking the countryside. Elsewhere in the building there are movie theaters, clubrooms, photographic darkrooms, and other recreation areas.

So much for the functional aspect of the building. As to its structure and visual effect, it is an original and overwhelming creation, despite the numerous debased imitations that have appeared since 1946. Its mammoth size—it is 550 feet long, 184 feet high, and 79 feet across—is enhanced by the rough texture of the cast concrete which reveals the patterns left by the wooden boards into which the concrete was poured. Elsewhere we see the texture of the concrete grillwork, and certain areas where the concrete has been sprayed on roughly. Each of the balconies which open out from three of its four sides has its walls painted in solid expanses of color, bright red, blue, green, and yellow. The form of the building is a simple rectangular block, but the feeling of heaviness is minimized by having this gigantic mass of concrete suspended on and cantilevered out from thirty-eight piers which seem massive when we walk under them, but appear surprisingly graceful from a distance (see fig. 54). This is because they taper downward and thus give the structure the appearance of standing on its toes, and also because they are set back under the building so that shadow tends to obscure their presence. These massive piers are actually hollow and contain the pipes and wiring for the villas.

The sides of the building show considerable variation in the size and proportion of the openings, again an example of ornamentation by the variation of whole sections of repeated and mass-produced units, because there are twenty-three different kinds of apartments for large and small families, plus the shopping area (which is louvered), and the elevator-stairway shaft. Moreover, the proportions of the various parts have been determined by the architect's Modulor system of ratios.

The north wall of the building is windowless. The villas on the south side have windows opening in several directions. All the rest of the villas stretch from the east to the west faces of the building. These long villas are the most interesting feature of the building, for each has a living room with a 16-foot ceiling, and a kitchen and bedroom ceiling just half as high. Two such villas are dovetailed together so that the bedroom of one is above the living room of the other, with space left at the center for a corridor (or "street," as the architect likes to call it). Together, every two villas form a rectangle two stories high, and only one "street" is needed for every two stories (see fig. 55). In one villa, therefore, the living room opens on the east and the bedrooms on the west. In the interlocking villa, the reverse is true. Otherwise, the villas are windowless. Each living room and each bedroom has a balcony or veranda which may be planted with flowers and thus serve as a little private garden. Each of these verandas is completely shut off from its neighbors, and each villa is sealed off from the adjoining villa by a system of lead boxes so that each is completely soundproof. More privacy is assured thereby than what the average homeowner enjoys in the ostensibly private houses of our suburban developments.

Figure 55 shows two such villas in both section and in plan, respectively. Each villa is quite narrow, measuring only 12 feet in width and 66 feet in length. We enter Villa A from the "street" and step into the large living room (L) which is 12 feet wide and 28 feet long. As in Wright's Robie House, this is not so much a room as it is an area. Its space runs under an 8-foot ceiling for 18 feet, and then opens to 16 feet as we approach the veranda (V). The space flows not only upward, but backward, over an interior balcony (B) which contains the dining area (D). A stairway on the south side of the living room leads up to this balcony and gives us a view over the living room and out through the veranda into the landscape. To the west of the dining area, in the center of the apartment, is the kitchen (K), the bathroom (Ba), and various closets and storage areas. Then comes the sleeping area of the villa (Br), which is divided into two spaces only 6 feet wide, 8 feet high, and, like the living room, 28 feet long. These spaces, which may, of course, be subdivided to suit the needs of each family, open onto a veranda that faces west (Vw).

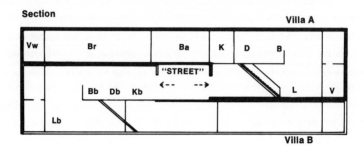

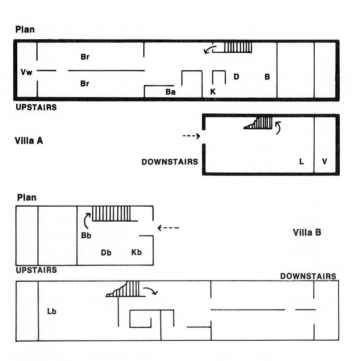

Figure 55 | Cross section and plans of two "villas" in the Marseille Apartment Block

The arrangement of Villa B has only two major differences. The front door opens on the second floor balcony (Bb), so that we must descend the stairs to reach the living room (Lb). The kitchen (Kb) is upstairs alongside the dining room (Db). The rest of the lower level is like that in Villa A except, of course, that its bedrooms face east.

Illumination in Architecture

The illumination of interiors has been a primary concern of the architect through the ages. In the Pantheon, in the Roman vaulted basilica, in the Early Christian truss-roofed basilica, and in the Gothic cathedral we saw various solutions for letting daylight into large interior spaces. But the architect must also control light, cut down on glare, and keep out heat. Arcades and porches are used in hot countries to provide shade in front of windows and doors. The courtyard and the patio serve to cool the interiors of houses in the Mediterranean world. For centuries, shutters, either on the inside or on the outside of windows, have served as means to regulate heat and glare. Still today, housewives in sunny parts of Europe close all the shutters on the east side of their houses and open them on the west during the morning hours, and reverse the process after noon. Louvers or horizontal slats on these shutters allow air to enter while shutting out the rays of the sun, as do our venetian blinds.

In cooler, darker Holland, houses often have two tiers of windows, the top range with fixed panes, the lower row with casement windows that open like doors (see de Hooch's painting in colorplate 8). The shutters on each tier—solid, louverless shutters, in this case—can be opened separately, so that a room can be lighted indirectly from above, directly from eye level, or both. Most shutters in the United States are nailed fast to the house on either side of a window, unfunctional decoration, intended merely to recall olden days. Front porches serve to cool the air and to shade the lower part of many houses in the English-speaking world, but here again, tradition sometimes overrides common sense. Houses on each side of an east-west oriented street, for example, have the identical kind of porches, although the sun in our hemisphere shines always from the south. The house with the porch on its north side is protected on what is its shady side anyway, while its rear smolders in the sun unprotected. One of the most functional systems of light control by means of the porch is used in the plantation houses of Louisiana, Haiti, and Santo Domingo whose fronts and sides are surrounded by continuous porches or verandas on every story. Thus the entire façade is shaded, and cool air circulates through the house.

Lighting has been both simplified and complicated by the advent of the steel skeleton, simplified because windows can now be placed wherever they are needed, and complicated because the fascination with large expanses of glass has aggravated the problems of heat and glare control. Actually, with the availability of electric lighting, buildings can be, and have been, built without any windows at all. It has been found, however, that people have a psychological need to look out of the building, so that at least some windows are desirable. Glass has been developed which filters out the heat-producing rays of the spectrum, and among the devices developed by the modern architect for controlling light is the giant louver. Working on the same principle as the louver on the traditional shutter, these modern louvers are generally arranged vertically, like gigantic venetian blinds set up on their sides, and are pitched at such an angle that the direct rays of the sun cannot penetrate. (See the seventh and eighth story of Le Corbusier's Marseille Block, colorplate 16). These particular louvers are fixed, but some are movable and pivot according to the brightness of the day. The headquarters of the Reynolds Metals Company in Richmond, Virginia, for example, has 880 louvers, each of them 14 feet tall, and each of them operated by an electric motor and controlled by an electronic eye. When the sun goes behind a cloud, all the louvers open automatically, and when the sun comes out again, they close to the proper position.

A simpler solution to both heat and glare control has been the grille, a device that has long been used in the Arab world and in India to let air in and keep heat out. Modern architects place grilles outside closed windows, however, so that they do not function to ventilate the building, but they still help cut air conditioning costs. Seeing through the grille is easy for those who are inside the building whereas passersby, farther away from the openings in the grille, are not able to look in. Since they are made of mass-produced, prefabricated units, grilles may be given interesting repetitive patterns and thus may become part of the building's ornamentation.

Le Corbusier for many years experimented with what he called *brise-soleils,* or sun-breakers, recessed spaces in the façade of a building which keep direct sunlight out of the living space. As we can see in the Marseille Apartment Block, these *brise-soleils* are not something added on to the building like porches or grilles. Instead, they themselves are the façade of the building, behind which each apartment is set back. Each *brise-soleil* functions as a porch, or like the veranda of the Louisiana plantation house. It also resembles the window system of the Dutch house in that each living room veranda is divided horizontally into two tiers of windows, each one about 8 feet high. These windows have curtains which function somewhat as the shutters do in the Dutch house. Each tier of windows may be darkened independently, so that light may come in directly from the opening on the floor level, indirectly from above, or, on a dark day, from both. This similarity between the Dutch house and Le Corbusier's villas is all the more interesting because it stems from the fact that the architects of both had a similar problem: lighting a house which was long and narrow. The shape of the Dutch house was determined by the scarcity of land in little seabound Holland. Houses were often built high in the air and on as few square feet of land as possible. For stability's sake, one house was built up against the next, so that the windows could be set only into the front and rear walls (except in corner houses), and these few windows had to provide light for the long, narrow interiors. The similarity to the Marseille apartments is obvious, and the reason behind this similarity is the same—the conservation of land.

Tradition, therefore, when used intelligently, can be a creative solution to modern problems. The unthinking perpetuation of tradition, on the other hand, is apparent all around us. The size of the glass panes in most of our windows, for example, was set in the eighteenth century when technology could turn out panes only nine or so inches high. Although modern glassmakers can now make whole walls of glass, we continue to set tiny panes laboriously into our windows and to crane our necks to see around the wooden mullions. We continue to build in styles of architecture originally imported from England although the climate in most of North America is hotter in the summer and colder in the winter than England's. We still build churches in the "Gothic" style, and we erect Cape Cod cottages in Florida and "ranch houses" in the crowded suburbs of our cities. Commercial concerns have eagerly made use of contemporary ideas of style and materials for office buildings, banks, and stores. They have found that modern construction is efficient and economical, and that it is good for public relations, lending prestige to the firm which uses it. Domestic architecture has been slower to adopt contemporary ideas in the design of buildings, and banks are reluctant to finance anything out of the ordinary. It seems as though the American homeowner wants an ultra-modern building to work in, but a house of traditional design, although when he goes on a trip he looks for a hotel or motel whose cantilevered balconies, walls of unbroken color, and vast panes of glass proclaim its contemporaneity.

256

Projects
1. Trace the change in the use of iron and steel in such buildings as the Bibliothèque Sainte Geneviève in Paris, the Crystal Palace in London, and the Eiffel Tower in Paris.
2. Examine as many photographs, diagrams, and plans as you can find of Le Corbusier's chapel at Ronchamp, Frank Lloyd Wright's Guggenheim Museum, Mies van der Rohe's Seagram Building, and Walter Gropius' Bauhaus buildings. What are the problems of illumination in each case, and how has the architect solved them?
3. Examine several photographs of Frank Lloyd Wright's Kaufmann House ("Falling Water") in Bear Run, Pennsylvania, the Johnson's Wax Company building in Racine, Wisconsin, Taliesin West near Phoenix, Arizona, and the Price Tower in Bartlesville, Oklahoma. Discuss each building with regard to the use of materials and to the relationship between the building and its site.
4. Visit three buildings in your neighborhood that incorporate contemporary ideas in their construction, and discuss them with regard to (a) structure and material, (b) esthetic effect, and (c) function and utility.

Suggested Reading

Alex, William. *Japanese Architecture.* * New York: George Braziller, Inc., 1966.

Blake, Peter. *Frank Lloyd Wright: Architecture and Space.* * Baltimore: Penguin Books, Inc., 1964.

Blake, Peter. *Le Corbusier: Architecture and Form.* * Baltimore: Penguin Books, Inc., 1963.

Choay, Francoise. *Le Corbusier.* * New York: George Braziller, Inc., 1960.

Doxiadis, Constantinos A. *Architecture in Transition.* New York: Oxford University Press, 1968.

Encyclopedia of Modern Architecture, ed. Wolfgang Pehnt. New York: Harry N. Abrams, Inc., 1964.

Giedion, Sigfried. *Space, Time, and Architecture: The Growth of a New Tradition.* Cambridge, Mass.: Harvard University Press, 1962.

Ishimoto, Tatsuo, and Kiyoko Ishimoto. *The Japanese House: Its Interior and Exterior.* New York: Crown Publishers, Inc., 1963.

Joedicke, Jürgen. *A History of Modern Architecture.* New York: Frederick A. Praeger, Inc., 1963.

Jones, Cranston. *Architecture Today and Tomorrow.* New York: McGraw-Hill Book Co., 1961.

Scully, Vincent. *Frank Lloyd Wright.* * New York: George Braziller, Inc., 1960.

Scully, Vincent. *Modern Architecture.* * New York: George Braziller, Inc., 1961.

Wright, Frank L. *Frank Lloyd Wright: Writings and Buildings,* * E. Edgar Kaufmann and Ben Raeburn. New York: Horizon Press, Inc., 1960.

*Available in a paperback edition.

Conclusion

In its simplest sense, style is one way of doing something that can be done in innumerable ways. Of all the countless ways of representing the human figure in sculpture, the African artist from Dogon, the Greek who fashioned the Zeus from Artemision, the sculptor from Moissac, and Michelangelo chose only four. Although the statue from the Sudan is unique—there is no other statue just like it in every respect—it shares its style with all the sculpture from the Dogon region made in the late nineteenth century. Even an artistic giant like Michelangelo is a product of his time, and shares both his ideas and his technique with his contemporaries. Style, therefore, is a product of the interaction between a person and a society. It is a fallacy, then, to think that the styles of the past which belonged to the ancient Greeks and Romans, to Titian, de Hooch, or to Goya can give adequate visual form to the spirit of the twentieth century, although Hitler and Mussolini thought so, and the Soviet artist is still compelled to believe it.

The percentage of the people in past ages who understood what the creative artist has tried to say has always been small. It was the princes in the Renaissance, not the general populace, who approved the works of their leading artists; it was the intellectual churchmen in the Middle Ages, the aristocrats in the Baroque and Rococo periods, and the upper middle class in seventeenth-century Holland. To those who complain that modern art is not understood by the man in the street today we may answer that modern art has never been popular in any age. As a matter of fact, the percentage of the population that goes to see works displayed in museums of modern art today is greater than the percentage which in any past time has viewed the work of its contemporaries. Still, one hears the opinion that the modern movement in art is a passing fad, a temporary aberration, or even a conspiracy perpetrated by talentless artists, unscrupulous art dealers, and scheming museum directors. If this is so, then there are hundreds of thousands of individuals who are being hood-

257

winked into liking something which is meaningless and empty. But if these individuals find something significant and satisfying in what they see, if a picture or a statue or a building communicates to them, then what they see is not meaningless and empty for them. And as we tried to show in Chapter 8, the basic definition of a work of art rests on its power to move the spectator, to help him understand himself and his world. If the art that is being produced today turns out, as the years pass, to lose that power, then it will cease to be art and become instead a document of our era, a little like the personal letter of a great writer which may be an interesting document but not necessarily a great work of literature. But if a contemporary work does communicate significant thoughts and feelings to a substantial number of people today, then we must call it a work of art, no matter how much it may baffle, shock, or annoy us personally.

Still, our task of understanding the contemporary artist may be more difficult than it was for people in the past to understand the artists of their own time, because, as we have noted, the language of art has changed so radically during the last seven decades. The Renaissance style—and in a broad sense this includes art from about 1400 to 1900—was based on the discovery of the physical world. "Rediscovery" may be a better word, because the Greeks and the Romans had based their art on physical appearances too. Today, however, most artists find no challenge in painting trees and clouds and people just as they look because this has all been done. It may have been a challenge for Filippo Lippi and for Leonardo da Vinci, each of whom helped discover how to depict the physical world in art. But today, this is common property, dispensed by every art school and exemplified by the pictures in every magazine and billboard. Copying nature today is a craft, not an art, (unless, of course, it serves to create the Surrealist's dream world or some other such expressive purpose).

Instead of depicting the world around us, most creative artists today are exploring the world inside us, not only the Surrealists, but the Expressionists and the Cubists as well. The lines, shapes, and colors of most modern paintings reflect not so much what the artist sees as what he feels. Sometimes the genesis of this feeling is more optical than intellectual, residing mostly at the sensuous level of expression, as in the pictures we call nonobjective, nonrepresentational, or total abstractions which depict no recognizable objects whatsoever. At other times, the artist's method of plumbing the depths of his inner world is to use the cognitive aspects of nature to explore associative levels in the sphere of the irrational, as Picasso did in his *Girl Before a Mirror.*

This inner world, psychologists and psychiatrists tell us, is not always very pretty. It is mysterious and sometimes frightening to us, full of demonic impulses and disturbing ideas, a little like the physical world was to medieval man. Yet once he has embarked on this voyage of discovery, the artist today is not likely to ignore it and return to the more comfortable paths which artists discovered and have exhausted for the past five hundred years. As art critic Herbert Read once wrote:

> In general, modern art, in spite of its strangeness and obscurity, has been inspired by a natural desire to chart the uncharted. If in such an attempt it has produced symbols that are unfamiliar, that was only to be expected, for the depths it has been exploring are mysterious depths, full of strange fish. . . . But if we persist in our restless desire to know everything about the universe and our-selves, then we must not be afraid of what the artist brings back from his voyage of discovery.[1]

1. Herbert Read, "The Psychopathology of Reaction in the Arts," *Arts and Architecture,* (September 1956), p. 34.

Colorplate 1
Jesus Calling Peter and
Andrew, a mosaic in the
nave of Sant' Apollinare
Nuovo, Ravenna, Italy.
c. 526 A.D. Approximately
48″ high, 60″ wide

Colorplate 2   GIOTTO DI BONDONE. *The Lamentation.* c. 1305.
One scene from a cycle of fresco paintings in the
Arena Chapel in Padua, Italy. 7½′ high, 7¾′ wide

Colorplate 3 HANS MEMLING. *Madonna and Child with Angels.*
c. 1480. Tempera and oil paint on wooden panel,
23$\frac{1}{8}$″ high, 18$\frac{7}{8}$″ wide. Mellon Collection,
National Gallery of Art, Washington, D.C.

Colorplate 5
above

TITIAN. *Venus with a Mirror.* c. 1555. Oil on canvas, 49″ high, 41½″ wide. Mellon Collection, National Gallery of Art, Washington, D.C.

Colorplate 4
left

FILIPPO LIPPI. *Madonna and Child.* c. 1440–1445. Tempera on wooden panel, 31⅜″ high, 20⅛″ wide. Kress Collection, National Gallery of Art, Washington, D.C.

Colorplate 6
EL GRECO.
*Madonna and Child
with Saints Inés
and Tecla.* c. 1598.
Oil on canvas,
76⅛" high,
40½" wide.
Widener Collection,
National Gallery
of Art,
Washington, D.C.

Colorplate 7 REMBRANDT. *Self-Portrait*. Signed and dated 1659.
Oil on canvas, 33¼" high, 26" wide.
Mellon Collection, National Gallery of Art,
Washington, D.C.

Colorplate 8   PIETER DE HOOCH. *A Dutch Courtyard.* c. 1660.
above   Oil on canvas, 26¾″ high, 23″ wide. Mellon
Collection, National Gallery of Art, Washington, D.C.

Colorplate 9   *Solomon and the Queen of Sheba,* a Persian miniature
right   painting. c. 1560. 13½″ high, 9⅛″ wide.
From a manuscript of poems by Jami. Freer Gallery of A
Washington, D.C.

Colorplate 10 CLAUDE MONET. *Woman Seated Under the Willows.*
Signed and dated 1880. Oil on canvas, 31⅞" high, 23⅝" wide.
Chester Dale Collection, National Gallery of Art, Washington, D.C.

東海道

五十三次之内

見附

Colorplate 11
HIROSHIGE.
Mitsuke. c. 1833.
Color woodcut print
on rice paper.
9" high, 12½" wide.
No. 29 from *The Fifty-
Three Stations of the
Tokaido Road.* Virginia
Museum of Fine Arts,
Richmond, Virginia

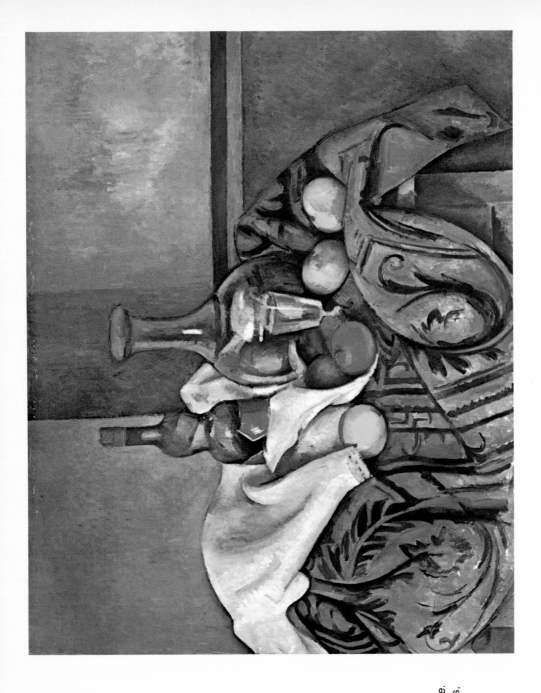

Colorplate 12
PAUL CÉZANNE. *Still Life.*
1890–1894. Oil on canvas,
26″ high, 32³/₈″ wide.
Chester Dale Collection,
National Gallery of Art,
Washington, D.C.

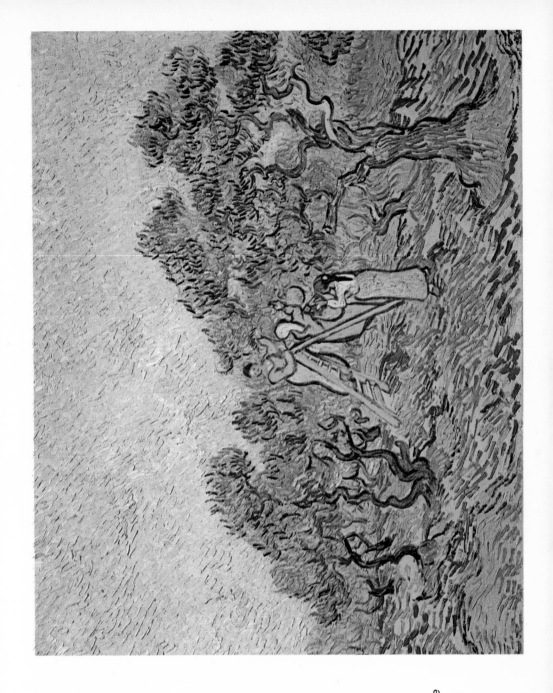

Colorplate 13
VINCENT VAN GOGH. *The Olive Orchard.* c. 1889.
Oil on canvas, 28³/₄"
high, 36³/₄" wide.
Chester Dale Collection,
National Gallery of Art,
Washington, D.C.

Colorplate 14   PABLO PICASSO. *Girl Before a Mirror.* 1932.
Oil on canvas, 63³/₄″ high, 51³/₄″ wide. Gift of Mrs.
Simon Guggenheim, Museum of Modern Art, New York

Colorplate 15
FRANK LLOYD WRIGHT.
The Robie House, Chicago
Illinois. 1909. Red brick
and white limestone

Colorplate 16
LE CORBUSIER.
The Apartment
Block in Marseille,
France. 1947–1952.
Reinforced
concrete,
184' high, 550' long,
79' wide

General Reference Books

Cairns, Huntington, and John Walker. *A Pageant of Painting.* New York: The Macmillan Co., 1966.

Capers, Roberta, and Jerrold Maddox. *Images and Imagination.* New York: The Ronald Press Co., 1965.

Cheney, Sheldon. *A New World History of Art.* New York: The Viking Press, Inc., 1956.

Fleming, William. *Arts and Ideas.* New York: Holt, Rinehart & Winston, Inc., 1968.

Fletcher, Banister. *A History of Architecture.* New York: Charles Scribner's Sons, 1961.

Gardner, Helen. *Art Through the Ages.* New York: Harcourt, Brace & World, Inc., 1969.

Gombrich, Ernst H. *The Story of Art.** New York: Phaidon Publishers, Inc., 1961; Oxford University Press, 1965.

Hamlin, Talbot. *Architecture Through the Ages.* New York: G. P. Putnam's Sons, 1953.

Huyghe, René, ed. *The Larousse Encyclopedia of Art:* vol. 1. Prehistoric and Ancient Art; vol. 2. Byzantine and Medieval Art; vol. 3. Renaissance and Baroque Art; vol. 4. Modern Art. New York: Prometheus Press, 1962–1965.

Janson, Horst W. *History of Art.* New York: Prentice-Hall, Inc. and Harry N. Abrams, Inc., 1962.

Janson, Horst W., and D. J. H. Janson, eds. *Key Monuments of the History of Art.* New York: Harry N. Abrams, Inc., 1959.

Janson, Horst W., and D. J. H. Janson. *A Picture History of Painting.** New York: Harry N. Abrams, Inc., 1957; New York: Washington Square Press, Inc., 1961.

Knobler, Nathan. *The Visual Dialogue.* New York: Holt, Rinehart & Winston, Inc., 1967.

Millon, Henry A., and Alfred Frazer. *Key Monuments of the History of Architecture.* New York: Prentice-Hall, Inc. and Harry N. Abrams, Inc., 1964.

Myers, Bernard S. *Art and Civilization.* New York: McGraw-Hill Book Co., Inc., 1967.

Pevsner, Nikolaus. *An Outline of European Architecture.** Baltimore: Penguin Books, Inc., 1960.

Robb, David M., and Jesse J. Garrison. *Art in the Western World.* New York: Harper & Row, Publishers, 1963.

Sewall, John I. *A History of Western Art.* New York: Holt, Rinehart & Winston, Inc., 1961.

Upjohn, Everard M., and John P. Sedgwick, Jr. *Highlights: An Illustrated Handbook of Art History.* New York: Holt, Rinehart & Winston, Inc., 1963.

Upjohn, Everard M., Paul S. Wingert, and Jane G. Mahler. *A History of World Art.* New York: Oxford University Press, 1958.

Watterson, Joseph. *Architecture: A Short History.* New York: W. W. Norton & Co., Inc., 1968.

*Available in a paperback edition.

Index

Bold numbers indicate works illustrated in this text.

1 2 3 4 5 6 7 8 9 10 11 12 13 14 15 16 17 18 19 20 21 22 23 24 25   78 77 76 75 74 73 72 71 70 69